DRAWING SOULS TO CHRIST

By
Rev. Stan Crookall

www.BibleArtMinistries.com

Dedication

This book is written with thanksgiving to Almighty God and to magnify His name. It is dedicated to the memory of Gwen Crookall. Gwen, my wife, life-long sweetheart, partner, helper and best friend asked me to write this book. We hope you like it.

When she knew death was approaching, Gwen said, "My work is finished, but yours is not. I want you to carry on and do what the Lord has called you to do." Just before she went to be with the Lord, she said to me, "The Lord said two words to me: 'Well done'!" What a tribute to a wonderful servant and gallant lady. I miss her more than words can adequately express, yet she does not seem far away.

You will read much about her in this book and her dedication to winning souls to Christ.

Gwen was a soul winner. She took a special interest in young women and taught them much about marriage and family. She was loved by so many she helped. She redeemed the time and invested her life in others. She was a true missionary to children, young people, and people of every age and walk of life. She was one in many millions. At her funeral, after her death on December 27, 2000, as they lowered her casket into the ground, I raised both my arms overhead and said, "Hallelujah, Hallelujah!"

My mother said of Gwen, "She is a brick," an old English expression meaning solid. She did not care who got the credit for whatever she had done that was good.

Once when Gwen was with me for a chapel service at Joyceville Penitentiary, near Kingston, Ontario, we arrived a little early and Gwen led a prisoner to the Lord before the service began. Later we were briefed to watch out for a certain prisoner who had attacked a priest just days before. When he was pointed out to us, it was none other than the young prisoner Gwen had just led to the Lord. General William Booth of the Salvation Army had a slogan, "Go for souls, and go for the worst." That was ever Gwen.

Gwen's good friend and helper with Pioneer Girls, V.B.S,

and Bible Clubs, Elva Moore said, "Gwen never had anything to prove and she was always the same."

For forty-six years Gwen marked December 10th on our calendar. It was the day our twins Peter and Ruth were born and went to be with the Lord. For some days before her home going, Gwen told me that she could hear her babies calling, "Mommy, mommy." She was looking forward to being with them.

Gwen designed what she called her family prayer circle and prayed for all the names on it each day.

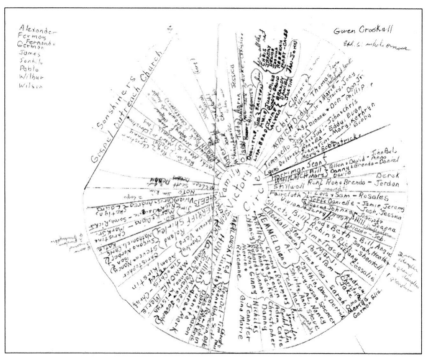

Gwen's Family Prayer Circle (one of three pages)

At her memorial service someone said, "Gwen was half of everything you did!" Also at her memorial service a handsome young man came to me and said, "I'm Robbie Kerr." Robbie Kerr was saved at six years of age in a house meeting in his parents' home at Aylmer, Quebec. He had driven 450 miles in bad winter weather that day just to honour Gwen and to let me know he cared.

But first is a reflection on "Grandma Gwen" by one of our grandsons, Jake Crookall:

Open arms, tight hugs, and freshly-baked lemon meringue pies were always the warm welcoming Grandma Gwen gave us during summer visits to their cottage. There is nothing more suited than memories of summer family vacations to describe her character. From the time we arrived at the Pentecostal campsite, excitement would grow inside as the expectation of excellent company and delicious desserts awaited! There was always a comfortable routine to our visits. As Grandma would be preparing the evening meal, she would always ask one of the grandchildren to "cook" Smokey's meal – hardly a laborious task, it involved adding a cup of water to a bowl of dog kibble – she would always supervise with a keen eye to help us out if we ran into any trouble. When it came to the evening, Grandma Gwen would be sure to add each of us to her prayers, just as she did every other day of the year. It was her constant concern for others that has lingered with me beyond those holiday visits. Throughout the years and wherever I went, it was a source of great comfort to know that every day Grandma was keeping you close in her thoughts and prayers.

Flyleaf Endorsement

Grandpa Stan

At a 2007 family reunion at the camp, Grandpa Stan was ministering with the paintings to some one hundred people. A grandson who at the time was studying at university said, "Grandpa,
they say that a picture is worth a thousand words – I think
that your way of using paintings is the best way to preach that
I have seen. As far as I know, you and Omar and German are
the only ones doing this in the whole world. Some sermons are
so boring that you can hardly wait till they end, but with the
paintings, the explanation is so interesting that it keeps everyone's attention all the way through, and it makes it so easy to
remember the Bible truths."

All the little kids were quiet because they were interested,
but it is great for every age. We had a great time of questions
and answers during the presentation. Five-year-old Nathan
said, "Uncle Stan is smart. He knows all the answers!" The biggest chuckle came from Uncle Stan.

Andrew Crookall, grandson of the author.

Acknowledgements

In the preparation of this book I am most grateful for the dedication and effort of Doug Pyle, the Associate Pastor at our church. Doug has helped me navigate the information highway, edit the book, and work the process. He is an inspiration to me.

I very much appreciate the work of my son Paul, who helped frame the book and edit my penultimate version. Where it is clear, you can thank Doug and Paul; where it is not clear, you can thank me.

This was written to be an inspiration and a blessing, and as a way of saying thank you to my God, my wife, and the thousands who have supported us in God's ministry.

You can read a copy of it on the web at
www.bibleartministries.com,
or you can order print copies from Xulon Press.

Contents

Introduction

"Stan, you have to put that story in writing." I was reluctant; I am an artist, not an author. But compelled by my wife's persistence, here is the story of how Art from the Bible has become an international ministry beyond expectations. We just stand in awe of the Lord.

Students and teachers in more than 10,000 schools across Canada, the United States, Jamaica, Colombia and Ecuador have been thrilled to see and hear this unique presentation. Many thousands have received Christ as their Lord and Saviour. To God be the glory – great things He has done! It has been an AWESOME ADVENTURE IN CHRIST!

The men and women of the Bible had many of the same needs and feelings that people have today. Sometimes they were happy and at other times sad. Some were heroes; others were cowards. It is up to each of us to choose between good and evil. The choices are as difficult today as then – real people with real problems. The same principles apply now as then: "They did not conquer by their own strength and skill but by Your mighty power and because you smiled upon them and favoured them." (Psalm 44:3)

Some of us have a tendency to revere Biblical heroes as super people thinking that these people lived on a higher plane than we can possibly attain. We also have a tendency to respect and revere some of the Lord's high profile servants today in the same way.

The Bible teaches that dependence upon the power of God and His anointing is the secret that produces answers to prayer and can make life an Awesome Adventure in Christ. It is not just for a privileged particularly holy few, but for all who simply, "Seek first the Kingdom of God and His righteousness." (Matthew 5:33)

When we realize our inadequacies and our utter helplessness to accomplish whatever the task is in our own strength – it is then that we learn to trust God to do what in our own strength cannot be done. We can also see how He deserves the Glory.

Gwen, my marriage partner, sweetheart and best friend for sixty years was the inspiration for this work and its existence is due to her vision and tenacity. She made me promise to write the book. Please read it in the spirit it is intended – it is our hope and prayer to honour God and bring blessings to you. Please read it prayerfully. A lifetime ago, in 1945, I read about the life of the Irish preacher Billy Bray. He taught by example how to pray about everything great or small. The value of prayer has been a constant in my life since then.

After Gwen and I had shared thirty wonderful years of life and ministry, we were about to gear down for retirement, but the Lord called us to begin Bible Art Ministries. That was in September 1976. This book tells the story of that ministry. But let me begin with how I found my partner, and the gradual unfolding of God's plan.

Chapter 1

Meeting the most wonderful girl

Gwen and I met in the summer of 1939. The world was just emerging from the Great Depression. War clouds were gathering on the horizon, but Chamberlain had assured us all would be well.

My brother had developed a sudden interest in attending Salvation Army services. This puzzled me, until I noticed the photo of a pretty girl on his bedroom dresser, and thought there might be a connection. He had not said one work to me about her. Nor had I asked. However, the next day I recognized the girl in the photograph amidst the crowd at the beach. I couldn't resist needling him about it.

"I saw your girlfriend today," I chuckled.

"What girlfriend?" Roy replied.

"The one in the photograph in your room." The cat was out of the bag now.

"Where did you see her?" he wanted to know. When I told him, he said, "She never goes there."

"She was there, you ask her," I said with confidence. The next day Roy said, "You were right."

Now that the secret romance had been discovered, Joyce became a regular visitor at our home. They invited me to go to a church picnic with them.

I was a little wary of the Salvation Army. My school chum Fred Barker's father was a Salvationist. One Sunday when Fred's father was dressed in his uniform and leaving for the service carrying his tenor horn. I suggested we go to the service. Fred replied, "What's the matter with you? Do you want to get saved or something?"

I didn't know what saved was, but from the tone of Fred's

voice, it didn't sound like a good thing. But going to a picnic shouldn't be that bad. Besides, there just might be another pretty girl there. That choice was the turning point in my life.

At the picnic, as we were finishing lunch, two beautiful girls came over to our table. They were sisters. They wore identical blue denim bib overalls with white blouses. They began talking to Roy, Joyce, and me. One sat down directly across from me. Her thick, wavy, honey blonde hair cascaded down over her shoulders. Her teeth were gleaming white and absolutely perfect. Her smile was beautiful, natural, and wholesome. She was joyful, bubbly, and so absolutely wonderful. It was Gwen. It was love at first sight. I knew with that first smile that this was the girl I wanted to be my sweetheart, life partner, and wife. I was seventeen and painfully shy. I could hardly speak to her.

The next day, Sunday, I knew I wanted to see her again, so I determined to brave going to church and risk being "saved." My brother and his girlfriend were a little surprised, but seemed pleased when I asked if I could go with them.

In that service my life was forever changed. When we arrived, I caught a glimpse of Gwen, but the only empty seats were right down at the front. That was where we sat. The guest preacher that night, a young Captain named Leslie Pindred, was destined to have a distinguished career with the Salvation Army, rising to the rank of Commissioner, and serving in key positions around the world. His message was just what I needed. I sat enthralled. Why, oh why, had no one told me this message before? I knew that the Lord Jesus Christ died on the cross, and I knew that I was a sinner, but I had never put the two facts together before. At last I realized what being a Christian was all about.

My mother was a believer and taught me the great stories of the Bible each night at bedtime. I knew all about Abraham, Isaac, and Jacob. I knew about David and Goliath, Moses, and Samuel, but I wasn't saved. I'm sure my mother thought I was, but somehow I hadn't grasped how to be born again. My parents had attended the Salvation Army when I was quite young. But my dad became a backslider – he no longer went to church, and didn't want mom to either. He lost touch with Christian values and behaviour.

I had been attending Sunday morning services and afternoon Sunday school at the Presbyterian Church just two blocks from home. Not because of any connection with God, but because it was the easiest way to get two points a week in Boy Scouts -- better than studying a lot of stuff and passing tests. I earned a Diploma, with a number of pretty seals on it for faithful attendance for several years. I learned respect for God and a lot of good things, but no one told me how to be saved, or if they did, I missed it. I can remember our big, completely bald, Scottish neighbour, Tom McNaughton, the church sexton, would reach down and twist my ear in a number of church services. He would say, "If you don't keep quiet, I'll have to throw ye oot!" He never did throw me "oot," but it was close.

When I was growing up, I tried to be good. Not always successfully.

But now the truth was being made plain to me. The sermon ended with an invitation to come forward to receive Christ as Lord and Saviour. My brother's girlfriend looked back over her shoulder and said, "Here comes Bert Morgan. He must be coming after Stan." I felt a little uncomfortable.

He was 'fishing' – a term Salvationists used for leading people to Christ in a prayer meeting. I was the fish.

I was sitting on the aisle seat. Bert knelt down beside me and put his arm around me. He asked, "Stan, do you pray?"

"Yes," I replied. I thought of how as I went to bed I often recited the old children's prayer my mother had taught me "Now I lay me down to sleep, I pray the Lord my soul to keep. If I should die before I wake, I pray the Lord my soul to take." It frightened me that I could die in my sleep at any moment. I also prayed when things got tough, like at exam time.

Bert interrupted my thoughts. "Stan, do you know the Lord Jesus Christ as your own personal Saviour?"

"No, I don't."

"Would you like to know Jesus as Lord and Saviour?"

"Yes, I would."

We went forward together to the penitent or mourner's bench. Bert led me in the sinner's prayer. He would say a phrase, I would repeat it.

"Dear Lord, I realize that I'm a sinner. I am sorry for my sins. I need your forgiveness. I want you to forgive me for Jesus' sake, because he died for me and took my place on Calvary's cross. Dear Jesus, I invite you to come into my heart and into my life to be my Lord and Saviour. In Jesus' name, Amen."

When I arrived home that night, my mother was anxious to know if I had enjoyed the service. When I told her about my conversion her eyes filled with tears. She had been praying for me.

As the days went by, I became aware of changes in my thinking and behaviour. I had been truly born again.

Prayers took on a new dimension and became a life-altering experience.

I began attending services at the Salvation Army three times each Sunday. I was sincere in seeking to live for the Lord and to learn how to do that. And sincere in my daily prayers that the Lord would bring Gwen and I together in marriage and in a life relationship with Him.

Gwen had been converted at age seven. She and her sisters Ruth (one year older) and Marjorie (two years younger) all went forward together to receive Christ in a Salvation Army service in Simcoe Ontario in 1931. All three served the Lord faithfully through their lifetimes. Gwen was there at every service along with her family. How wonderful it was to see her each week – but I was so shy I didn't know how to approach her other than to say hello. I felt so unworthy of her. I knew it would take God's intervention if we were to become friends and sweethearts. Boy, did I pray.

I wasn't very handsome, and there were better looking fellows interested in Gwen. What I didn't know was that Gwen had never dated anyone and that she was not quite sixteen. She looked older. She was her father's favourite daughter, and he didn't want her dating anyone. She was the most beautiful girl in the world to me.

How wonderful it was to see Gwen each week at Salvation Army meetings, but how frustrating to be so shy and unable to get to know her.

This went on for seven months. Then, one Sunday, a dozen of the young people's group got talking about the local Pentecostal church. We wondered if they really did roll on the floor and hang from the chandeliers. Someone thought it would be great to go as a group to find out. Gwen was interested in going and I realized this might be the opportunity I had been waiting and praying for. I could hardly wait.

We all walked together from the Salvation Army Hall to the Pentecostal Church. I made sure that I got close to Gwen. I summoned my courage. Sixty years later she remembered my words, "May I have the pleasure of sitting beside you?" Hers was: "Sure." And a great pleasure it was.

The people didn't roll on the floor nor hang from the chandeliers. They were very much like we were.

One song stuck with me:

> "Telephone to glory, oh, what joy divine,
> I can feel the current, moving on the line,
> Made by God the Father, for His loved and own,
> We may talk with Jesus, on the royal telephone."

God was answering prayer. I was connecting.

When the service was over, I asked Gwen if I could walk with her on the way back to the Salvation Army hall. She smiled and said, "Yes." Wow! I was thanking the Lord.

As we got within a couple of blocks from the Salvation Army Hall I knew it was now or never to take advantage of the opportunity the Lord had given me. I prayed. Would I be rejected? Would she say yes? I had to ask. Finally, somehow I was able to say it, "Can I come to visit you at your home sometime?"

Gwen's answer shocked me, "You will have to ask my mother." This was a formidable task for a super-shy 17 year-old. At least it wasn't a "No." And she hadn't said, "Talk to my father," which would have terrorized me. She was really saying yes. Double wow! Her mother said yes, too. Hallelujah! Thank you Lord!

The Lord had given me favour with Gwen and with her mother as well. Gwen's mom faced a real hurdle getting an okay from her husband. Even broaching the subject took real courage and finesse. The Lord gave Gwen's mom wisdom about our "date." She arranged a party with several neighbours and myself invited. Two of the local farm boys showed real interest in Gwen, and I was beginning to burn, especially when one of them took her outside to "count the stars" as a forfeit in a game we played. I was thinking "This is my date, and he is out there kissing my girl." Much later I found out they really did count the stars and didn't kiss at all. Her first kiss would be reserved for me. Oh, how I thank the Lord for that. What a treasure!

Gwen was just so wonderful to be with. Her hopes and dreams so mirrored mine. We talked about putting the Lord first, about our dreams for marriage, a family and a little white house. But we were now a nation at war. Gwen's older brother Bill was in the Army. My brother had joined the Navy. It would soon be my turn to serve.

When I turned eighteen I went to the Navy recruiting centre. They laughed at me. I was like the 97-pound weakling in the old Charles Atlas ads. How humiliating. They told me to go home and grow up. I took their advice – lifted weights, bulked up, and dated Gwen.

Gwen and I were born on the same date, two years apart. On our second birthday together I gave her an emerald ring. We knew it was an engagement ring, but didn't tell anyone. We were just 17 and 19. Later I replaced the emerald with a diamond.

When it came time to ask Gwen's father for permission to marry her, I knew it was possible that he might kill me. He was a powerful man, with a great temper. The first time I met him, he met me on-the-run, as I came up the sidewalk. He tackled me, gouged me, twisted me, thumped me, supposedly in fun. But I was getting the message, "Don't come back." No one would have been good enough for his favourite daughter. Even worse, Gwen's parents thought her older sister Ruth's boyfriend Len Goddard was the fair-haired boy. Len knew how to meet and get along with people. I was from the "north end" and my communication skills were sadly lacking.

Well, I made an appointment to talk with Gwen's dad. You can believe I did a lot of praying. We sat opposite each other about ten feet apart. I began, "Mr. Aspden, I think you have a wonderful family. You have done an excellent job raising your children, and I think Gwen is the best one." I blurted out the rest of my memorized speech. "I want you to know that I love Gwen with all of my heart. I promise you that I will honour her, be true to her, protect her and never do anything to hurt her. I would like to ask for her hand in marriage. I hope you will approve of our marriage."

There was a brief moment of silence, and then Gwen's dad rose to his feet and moved quickly towards me. I really thought he was going to fill me in (a Navy expression for beating me up.) Instead he reached out his arms and embraced me. He kissed me full on the lips. I was embarrassed, greatly relieved and happy beyond words.

Drawing Souls To Christ

Gwen was waiting just outside in the hallway. She cried with joy. Again God answered prayer.

We were married Saturday, April 04, 1942 at 4 p.m. at St. Andrews Presbyterian Church in Hamilton, Ontario. Gwen and I had attended several Salvation Army weddings. To us, they lacked the dignity of the church wedding. Our wedding was everything Gwen and I wanted it to be.

We had a few wonderful months together before the Navy called me to active service. Leaving my new bride and heading alone for the East Coast was a shock. We didn't know if we would ever see each other again, or if I would ever get to hold the child we had conceived.

Chapter 2

World War II, the Canadian Navy

Gwen and I wrote to each other every day, sometimes twice. We prayed and prayed and prayed.

When we were at sea, I would sometimes go for weeks waiting for mail call, then get twenty or thirty letters at once. Gwen numbered the letters so that I could read them in sequence.

On July 9, 1943 I received an alarming telegram. There had been severe complications in childbirth. The doctors did not expect Gwen or the baby to survive. They requested immediate compassionate leave for me to come home. I had felt uneasiness about Gwen's pregnancy and had previously talked with the Navy Chaplain about this. He knew all about the situation and granted immediate leave. Within hours I was on the train from Halifax to Hamilton, a 28 hour journey. I prayed non-stop all the way. Gwen was just nineteen.

When I arrived home in Hamilton I could not see anyone I knew at the station, but suddenly Gwen's younger sister Marge jumped on my back and shouted in my ear, "Gwen is O.K. and your daughter Marjorie is O.K." God had answered prayer. That was where I really learned how to pray. Somehow I believed they would be okay. I don't remember crying until I knew they were okay.

I went immediately to the hospital to see Gwen and Margie. Now we were three. How wonderful it was to see Gwen's beautiful smile again. She had been in convulsions with toxemia and unconscious for 48 hours. Margie weighed in at 10 pounds, 2 ounces. It had been a forceps birth. Gwen had really suffered, but she didn't say one word of complaint. That was Gwen. She just smiled. How glad we were to be together. It would be a month before she could walk again.

My ten day leave was quickly over. Gwen insisted in getting out of the hospital the day before I left. She cried until they allowed her to leave. It sure was hard to return to the Navy.

When I got back to Cornwallis Naval Base, I learned of an Engineer's Writers Course in Toronto. It was a 12-week course. Wow! Twelve weeks in Toronto just fifty miles from home. I applied immediately.. I really didn't care about being an Engineer's Writer. I thought that was kind of sissy stuff, but I wanted to be with Gwen.

When my request came before engineer officers Lieutenant B. Booth and Warrant Engineer Johnny Jones, they asked me about my ability to type 60 words per minute and write letters, etc. They looked at each other and nodded – then said, "Come up to this office at 1 p.m. tomorrow. We will try you out and then see about you attending the course."

The next day at 1 p.m., I was there with bells on. I knocked on the door and a Stoker opened the door. "Oh, you must be the new man."

"No, I am not the new man. I am here to see about getting the Engineers writing course."

"Oh, no, you are not. You are taking my place and I am going to Halifax." What a revolting development! Those stinkers! The last thing I wanted was to be stuck in a shore job at Cornwallis. I hated the place.

As the weeks went by, Gwen got stronger. I realized if they moved to near the base, I could live with them ashore when I wasn't on duty.

I prayed a lot about it, and the Lord led me to accommodation in a farmhouse about a mile from the Naval Base. Mrs. Henshaw was a fine Christian lady, and she was good to us. Each Sunday we had a wonderful dinner with her and then sang hymns around the old organ as she played.

HMCS Cornwallis was the biggest naval training facility in the Commonwealth, so many friends from Hamilton came through for their orientation. They were always welcome at our place. Gwen's dad enlisted as a chief motor mechanic and he enjoyed his visits to our place.

Later, my two bosses were assigned to ships. No longer needing my services, they got me into the Engineer's Writer's

Course. So it was back home for Gwen and Margie and off to Toronto for me.

In Toronto I went door-to-door looking for a place for my wife and daughter to stay. I was praying continually. A young war bride talked her mom and dad into letting us stay with them. The Banks were like family to us. God had provided an answer to prayer.

After my course was completed, I went to sea as part of the commissioning crew of the frigate HMCS Sussexvale! That was another adventure in Christ.

During wartime you always face the unknown. You never knew if or when you will get home again.

Gwen and I took advantage of every possible opportunity to be together. One time my ship docked in Saint John New Brunswick. I got a 48 hour leave, spent 44 hours on the train and four with Gwen. It was worth it.

Life onboard a ship on active duty is tough enough. Living openly as a Christian brought additional conflict. Just as children ridicule and bully someone different, so a group of unsaved men react to one who stands for God. Boots tossed at those who kneeled to pray were a favourite, or unexpected jostling. One night a Leading Stoker named Leclair, a professional wrestler in civilian life, came aboard ship drunk and threw a vicious elbow smash into my hammock. He couldn't tell and didn't care whether I was in it or not. I thank the Lord that I was sitting on a locker at the time, but I saw it. I wondered why he did it. I really liked him and had tried to be a friend.

In the Salvation Army you were taught to "show your colours," to stand true to the Lord. So I knelt at a lower bunk to pray. Within minutes my fellow sailors were shouting against me and throwing things at me. I went to see a Navy Chaplain about it to ask his advice. He said, "Why don't you just pray in your bunk so that no one knows what you are doing?"

In contrast, when the Commanding Officer of HMCS Stadacona barracks in Halifax heard that a sailor who knelt to pray was ridiculed, and had boots thrown at him, he went to the barracks and called all the men together. "I understand that there is one amongst you who kneels to pray each day. Will that man please step forward?" The man stepped forward not knowing what to expect.

Then the Commanding Officer said, "I think your praying is

highly commendable. We all need prayer. Would you be so kind as to pray for all of us right now?"

What a beautiful gesture! There was no further problem for him.

At Bon Echo Provincial Park in 2001

Recently I was preaching at Bon Echo Provincial Park and mentioned this story. Afterwards a man came to me and said, "I was one of those who threw boots at people like you in the Navy. But it convicted me of my need of Christ and led me to the Lord. I have been a preacher now for fifty-five years."

Life at sea had its ups and downs, especially in rough weather. North Atlantic storms usually last about five days. There was one blessing; enemy submarines stayed deep, they couldn't operate at torpedoing depth in heavy seas. During the worst storms the entire crew would be seasick. Some mess. Even our captain 'The Mad Spaniard' got seasick.

My "station" was in the engine room. I had to record each order that came from the captain at the bridge and the time it was obeyed. When the Captain phoned he mumbled as though his mouth was full of marbles. The E.O. (Engineering Officer) would cover one ear and answer. He was hard-of-hearing. He would listen for about a sentence then hand the phone to me to decipher. Oh joy! Somehow I had to pick up on what had already been said and relay the message to the Engineering Officer. I did a lot of praying and guessing. As far as I know I never guessed wrong. We all survived.

Action stations can go on for hours or days. It was a continual fireworks display up top, but we could not see it. We could only smell it and hear it in the engine room. Our twin 4.7 forward guns made a nice boom, boom. One fired an armour piercing shell and the other a high explosive round.

Directly above us was the rear 12 pounder. It just went BANG. The air scoops above deck sucked in the smell of burned cordite and the noise reverberated in them. You covered your ears if your hands were free and stretched your jaw to lessen the danger to your ears.

Then when we laid down a pattern of depth charges, the explosions nearly lifted the stern of our ship out of the water.

Once in a while I would sneak up the ladder and take a quick peek to see the display.

We were at sea three to five weeks without seeing harbour. We were refuelled at sea, but not re-provisioned. Seasick cooks short on supplies don't do too good a job.

Every Friday when we were in harbour we had fish and chips. What a scramble for the grub there was that day. But there was no ketchup. Some of us chipped in and bought ketchup ashore. For some reason, those who did not help to pay for the ketchup seemed to use more than those who did.

My hammock was with 43 others in the Stoker's Mess. It was in the bow, below the water line, a pie shaped space the size of a large living room. Our lockers doubled as seats during the day. When we cut through ice it made an interesting scraping sound.

Once, near Bermuda, we escorted the hospital ship Louis Pasteur onto a coral reef. We banged our own ship up so badly that we were in dry dock in Bermuda for almost a month getting repairs. Being cooped up at sea is bad enough, in dry dock it is worse. One night the discussion turned hostile towards me, because of my faith. I prayed "Lord, please help me!" God's answer was immediate.

Pickard was the biggest man aboard, well over six-foot with almost three feet wide shoulders. He was blonde and looked like Joe Palooka the boxing champion in the comics. He commanded respect and attention. He was a man of few words, but when he spoke he meant it.

"OK, you guys, you are making fun of Crookall because he prays. When we were over in Portsmouth harbour and "Jerry" was dropping bombs on us, which one of you did not pray?" Silence replaced the jeering. No one spoke.

"OK then, I want you to know that I stand with Crookall. If any of you have anything to say to him, you say it through me. Get that?" Wow, that ended the matter for as long as I was aboard that ship. Thank you Lord!

Pickard was from Hamilton as I was. After the war, he owned and operated a driving school. I went to see him and thanked him again. He said, "It was not anything." I told him it sure meant a lot to me.

Aboard ship I shared an office (about four feet by eight) with the Engineer Officer. It was a place of refuge and a storm shelter for me. When it got real rough at sea, I slept there on the floor. Being closer to the middle of the ship than my bunk, it was a little smoother ride.

After taking the Engineers Writers Course in Toronto I was now a Stoker 1/C E.W., or Engineer Writer. I was the E.O's secretary and right-hand man. It was a good job. There was only one E.W. per ship. It was also a position of confidence for I was in the know about almost everything the Engineer Officer knew.

One day, as I was praying, I told the Lord that there were not many Christians in this Navy. Not long after this, we were in Halifax harbour. It was 11 p.m. We were to set sail at midnight for Londonderry, Ireland. Suddenly a signal was received. I was to be drafted off the ship immediately. Wow! It took some scrambling to get my gear together. I was sorry to leave my fellow shipmates especially when I had no idea where I was going. Little did I realize what adventure the Lord had in store for me.

When I got to the manning depot, I was surprised to find another E.W. was on the draft with me. Harry and I were bewildered. Which ship would require two Engineer Writers? It must be a capital (large) ship and probably headed for Japan and a whole new war over there. We looked out in the harbour and there were two capital ships, the cruiser Uganda and an Aircraft Carrier. It would be one or the other!

The Stoker Petty Officer in charge of the drafting office was Stan Rosart from Hamilton. His brother Ray was married to Gwen's best friend Barbara. I knew Stan. I had looked him up aboard the old American four-stacker destroyer HMCS Hamilton a year or two ago. But Stan could not tell us anything.

The next day the Cruiser was gone. It had left during the night as most ships did to avoid submarine detection. It was March 1945 and the War in Europe was looking better for us. So we figured we were going to be redeployed to Japan on the Carrier. Wrong!

When Stan Rosart handed us our assignment papers, we could not believe it. We were going to Ottawa to work at Naval Service Headquarters. We would work nine to five in an office each day and live ashore. It might just be possible to have Gwen and Margie come to live with me. Wow!

At Ottawa I was placed in charge of compiling a list of all ships in the Canadian Navy and making up charts to show the days at sea and in harbour for the period of hostilities from September 1939 until the present. Harry was to be my assistant. We had to work in a huge office with about a hundred women. Harry thought he had gone to Heaven.

Later I was moved to the main Engineers' Office where I worked with Captain Porteous, Commander Wood, Lieutenant Herbert Thomas and Warrant Officer Ernie Brown and two secretaries. It was the top job in the Navy for an Engineer Writer. Why me? Was this part of God's plan?

An even bigger surprise came on the morning I started my new job. I overheard Lt Thomas say to a visiting Engineer Officer, "May I ask you a personal question?"

The officer said, "Why certainly, go ahead."

"If you believe the Bible to be true and you live according to its teachings, then at the end of life you find out that the Bible is not true, would you have lost anything?" (I almost fell off my chair).

Drawing Souls To Christ

The answer came slowly and deliberately, "Why no, I would not have lost anything."

Then Lt. Thomas said, "Now let's look at it this way. Supposing you don't believe the Bible is true and you don't live accordingly to its teachings. At the end of life you find out that the Bible is true. What then, will you have lost something?"

Again the answer came slowly and thoughtfully, "I will have lost everything."

I could hardly believe my ears. I was in the highest office of the Engineer Room Branch of the Canadian Navy. I was hearing an Engineer at the top witness for Christ to a fellow officer. God was showing me that He had His people at the top. God had answered my prayer so beautifully. But there was more.

As soon as Lt Thomas was finished I almost climbed over my desk to get to him. "Sir, I could not help overhearing what you said to that fellow officer. I am thrilled to know that you are an active witnessing Christian."

"Oh, tut, tut, Crookall, Captain Porteous is a devout Roman Catholic, and Commander Wood is an evangelist. He spends all his spare time preaching in evangelistic crusades around Ottawa."

I reported to Warrant Officer Ernie Brown. I liked him. One day he was rushed to the hospital with a burst appendix. Peritonitis had set in. His life hung in the balance. I thought, what if Ernie dies and does not know the Lord Jesus Christ?

After prayer, I decided to go and see Ernie in the hospital. Ernie's wife was there. That did not make it any easier. Remember I was super shy. I asked the Lord to help me and I began to witness to my superior officer. Suddenly he exclaimed, "Crookall, are you a Christian?"

"Yes, Sir, I am."

"And you are trying to win me to Christ?"

"Yes, Sir, I am."

Then a big smile, "I am a Christian; you don't have to win me." Wow! A load lifted off my shoulders. All five officers were outstanding Christians. God does have a sense of humour. God is concerned about the little people. He answered my prayer so gloriously.

I prayed with Ernie and his wife in the hospital. Again God heard the prayers of His people and Ernie Brown was restored to health quickly. In those days that was a miracle. Most did not recover from peritonitis, and we all knew it. To God be the glory!

In Ottawa it was almost impossible to find an apartment to rent. Someone at Headquarters told me about a place. I got it, and Gwen and Margie moved to Ottawa to be with me. Margie was now two. I had been away so long she didn't know me. That hurt. But it did not take long till she was calling me "Daddy Boy" and all was well.

We found Ottawa III Corps of the Salvation Army to be a very special place. Worshipping there, I was challenged to commit my life to serve the Lord full-time when the war was over. But I had different plans. Gwen and I wanted to settle down in Hamilton with a little family and roam no more. I had seen enough of the outside world. I wanted to go home.

While at Digby Nova Scotia, I had preached my first sermon. When I got home they had heard about this and asked me to preach at our home Salvation Army Corps (church).

When I gave the altar call (an invitation to become a Christian) two people responded and came forward to kneel at the front and pray. As they came forward I heard the Lord say; "This is what I want you to do." The tears came. It was such an honour to be called. Yet I was not ready to say yes. It would be a struggle for several months. Then one Sunday morning when I was alone in our little Ottawa apartment, I knelt and surrendered to the Lord to go wherever He wanted me to go and do whatever He wanted me to do.

Immediately my heart was filled with peace and joy. I was on cloud nine for weeks. Gwen was willing to support me in whatever God called me to do.

George and Elsie Heron were in the Air Force. They were planning to enter the Salvation Army Training College in Toronto in September 1945. My discharge had not come up yet. Could we make it, too? Again we prayed.

Lt. Thomas spoke to me about staying on at Headquarters when the war was over. "You have four years war time service which counts for eight years. Twelve more years and you will have a pension for life. We will give you a good job here and a higher rank and better pay. How about it? "Well, Sir," I began. "I appreciate your kind and generous offer, but I feel led of the Lord to go to Bible school and become a minister of the Gospel."

Drawing Souls To Christ

Lt.Thomas was surprised and moved. "By all means, Crookall, ministry is the highest calling. Do that with my blessing."

Come September, my discharge wasn't through. My boss arranged for me to be transferred to Toronto to HMCS York and have leave to attend Bible school until my discharge came through three months later. What a blessing!

Stan and Gwen Training College Graduation

Chapter 3

The Salvation Army

Training College

Our first day at the Salvation Army Training College was nearly our last. Adjusting to the Salvation Army made the Navy
look easy. In the military, if you want to question something,
you begin with "Permission to speak freely, sir." In the Salvation Army (back then) it was obey without question.

Gwen and I entered training together. Children were not
allowed in residence, we had to leave our daughter with her
grandmother, and see her every second Saturday afternoon. It
was going to be hard.

**(left-to-right) Grandma Aspden, Margie, and Gwen
at Training College, Toronto, for her bi-weekly visit**

Glen, a fellow student, and I helped out at one of the Toronto churches. We got to know Henry, who had played in the Salvation Army Staff Band in London, England, but who no longer served the Lord, and rarely attended church. We prayed for him and decided to visit, to bring him back to the faith. .

Well, the Major in charge of that church said "NO." Instead of taking us to Henry's house, he dropped us off at a street of his choosing, and told us to go door to door, then he drove off. Glen and I looked at each other and decided to go and see Old Backslider first.

The next day we were both on the carpet at the College. The major had reported us. We were learning. I was twenty-two and Glen was eighteen. I felt it was my fault. We just did not want to see that loveable old character go to Hell. He had told us about things General Booth, the founder of the Salvation Army, had said. Things I remember to this day.

We would learn that the informer system was far more extensive than we imagined.

As a boy I had grown up in the tough North End of Hamilton. We did not honor squealers. That was not the way I would have treated the insubordination if I were the major, but I guess he was protecting his own hide too.

Did I have to adjust my thinking? I certainly had to be more careful and think things through before taking action. It all seemed like small potatoes after dealing with life and death in the North Atlantic.

That was not the last time I was on the carpet. One staff, Colonel (then Major) Arthur Moulton, was a real help, and became a life long friend. Whenever I was on the carpet, he would tell me "Don't take it too seriously. The Army is changing and things will get better. Just hang in there and smile." He made me feel that he was on my side.

Becoming a Gospel Artist

The world is shocked when great Christians fail. We all fail at times, but in different ways. Our lives may be shattered temporarily or permanently by the injuries inflicted by believers whom we loved and respected. We can allow these experiences to break us or make us stronger.

Sometimes God allows us to see failure in great leaders so that we will get our eyes off them, and realize we must trust the

Lord and depend wholly upon Him.

After graduation, I looked to my new Divisional Commander to be a mentor and encourager. I had great respect for him and his abilities as a preacher. The way he read the Scriptures in a service influenced me to read the Bible and give emphasis to it as it was the most important part of the meeting. I will be forever grateful to him for that.

But beyond his skill as a preacher, he was a thorn in my flesh and a constant source of discouragement. He blasted me once a month for the fifteen months I served in my first Salvation Army Corps. It seemed he thought that everything I did was wrong. I remember not a single word of encouragement, and he never prayed with me during that time.

Each time I took my monthly report to the Divisional Office, Gwen knew that I would come home discouraged. I tried to sneak in, drop off the report with the secretary, and get out before the Divisional Commander knew I was there. It never worked. Sometimes I wondered if the secretary had a hidden buzzer to warn of my arrival, like bank tellers have to report robberies. The Divisional Commander would come to the door of his office, and say, "Oh, Captain I want to see you." Shudder. "Come into my office! Shut the door! Sit down!" Then he would blast me. "Blast" is a naval term for scolding.

The Divisional Commander seemed to have a system of informers the Kremlin would die for who revealed to him my every move -- except what I did right. In addition to this, my monthly reports were compared with those of my predecessors and circled in red where mine did not measure up.

One day our dear old Corps Sergeant Major said, "Well, Captain we have more people attending our services now than any time in the past fifteen years."

"Oh, no, Brother Brown, you are mistaken about that!" I said.

Brown replied, "How do you know? I was here and you were not."

"But the Divisional Commander's statistics show otherwise" I countered.

With a wry smile the Sergeant Major said, "They must have been counting ears instead of noses."

Wow! I really was not a failure after all. I included this in my next monthly report. My boss still wasn't impressed.

It is unlikely to happen today, but in my first church, the congregation asked me to make the services longer. Rather than more sermon, I turned to chalk drawing. I tried stick-men Bible stories and never looked back. I didn't have to jump off the platform like my predecessor that the boss so liked. I was myself as a chalk-drawing evangelist. My stickmen would do the jumping for me.

I used coloured chalk on white flipchart paper. Other artists were using white chalk on blackboards. It was fun and I found a natural humour in the stickmen drawings which brought new life into old stories and with God's blessing made them unforgettable.

Don't Rock The Boat

Growing in grace takes time and I had a lot of growing to do.

Most Salvation Army officers had grown up in the Salvation Army. Many were the children of officer parents. They knew the rules. Don't rock the boat. Obey orders without question.

I had taken many orders in my four years in the Navy, and most of them made sense. If an order was good, I obeyed it. If it didn't make sense or was down right stupid, I questioned it. I rocked the boat. For example, my commander planned a meeting of the four Salvation Army corps (churches) for Christmas Sunday evening. He told me to be an usher. Then the minister from the largest Protestant church in Saint John asked me if I would preach at his Christmas Sunday evening service, to be broadcast province-wide by radio.

I accepted. Preaching the Gospel in a liberal church with 1,000 people attending and thousands listening in by radio seemed to me a better way to reach souls for Christ than being an usher – plus it would give the Salvation Army recognition.

I expected the Divisional Commander would be excited when I told him. Indeed, he was: with anger. "Captain, it is more important for you to be an usher at our service than it is for you to preach at their service."

I knew if someone else from a liberal church preached that night there would be no Gospel in the message. I saw it as a great soul-saving venture. I was reluctant.

I said, "Brigadier, would you phone the minister and explain that to him?" There was a spluttering at the other end of the line as the Divisional Commander emphatically said, "Certainly not." My response was, "Then I just can't tell him either, and I will go to that service to preach and arrive at your service one hour later, in time to take up the offering."

At the Salvation Army training college, two top radio announcers had taught us how to speak on the radio. As "extra duty" I did morning devotions on the radio,, and really loved it. I also participated in the weekly interdenominational ministerial meeting . I was the only war veteran, and the other ministers were intrigued by and appreciative of my war service record. They were more helpful to me than my Divisional Commander was.

It was a great service with a huge church packed full of people, and that vast radio land audience. I was able to get back in time to work as an usher at the Salvation Army meeting.

SAILORS' NIGHT

Part of my reward for this adventure was to be reassigned to a smaller, more out-of-the-way parish – the church equivalent of being exiled to Siberia.

Parrsboro, Nova Scotia, was a quaint little seafaring town of 2,000 souls. In the Nineteenth Century, it had been a busy seaport famous for the three-masted schooner ships built there. But now the harbour was a place of desolation. Most men worked at the coal mines fifty miles away at Springhill or at the lumber camps and just got home week ends.

The small Parrsboro Salvation Army Corps had amazingly sent three cadets to the Officers Training Gwen and I were on. One was Ed.Read, who became a Commissioner in time and well known and highly esteemed around the world. He would probably have been considered for appointment to General and leader of the Army world wide if his health were not in question. This was indeed an amazing accomplishment for anyone from Parrsboro. The rank of Commissioner is equivalent to a Four Star General in the Army.

Parrsboro Corps had not had a married couple as Corps Officers for some time as finances were poor. The Divisional Commander was aware of this, but made no effort to help. Our total salary as Captains was $17.50 per week, in 1948. We paid all expenses from the offering before we could draw any salary. There was no contribution from head office. In two months, our total take-home pay was six cents. When discharged from

Drawing Souls To Christ

the Navy, I had $1500.00 saved, enough to purchase a brand new Chevrolet. When we left Parrsboro we were considerably less affluent. We had 2 small children, Margie 4 and Paul just three weeks old, when we arrived. We lived on boiled beans and bread. About once a month we were invited out to dinner. How we looked forward to a good meal.

Food was not our top priority, ministry was. We felt a burden for the people, but how could we reach them? Gwen and I prayed about what we should do. Finally, we thought about a special "Sailors' Night" service. We couldn't afford to pay a preacher so we decided to announce a mystery guest speaker, a former member of the Canadian Navy who would preach in full navy uniform. That would be me. We hoped they would not guess right. And no one did.

There were four or five old retired sea captains from the town's boom days. I called to see each one and borrowed port and starboard lanterns, flags, oars, a ships bell, etc. I borrowed a beautiful painting of a navy corvette (a smaller version of a battleship) from the local post office and painted a replica about 8 feet long to decorate the front of the platform. There were life preservers, crossed oars on each post. We advertised, including a large sign in the town's only drug store. The town was buzzing.

Sailors' Night, Sergeant Major Mrs. Lovelady, Captain and Mrs. Stan Crookall)

Finally, sailors' night arrived. It was snowing and windy. I wore my navy uniform, but with my Salvation Army trousers, cap and overcoat, and went out to the open-air street service that preceded the church service. We all then went back to the church, and I rushed upstairs to our living quarters above the hall and donned my Navy bell bottom trousers and cap.

We had a full house, for the first time in many years. As I walked down the aisle the devil was suggesting to me that this was the most stupid thing I had ever done. I was wishing there had been a place to hide. I prayed silently. I rang the ship's bell to begin the service, and turned around to face the congregation.

A reporter from the Halifax Herald newspaper was positioned in the centre of the sanctuary--a big impressive man. He jumped to his feet and began applauding. In seconds everyone was standing and doing the same. Hallelujah! That broke the ice so to speak for me. I was now able to relax and lead the service. Of course we sang the sailors' hymn, Eternal Father, Strong to save......

My sermon text was Acts 27: 29 "Then fearing lest they should have fallen upon rocks, they cast four anchors out of the stern, and wished for the day." The four anchors I preached about were GRACE, FAITH, LOVE, and HOPE.

Bless the Lord! The Lord made it a great service. I am confident that those who attended will never forget it. When the invitation to receive Christ as Saviour and Lord was given, a sailor was one who responded. How many others did only eternity will reveal.

From that night on, the attendance at Sunday evening services doubled. The Halifax Herald and the Salvation Army WAR CRY carried Photos and reports. Our Divisional Commander phoned to express his appreciation. To God be the Glory!

I got to know the reporter. By this time, we couldn't afford to have a car, so he loaned us his new Mercury every Wednesday to do errands.

Gwen was able to lead a young mother who worked at the hotel next door to receive Christ as Saviour. Gwen also spent time with the teenagers and we had a small but great group. I wrote a play on the book of Esther that our teens just loved. We had a number of rehearsals and then the performance. It was something that we all enjoyed along with those who came to see the production.

Drawing Souls To Christ

Every young pastor learns some things the hard way. Looking back you can see the stepping stones in God's great plan for each life.

After nine months at Parrsboro we were told we would be moved to Sackville, New Brunswick. where we could receive our salary again. The townspeople at Parsborro took up a petition requesting that we be allowed to remain there. Wow! This must have come as a real surprise to the Divisional Commander. It certainly did to us. The D.C. asked me to arrange a meeting with the people involved. At that meeting the D.C. told the crowd that we were being moved so that we would get our salary at the Sackville Corps--but if they would commit themselves to support us in Parsborro, he would allow us to remain there. A vote was taken and the people decided they could not make that commitment. It was part of God's plan.

What did we learn at Parrsboro? Many things. When you pray and mean it, for His Glory the Lord will make a way where there is no way. We also learned that as you pray the Lord will lead you in doing the thing that will reach the people where you are "drawing them to Christ."

GOD'S PLAN FOR US AT SACKVILLE

How could two towns 70 miles apart be so different? Parrsboro was struggling to stay alive, Sackville, home to Mount Allison University, was alive and well. The Salvation Army hall with living quarters above was smaller at Sackville, but warmer and cozier. The town was vibrant with university students, one of whom was my cousin Lorrie Wragg from Oshawa. Lor went on to become coroner in Chicago and later a family physician in San Francisco.

Our main evangelistic outreach was to university students downtown at the Four Corners in front of the drug store. Each Saturday evening we drew stick-men chalk drawings to tell the Bible story. Crowds of students gathered and listened with great respect. Some of the theology students stood with us. Some students came to the Sunday services. One became a missionary to France and was supported financially by Evangel Baptist Church in Hamilton, Ontario where I would become pastor some ten years later. What a surprise that was.

At the same time Pastor Perry F, Rockwood, of a Presbyterian church in Halifax, N.S. left his church to start The Peoples

Church. Perry denounced liberalism in the church and was defrocked by the Presbytery. He became a radio voice reaching multitudes for Christ even today in his old age through The Old Time Gospel Hour. He ministered with tears in his voice and fearlessly preached on an ever expanding radio network. It was my privilege to meet Perry F. Rockwood at his church in Halifax while I was with Gospel Light in the mid 1960s. The Greek word "doulos" (Bond servant) really applies to his life. I wish there were more like him.

Ken Martin, a theology student and World War II veteran attended our Saturday open air services, and became a regular attendee at our Salvation Army Corps. Ken personally challenged each of his theology professors at Mount A and found that not one was born again. Several theology students transferred to Evangelical Seminaries and Bible Colleges.

At Sackville I met Dr. A.K. Herman, pastor of a large Baptist Church there. He was like a father in the faith to me. A chalk artist evangelist had ministered in his church and I asked Brother Herman if I could see some of the drawings he had left behind. Pastor Herman invited me and our congregation to attend a Missions Week with the Rev. Harold Germaine and Gordon Bishop of the Sudan Interior Mission. They would show a film each night. Most missionaries I had heard were dry as sticks, but the films sounded interesting. I was not prepared for the sacrificial challenge they would give.

The Salvation Army book of Doctrine stated: With respect to the heathen, we can safely leave them to the mercy of God. They did not believe that the heathen are lost. The S.I.M. boys sure did. Here were two talented, dedicated men who left family at home to go to the heart of Africa to declare the unsearchable riches of Christ. I was blown away by their challenge. I could never be the same again. When I got home and told Gwen all about what I had heard she too was shaken. The next night Gwen went with me. Ken and Verna Martin went too.

No one could sing like Harold Germaine. When he sang,
"Is your all on the altar of sacrifice laid?
Your all does the Spirit Control?
You can never be blessed, or have peace and sweet rest
Till you yield him your body and soul!"

Drawing Souls To Christ

We could not hold back the tears. People were saved each night. Believers were challenged. Ken and Verna Martin and Gwen and I attended each service. We knew that on the closing night there would be an opportunity to respond to the challenge to be willing to serve the Lord wherever He called us to serve. Both couples had been very seriously praying about this commitment and were prepared to make it publicly. It was not an easy decision. It involved the possibility of great sacrifice. It involved the possibility of having to leave our children at home in Canada while serving as missionaries in Africa for a five year term. Both couples had two small children.

When the invitation was given on the last night of the meetings, all four of us responded. There was a prayer of commitment and dedication.

Early the next morning there was a phone call from our Salvation Army Divisional Commander. Someone had called him from Sackville. He was angry and felt we had disgraced the Salvation Army by responding to the altar call to show our willingness to serve the Lord in Africa. He demanded that I take the train to Saint John to discuss the matter immediately.

Next day, on the carpet again, I told the D.C. that we felt led of the Lord to apply to be missionaries. If accepted, we would resign from the Salvation Army. The D.C. told me that it didn't work that way. We would have to resign. first before we could apply to the mission. I replied that we would pray about the matter for two weeks and then respond as we felt led of the Lord and according to the Salvation Army rules.

In the mean time, there was an Officers' Council coming up in Halifax with the Canadian Chief of Staff Commissioner Baugh. The former Commissioner Ben Orames was a gentle, Godly man. The new one was abrupt and irritable. He had a wooden leg that did not bend, and a disposition to match. There was a question box provided at the meetings. You did not have to give your name. But our question would identify us easily. It was; "If an officer is interested in missionary work with the Salvation Army in Africa, what is the proper procedure to follow in making application?"

Commissioner Baugh read the question, and then he sort of growled, cleared his throat and stated, "It is not up to this officer to determine where he will serve. That is up to us at headquarters to decide. We may decide to send him to China or

Japan or India etc. The officer should present himself for missionary service and leave the choice as to where he will serve up to us."

Gwen and I thought about the Salvation Army's lack of concern for our personal welfare at Parrsboro. We wondered about similar treatment in a distant land. Our burden was for Africa not somewhere someone else may select. As we prayed, we concluded that we should do what our D.C. stated, so we wrote a letter of resignation to the Salvation Army and a letter of application to the Sudan Interior Mission.

We got an immediate frantic reply from our Salvation Army divisional commander. He did not want to accept our resignation. He urged us to reconsider. Then we began to hear from the Field Secretary and others. Brigadier Green offered us a corps in the Hamilton Ontario division real close to home. His daughter Marion was a good friend in our college days. She probably put in a good word for us. The Sudan Interior Mission's response took longer, and was negative -- we failed the medical exam. We were deeply disappointed. Our families were greatly relieved.

We realized later that Africa was for us like Abrahams test to slay his son Isaac -- a test of commitment and faith, but the sacrifice was not required.

I shall be eternally grateful for what the Salvation Army taught me about evangelism and getting out into the market place to win the lost to Christ. I also learned that Christian leaders need to be good leaders, not just good preachers.

Chapter 4

The challenge
of missions

In 1946 while in Bible College in my daily devotional reading this verse, Isaiah 1:25, stood out to me one day. "I will turn my hand upon you and will surely purge away all thy dross and take away all thy tin."

I didn't understand it. As I checked the Bible commentaries, I learned that it revealed God as the refiner, like a refiner of silver. Great heat was required to melt the metal so impurities would come to the surface to be drawn off. This would leave the metal pure and fit for use. Wow! I shuddered. What would I have to go through in order to be fit for the Master's use?

How many once-great Sunday school teachers, choir members, and Christian workers of every kind have you met who could not stand the fire and quit? The bitterness they retain festers into a self-destructive force bringing gloom and heartache. But if we allow ourselves to be "refined," we experience joy, love and hope.

Having resigned from the Salvation Army, we were back at home in Hamilton. It was 1949. My brother Roy had a taxi business and I tried that for a few weeks, but both he and I soon realized that was not for me. I worked at a gas station, and then got a good job at Westinghouse. We still felt called to be missionaries.

FINDING A WONDERFUL CHURCH –
PHILPOT TABERNACLE

By this time we had found Philpot Tabernacle. The prayer by Dr. Peter Hoogendam, their pastor, at a Youth for Christ Rally led Gwen and me to a Tuesday evening prayer meeting at Philpot. It was the prayers we heard there and the preaching of the Word that led us to leave the Salvation Army and join Philpot Church. We thank God for that great privilege. When Pastor Hoogendam stood in a Sunday service to pray and looked heavenward beyond the beautiful glass dome of the sanctuary it was like a glimpse into the glory of Heaven itself. To sit under his teaching and preaching ministry was better than attending a seminary. He always spoke for exactly 30 minutes and you wished he would never stop. Peter and Millie Hoogendam both loved Gwen. They recognized her for the treasure she is. We felt that was where we belonged.

The church's founder, Dr. P. W. Philpot had served as a Salvation Army Officer for many years, rising to the rank of Colonel. He was awarded a gold watch for outstanding service by people in the community where he ministered. Those over him in the Salvation Army told him he could not accept the watch. This was just the final straw of restrictions that hindered his ministry, so he resigned from the Salvation Army and began work fulltime as an evangelist. He would conduct tent meetings which lasted several months. In each area there were so many converts that new churches were formed to serve them. These new churches became a new denomination known as "The Associated Gospel Churches of Canada."

The music and singing under the leadership of Bill Lawson was as good as it gets, with piano, organ and orchestra. When we sang "At Calvary," written by a former pastor of the church, it was a never to be forgotten experience. This is what Church should be like. We looked forward to every service and did not want to miss any.

THE INCORRIGIBLE BOY'S CLASS AT PHILP0T

I became assistant superintendent of the Sunday School at Philpot, and was given a class of boys that everyone else had given up on. There were 12 of them, aged, 12 to 14, whose purpose in attending seemed to be to make the teacher's life miserable. They would test anyone's commitment. I sensed that the Superintendent could hardly wait to see what would happen. The boys were from the neighborhood, which was downtown and rough. They were not from Christian families. It would require a lot of prayer and Divine Guidance. It was clearly a challenge. They would need a lot of love. They needed to learn that the joy of the Lord is more fun than mischief.

We used the first session to get acquainted and plan. I asked what they thought the class should be like? What our objectives should be? What about special reward times for good attendance and progress? Would they like to go to a hockey game, play baseball, etc? They decided that when it was fun time we would have fun and parties, but when it was Sunday study time we would study the exciting Bible lessons and learn about prayer and how to apply the Bible to daily living. We planned our first party for just a few weeks away. Our goal was to be the best class in the Sunday School. Wow! They were excited.

We also agreed I would visit each home. If a boy missed a Sunday I would phone the parents. If he missed two Sundays I would visit at the home. Attendance was no problem. We took in a great hockey game as a class. We had hotdogs, pop, ice cream, cookies etc. after the game at our house. We had some great Sunday School lessons. Within a few weeks Evangelist Dr. Hyman J. Appleman came to our church and spoke to the Sunday School and the whole class got saved. To God be the Glory! How great is our God!

A Sunday School class involves sacrifice of time and effort, but it is worth doing well.

We had not been baptised, since The Salvation Army does not practice baptism or communion. So we were baptised at Philpott. Soon after, I asked Pastor Hoogendam to help me get back into full time ministry. He came up with an offer of the Church supporting us with the Rural Life Mission to minister in Northern Ontario – a mission field in Canada – no medical exam needed.

O'Conner Vacation Bible School 1952 Paul is centre front in white Gwen is back right

Our Slate River home

The Jonesville church

Stanley Sunday School

Our Rural Life Mission truck

Drawing Souls To Christ

RURAL LIFE MISSION

Miss Mae Brooks was founder of the Rural Life Mission. She came once a year to speak and raise money. She talked through her teeth almost with her mouth closed. She maximized the hardships and had coloured slides to prove it. She showed a tar paper shack covered in snow and said, "This is where the missionaries live, heh heh, its three rooms and a path, heh heh." She made it sound so bad you sure didn't want to go there, but you would gladly give some money so that somebody else could. Strangely enough if you were a prospective missionary there was another side to the story that was not quite so difficult.

Mae was at this time forty years old. She had worked with the Sunday School Mission and decided to branch out in a mission of her own. Both ministries worked in the Thunder Bay area but in different sections so they did not overlap. This was good. But Mae was frugal to the point of being stingy and created financial hardships for married workers. You had to sign a pledge that you would work for three years. The mission made no pledge or guarantee to you. The climate was severely cold. Forty degrees below zero was common and sixty below in Geraldton. Mae could make and break promises. She had a great Board but their decisions were disregarded if they did not agree with hers. She seemed too good to be true, and was pretty slick at getting what she wanted. Mae spent most of the winter in Southern Ontario at her parent's farm home in Hagersville.

As Gwen and I considered the challenge of the Rural Life Mission and prayed about it, we felt led of the Lord to accept this opportunity to serve. Not in the heat of Africa, but in the frigid cold of far northern Ontario.

There was one problem, we weren't free to go. Gwen and I had moved into the home of a friend from the church whose wife had been institutionalized at the psychiatric hospital. It was so bad that when her husband took photographs of the children to show her, she ate the photographs. Gwen looked after the couples' two young children. How could we leave them? As we prayed and others prayed with us, God did exceedingly abundantly above all that we could ask or think. Suddenly, the mother was well and released from the hospital. Now we could go north and serve the Lord in the Rural Life Mission. God answered prayer in ways past finding out. To God be the glory!

So we were off to Port Arthur, and Faith Chapel. Our duties included: Pastors of Faith Chapel, Sunday School 10:00, Service at 11:00 and 7:00 pm; Wednesday evening prayer meeting; Finnish English Radio Program 9 a.m. Sunday CKPR Fort William; South Stanley Schoolhouse Sunday School 2 p.m. (50 mile drive). Plus, we presented the religious education period in twelve different rural one-room schools. In the summer, we were camp directors at Round Lake for four weeks, supervised a dozen summer workers, and led Vacation Bible Schools.

While I was Pastor of Faith Chapel we had planned a church annual meeting. Mae arrived ahead of time and always just before supper. She said, "I hope you have decided the outcome of all the issues before the meeting". I replied that I thought this was the purpose of the meeting in order to have a democratic vote. "Oh, no! You decide, not them. It just does not work the other way."

ROUND LAKE BIBLE CAMP

Round Lake Bible Camp was one of the most exciting outreaches of the Rural Life Mission. Most campers were students in the one-room public schools we ministered to once-a-week. In a sense, Round Lake Camp became "harvest time" for the sowing of the Word all year.

For recreation we played baseball, swimming, boating, fishing, hiking, etc. Hardly ever did a camper leave unsaved. We had a truly happy time.

An example of Mae's ingenuity took place at Round Lake Camp one day. Gwen and Mrs. Helseth were the cooks. Mrs. Helseth was a senior member of Faith Chapel. She was so much like my Mom. We just loved her. They were both excellent cooks. The problem was Mae ordered the food. Well, Mrs. Helseth was concerned about too many wieners. She suggested to Gwen that she talk to Mae about better quality food.

Gwen knew better than to ask herself, but thought Mae might just listen to Mrs. Helseth. So Mrs. Helseth asked. "Mae, we are concerned about the children's diet. Too much baloney and wieners is not good for them, what do you think about it?" Mae's reply was priceless, "You are absolutely right--just give them one wiener instead of two."

While the campers lacked in nutrition they did not lack in good spiritual food. We had such a good Bible teaching program and prayer and worship that it was indeed rare that any camp-

Drawing Souls To Christ

er returned home unsaved. We taught the great old hymns that were rich in doctrine. The kids sang them with enthusiasm and great joy. We used Gospel Light Vacation Bible School curriculum. All of our teaching sessions were joyous occasions. No one wanted to miss a session, or to be late. For the boy's meeting we had four men participating in each session. We used flannel graph, chalk drawing, object lessons, and hand puppets. My heart warms as I think of those precious moments. We encouraged the campers to lead in prayer and personal testimony.

I was also a cabin leader. How could I quickly quiet ten kids and get them to sleep at a reasonable hour? As I prayed the Lord gave me an idea: if I was able to get to sleep by ten, I would take whoever wanted to fishing at six. It worked. The four or five boys who wanted to fish made sure the others got to sleep, or at least were quiet. Round Lake was teeming with Northern Pike. In half an hour we caught two big ones. When Mrs. Helseth saw the pike, she figured four more would feed the whole camp. So we prayed and went back out and got a meal for everyone. Wow! That was exciting.

At senior boys camp, we had one younger boy who came with his older brother. Not a good idea. A bigger bully from another cabin slugged him – really hurt him and made him cry. I took the bully aside and talked with him about what he had done. I gave him a lecture on fair play. Then I put him across my knee and gave him a spanking not too hard but enough to feel it. An hour later the bully was missing, we learned he planned to walk home. Several of the men went after him. I did not go because I thought he would have nothing to do with me. When the staff caught up to him, the bully said he would come back to camp -- only if he could move into my cabin. I'm still thinking about that one. He also committed his life to Christ. Hallelujah!

Ken H. was a counsellor one summer. He was eighteen and training in Bible School. He was good looking, had a great shock of curly red hair, and was big and strong. The young women all appreciated him.

Well, Ken was making a point in his sermon one evening. He told us how his mother made him write out a certain scripture verse five hundred times. He said "I wrote it so many times I almost memorized it!"

We had beautiful camp grounds. The buildings were primitive, but by northern standards O.K. Our dining hall chapel was an old log building. It had been a lumber camp. We had no electricity. Cook stoves were wood burners. I had to supply the wood from dead trees in the woods. If I could get someone on the other end of the five foot crosscut saw, it helped, otherwise it was hard work.

We had an icehouse. Blocks of ice were cut from the lake and packed in sawdust. Someone else did that. We just had access to it.

Round Lake was one of about six lakes in a chain connected by rivers. It presented an ideal canoe venture. A small mountain shaded most of our camp until about 10 a.m. each day. That is when the ice which formed on the water bucket overnight melted. This is the NORTH, THE FROZEN NORTH. Oh yes, I was also the lifeguard. I prayed that no one would get into difficulty because I did not want the jump into the ice cold water.

At Thunder Bay the Mission had a 1939 Plymouth car known as the Blue Vision. It was painted a Hideous Blue. It was definitely one of a kind. No one knew how many times the odometer had rolled over the 100,000 mark, or been hoisted out of ditches and frost boils. The '39 was good model, but after 11 years of hard service, this one was ready for the scrap yard. The car was shared by two women missionaries and Gwen and myself.

One of its uses was to pick up Oscar and Velma Drugy, a wonderful Swedish senior couple, with a beautiful lilting accent. One day, a rear door was stuck shut. Oscar got in first as his wife was crippled with arthritis. When we arrived at the church Velma was struggling to disembark and I was trying to help.

In desperation Oscar said, "Vhy don't you yust yump out?"

Whereupon his wife replied, "Yump, Yump, Yump out? Brother my yumping days are over!"

The Drugys never missed a service. There were some great people at Faith Chapel.

We needed an additional vehicle. We were praying, and Mae was sharing the need in her meetings in various churches. Suddenly we got word that an automobile dealer in Acton, Ontario had given the Mission a brand new G.M.C. pick up truck, and we were to go down to get it. Hallelujah! We picked it up in Hamilton. We needed a box on the back so that we could carry passengers to Sunday school. Again suddenly there it was with a for sale sign on it. It was custom made, stained brown complimenting the truck's light yellow. It was perfect. Only $150.00. From then on when we sang "Count Your Blessings", we sang "Count them ton-by-ton (Or half ton)." How great is our God!

WHY STEWART QUIT GOING TO SUNDAY SCHOOL

With the new truck with the benches in the back (this was years before seat belts), we often picked up a dozen or more kids for Sunday School. Stewart had been a regular, but now didn't want to go anymore. I called to see his Mom. Stewart had bulging eyes. You guessed it, some of the kids called him bug eyes. I promised that I would do what I could. The most important thing was to pray.

The next Sunday I stopped at Stewart's house, but Stewart wasn't going to Sunday school. I talked with the kids in the truck.

"Do you have any idea why Stewart stopped going to Sunday school?" They knew: "We called him Bug Eyes.", and they hung their heads in shame.

The next question was, "Would you like to have Stewart come back?" "Yes" from everyone. We prayed and asked God's forgiveness.

I talked with Stewart and his Mom. They would think it over. The next Sunday, we were praying as we drove to Stewart's house. Suddenly the door opened and Stewart came out. A great cheer went up from all the kids. It was a good feeling. But there's more. Stewart's Mom began to come to church. Wow! And she loved it. How wonderful it was to see them both come into a vital relationship with the Lord. To God be the Glory! God loves to do the exceeding abundantly in answering prayer.

WELCOME, MR. AND MRS. JACK LONGLEY
TO THE LAKEHEAD TEAM

The Longleys were alive, active senior citizens who, on retirement, wanted to serve the Lord. They were to begin a new outreach in the more rural isolated places. They had a GMC pick up truck just like ours but dark green. Adapting to Thunder Bay weather and driving was difficult for them. As Gwen and I thought and prayed about it we felt that if the Longleys were interested in taking over the ministry of Faith Chapel we could do the new isolated mission. Everyone including Mae Brooks thought it was a Great Plan.

For Gwen and me the establishment of local churches where there were no churches was more what we were about. We found a cute little house in Slate River right on the main highway. The snow plows came through there first. We were just 15 miles from Fort William. Our house did not have a bathroom or running water, but we managed okay. I think the rent was $20.00 per month. Shovelling out the driveway after a snow storm was interesting.

Soon we had established regular bi weekly church services in the tiny villages of Sunshine, Stanley, South Lybster, Conmee, Oconner. We conducted services in many other places several times each year. Preaching in a lumber camp was the toughest. First it is tough enough just arriving. Then you have to preach while they gobble down their food. You have about 15 to 20 minutes.

Our Sunday morning radio broadcast The Finnish English Radio Hour on C K P R Fort William reached far-and-wide. We were invited by a couple in the railway town of Schriver to conduct services there. We rented the town hall and got permission to visit the schools to invite the kids. We advertised on our radio program. More than 200 kids showed up. They called it a concert. They pleaded with us to come back. We did. Then Mae Brooks sent two good experienced young women to take over and a church was established. I also conducted morning devotions on CKPR once a month.

Walter Kotanen, a volunteer whose brother Tauno married a missionary, was our faithful Finnish interpreter. Walter just loved to go with us and share the unsearchable riches of Christ with the Finnish people. Quite often he brought a large bag of potatoes for us. We repaid him by helping on the farm when needed.

As I look back on sixty years of ministry, I can see how God was refining and teaching us, preparing us for a greater ministry that we were totally unaware of.

SCHOOL HOUSE CHURCHES

Our mission was now to establish churches in remote communities, as most had no church. The only public building was the schoolhouse. Usually just one room and many were without electricity.

Drawing Souls To Christ

In the winter, often at 40 below zero, the first one there had to light the Coleman lamps, then light the wood fire in the barrel type stove, and by the time the congregation arrived, it was warm.

Nearly everyone in the village would come to the services. We took Walter Kotanen with us to interpret for the Finnish people. We tried to learn Finnish, but we were never fluent in the language.

Congregations ranged from 15 to 100 depending on the size of the village.

Once we took a quartet from Briarcrest Bible Institute with us to Sunshine. The boys could not believe how the crowd filled the schoolhouse. They said, "You must have done some great advertising." They were amazed when we told them that the people did not even know they were coming.

Another time Phil and Louis Palermo visited the Lakehead and they joined us for a meeting. Wow. We were in the big time. Phil and Louis traveled around the world singing for Billy Graham. They were precious. Years later they came to Peterborough and while there had dinner with us. Gwen cooked them fish-and-chips. They loved it.

The Lord enabled us to establish schoolhouse churches in Sunshine, South Lybster, Nolalu, Stanley, Conmee, Oconnor, Tarmola, and Kekabeka Falls.

Lena K, in Stanley, heard our broadcast. She was staying with her sister and working in the kitchen at her brother-in-law's hotel. She asked me to visit. When we were praying, her brother-in-law walked in. He later told her that if I ever came there again he would shoot me.

Lena phoned. "Don't come."

I said, "We will come, the Lord will look after us." Lena's brother-in-law was sitting on the hotel steps. If he had a gun he did not shoot me. Thank you Lord!

Photo of Lena and her daughters Peggy, airline stewardess, Rose, with her husband missionaries to Morocco, mother Lena, Christine married to a jeweller in San Francisco

But another day when we were travelling from Stanley to South Stanley school, we passed the hotel and Lena was sitting on her steamer trunk on top of a six foot snow bank crying. She had been thrown out of the Hotel. We picked her up, threw her trunk in the back of the truck, and took her home with us to Slate River.

Lena became our baby sitter. She lived with us for three months, and then went to live with her daughter in Toronto. When Lena prayed, she always concluded her prayer, "In Jesus precious, precious name."

Lena made the best cabbage rolls and perogies you ever tasted. She taught Gwen a lot. Lena had one daughter who was a missionary in the Middle East. Another was an airline stewardess, and the third was married to a jeweller in San Francisco.

We kept in touch with Lena for many years until she went to be with the Lord. She is precious.

Taking the Bible Story to different one-room schoolhouses and one four room schoolhouse each week was a real delight. It was fun. It also was strenuous.

Paul, aged three, accompanied us as our song leader. He could do it well. The kids just loved him. Here was a precious pre-schooler with God given ability being as natural as could be doing a work for the Lord. God was indeed in our midst in blessing as we sang His praises.

One Father's Day I arranged for Paul to sing "It is no Secret What God Can Do" on the radio broadcast. He practiced with Eva Mackonen at the piano, and all went well. But during the live broadcast, he started out well, and then began to speed up. He sang so fast that Eva had a hard time trying to keep up with him. So much for showing off my son! It must have been hilarious for those listening. It was not for me.

In the schools, Gwen would have a session with her favourite hand puppet "Nosey Boy". Wow! The kids sure went for that. I usually taught the Bible lesson or Bible story with special flannel graph figures I painted myself. Often I would draw stick-men to tell the Bible stories. That is where stick-men really developed.

At one school there was a Jehovah's Witness family. They went to the cloakroom for the duration of our session. But you could see them looking through the cracks in the partly open door, and they got the message with as much interest as the others.

The arrival of the Blue Vision (our 39 Plymouth) sent up a cheer in the schoolyard when we arrived. It was a happy time, just as it should be.

Many of the villagers were solidly Finnish and others had a few Swedes thrown in. The accents were interesting. One schoolteacher was Polish and spoke English with a strong accent. Each student spoke as he did. I recall on our first visit to that school, I looked over at the teacher, a likable friendly man, with a big smile trying to keep from laughing. He smiled back. He understood perfectly what I was thinking and shrugged his shoulders, almost laughing himself.

As time went on, we got to know people in the various communities. At Nolalu, Into and Helen Klamie became our dear friends. They owned and operated the General Store. Into also had trucking business and was the largest hay merchant at the Lakehead.

Into was Finnish and Helen Swedish. They were a delightful couple, perhaps 15 years our senior. They loved the Lord, they loved each other, and it showed. They had a lovely, warm, cozy home and big smiles no matter how busy.

Helen could whip up a delicious meal at a moment's notice. Their home was like a home away from home to us. They adored Paul with his fluent vocabulary and laughed heartily at his words of wisdom.

Once, Helen looked after Paul while his mother was in the hospital for a few days. They kept him busy stacking canned goods and things in the store. He drew a face and Helen said, "That face looks awfully sad." Where upon Paul replied with a whimper, "That is just how I feel!" Time to do something else.

Helen played the organ. They had a small portable organ and Helen would play at School House Churches we established in the area. Fifty miles meant nothing to them when they could come and help us in a service. Later when we moved to Geraldton, they would come about once a month and bring the organ to play at our Church there. That was a round trip of more than 200 miles.

GERALDTON

Geraldton was as far north as you could go by road in Ontario. There were eleven gold mines in the area, and a town of two thousand. Temperatures of forty degrees below zero were common, and sometimes sixty below. Summers were short.

One day as we were closing up Round Lake Camp, Mae Brooks told us that the missionaries at Geraldton had wanted to quit, so she had promised them that they could take over our work and we would be sent to Geraldton. She said it was the Board's decision and that we would go to Geraldton or else. I wish I had asked her what "or else" meant. We had about nine months left to go on our pledge to stay with the Rural Life Mission for three years. We decided to go to Geraldton and if we did not like it, leave from there when our pledge was fulfilled.

We had no desire to move to Geraldton and were not happy about the way the move was arranged without any input on our part.

Mae Brooks attended our final meeting at South Stanley School Church. The villagers were really upset that we were leaving. One who was on the School Board told her that he had worked hard to get the Board to approve painting the Church (School) and now the pastor was leaving.

That night I preached about the twins Jacob and Esau. Mae was quite impressed by the service, the people in attendance, and their reaction. She said, "I wish the Crookalls could be twins, too, so that one could go to Geraldton and the other would stay here."

If we had not been forced to Geraldton, I don't think we could have left the churches the Lord enabled us to plant at the Thunder Bay Area. Was God in all this?

When we got there, the mines were starting to close down, but lumbering was going strong. It was a real tough place. Our friends, the Klamies, sent one of their trucks to ship our household goods. It was a soggy foggy day. Geraldton looked awful. Even when the sun shone it looked awful. A forest fire had left its mark and burned trees are not pretty. But awful was not new to us. It was so much like Parrsborro, only much, much colder.

But guess what, our friends, the Burns from Slate River, had moved to Geraldton. John Burns had been principal at Slate River School where we became good friends. Se we were not alone. John's school at Slate River was four rooms. He had persuaded me to be coach of the school hockey team and later leader of a Boy Scout troop in what little spare time I had.

Our home at Geraldton was actually one mile out of town at Jonesville. It was small, with a wood stove. There was a wood shed with wood neatly cut and stacked.

There was a small church building made from two railway bunkhouses joined together. It was about fourteen feet wide and forty feet long. It had been located in a great spot right down town, but the missionaries lived at Jonesville about a mile out of town. It seemed to the missionaries that it would make things easier for them to move the church to Jonesville just across the road from their house. After all hardly anyone came to church anyway. Amazingly Mae Brooks had approved of this move. She told us that these missionaries had been faithful. That meant did not object to anything she said or did. It was implied that we were not.

Moreover the church had been set up on supports and needed to have posts placed beneath it. What a prospect! I told her that I did not know what Charlie (the previous missionary) had in mind and I needed him to supervise the job required. She agreed. What a relief! Charlie was small, but mighty, and that part was good.

We dug the postholes by hand and slid the posts into place underneath the building. We somehow managed.

Later when I tried to paint the building, when I applied the first brushful, the old weathered wood gave a slurping sound and swallowed the paint in one gulp. It took several coats, but I finally got it finished. It did not look great, but it looked better.

We ordered tongue and groove strips of wood to close in the crawl space. I suggested we get the wood pre-cut to three-foot lengths. "No, brother", said Charlie, "that will cost too much. We will cut each board with a handsaw." It took the best part of a week. Charlie was in charge so that is what we did.

There were no adult services. No one would come. About ten or twelve kids came to Sunday school and Wednesday night Bible Club. There was a Sunday School at the school at the mining townsite at Little Long Lac. That was it. We had no transportation – Charlie got our mission and our truck. We traveled to Little Long Lac School twice a week by taxi. It was a big adventure.

Geraldton had four churches: Presbyterian, Anglican, Roman Catholic, and Lutheran None was evangelical.

This would call for much prayer. I became burdened for the miners and how we could reach them.

After about three months we had a Lumberjack's Night. This was similar to Sailor's Night in Parrsborro. We had a packed church of eighty-four people including kids sitting on the floor. But how could we reach two thousand?

SHEPHERDS OR WOLVES

Margaret was a young Christian nurse. She was an American and came to work at Geraldton's tiny hospital. She found our church and attended faithfully. She called in often to see us.

One Sunday afternoon she had walked across the frozen lake. She wanted to know who owned all the German Shepherd dogs that accompanied her on her walk. She did not know they were wolves. There was not a Shepherd in Geraldton.

After ministering at Geraldton for some weeks one night at Bible Club, thirteen kids got saved. Wow! These were our first converts at Jonesville Geraldton Church.

The next week we were teaching these converts how to pray. Little Judy McInnnes prayed a nice little prayer and ended with "Lord, bless everyone 'cept the devil. Amen."

Drawing Souls To Christ

DON'T MISS THIS STORY

The largest building in town was the movie theatre. After weeks of prayer, I approached the manager to rent the theatre for a rally. He said, "I don't want you in my building." That was disappointing. Then Rev. Grey of the Anglican Church came to see me. "We are planning our annual Combined Christmas Service. We have never invited your church before, but we would like you to join us this year. We would also like you to preach for twelve minutes. We don't want to tell you what to preach, but the title is 'What does Christmas Mean, Today, Tomorrow, Next Week?' The service will be held in the theatre." Wow!!! That was Christmas 1952.

God had not failed to answer. He just did it in a better way.

As I prepared my twelve-minute message, I began with something the people would understand. It was a Christmas carol that was sung that night. "Hark the Herald Angels Sing," focusing on "Born To Give Them Second Birth." Then I linked John 3:16 and explained that this is what Christmas is about. This is what Christmas means. God's Gift of Salvation to all who will receive.

As I stepped forward onto the centre stage at the theatre and began to preach, it seemed that the entire congregation was suddenly moved by the Lord and leaned forward in their seats. The Lord gave me liberty and freedom to preach. It was truly a message the Lord had given me for them. I was not at liberty to give an altar call, but I explained the sinner's prayer and invited them to pray it with me. I had delivered my soul. From the burden of my heart I had shared the message of redeeming grace. I had told them of my own experience as a seventeen-year-old who had attended church and Sunday school, but did not understand how to be born again.

Suddenly I saw the Anglican minister, who had invited me to come and preach, making his way through the crowd towards me. His face was set. Was he angry? Was he upset by what I had preached? As he got closer, I could see the tears streaming down his face as he stretched his hand towards me. "Stan, I want to thank you for that message. Personally, I want to thank you!" Then he turned and walked out of the building without speaking to anyone else. Bless the Lord!

The theatre had been packed with people that I would never have drawn there on my own, we didn't need to pay rent, and bonus, I received $25 of the offering. God is good. His ways are past finding out.

From that moment on Rev Grey was my very special friend. He would phone me from time to time and say, "I am sending someone to see you. I told them to go down to the mission (our church) and see you. You will be able to help them better than I can."

GOSPEL NEWSPAPER

GOSPEL NEWS 1953

Published by the Rural Life Mission Inc.
Edited and arranged by Rev. Stan Crookall

Stick men tell a Story

Do you know the story? It is found in Luke 15:11-24.

Although the theatre was packed, we still had not reached our objective of witnessing to every family and person in Geraldton.

As I prayed, the Lord led me to prepare a special Gospel Newspaper that I planned to deliver personally door-to-door throughout the town.

The editor of the local newspaper "The Nugget" (it was a gold mining town) was all for it. He was about my age and helped me to set up the paper and illustrate it just right.

The Gospel News contained an article "Why the Book Ben Hur Was Written," a sermon about Paul and Silas in prison, a stick man illustration story of the Prodigal Son and how to receive Christ as Saviour and Lord.

When it came off the press I began taking it door-to-door. I felt it was my burden and my personal mission to accomplish. I felt that when this was completed I could leave Geraldton and the Rural Life Mission. That is what we did. I talked personally with everyone I could about the Lord

John Harvey was a quiet dignified mature man respected by

all that knew him. He was a Baptist minister who worked for the Upper Canada Bible Society as a colporteur (or Bible salesman).

John phoned from his home in Port Arthur one day and asked if he could stay with us for a week while he worked in the Geraldton area. Was it an answer to our prayers for guidance?

Each evening Gwen and I talked with John about his ministry and the Bible Society. Finally John said, "Would you be interested in working with the Bible Society? We have an opening for a Colporteur right now. I would be glad to recommend you."

Gwen and I thought and prayed about it. It was real missionary work, calling from door-to-door, trying to lead people to Christ along with selling Bibles.

Marjory, Gwen, Stan, Paul in Peterborough 1956

Bill and Isabelle Spinks

Edinborough Castle in Peterborough

Paul and Margie in front our first house trailer

Chapter 5

Beginning with the bible society

We felt the Lord was leading us so we made contact with Bible Society in Toronto. They sent their district secretary, a minister from North Bay, to see us. It did not take long. The Bible Society assigned the Eastern Ontario area to me -- from Oshawa to Kingston and from Lake Ontario north to Algonquin Park. I would be on probation for three months and on permanent staff after that if I was successful.

They provided a 1950 Chevrolet sedan delivery van to drive, along with a load of Bibles. It would be another chapter in the "Awesome Adventure in Christ."

We moved back to Hamilton. Gwen and the children stayed with my mother and father while I traveled through my territory working Monday to Friday and coming home weekends.

MEETING THE PRIME MINISTER

One day when Paul, who was four at the time, was with Grandpa Crookall, they met Prime Minister Louis St. Laurent, who was visiting Hamilton. The Prime Minister looked at Paul, who was wearing a hat inscribed "ANAVIC," and asked "ANAVIC. What does that stand for?"

Paul piped up, "Army, Navy, and Air Force Veterans in Canada."

"Oh, I see you are reared from good stock," the Prime Minister replied. "And what does your father do?"

Paul's reply was monumental: "My father is a minister, but not a prime one!"

There was no baby-talk at our home. Our children had a great vocabulary at two and three years of age. We took time to teach them, and Gwen was a great mother.

When our son Tim was less-than two years old, we had a

church banquet at my ordination. Tim was enjoying a choice piece of ham when my good friend and mentor, Dr. Merle P. Estabrooks, asked, "Is that good, Timmy?"

Tim's reply was, "It's delicious." That both of our sons became pubic speakers is really no surprise. God has promised to bless our children, and He does.

BACK TO THE BIBLE SOCIETY...

It was early summer, 1954. The Bible Society asked me to begin in Haliburton, which I did. But my first two days I spent in Oshawa. I saw Church Street and thought that might be a good place to begin. My first day on the job was discouraging and I began to realize how only God could give success in this new venture. I began to pray without ceasing. I prayed as I went from house to house. I did not actually sell a single Bible that first day, but I did get a few orders. When I delivered them a few weeks later, I realized that the day had not been a failure. There had been the opportunity to share the Gospel verbally with many, give a Gospel tract and helps for Bible reading, as well as have an encouraging word with those who were believers.

In Oshawa I stayed overnight at my Uncle Tom and Aunt Jenny's house. On Saturday, just before I left, my Aunt Jenny bought a $6.00 Bible. A sale at last! Things were picking up. How kind of Aunt Jenny.

Then on my way home I stopped to see Ken and Verna Martin and they bought five Bibles. Wow, my sales were up to $60.00. I went home happy and Gwen rejoiced with me.

My Dad did not think much of my new job and the first thing he asked was, "How much did you sell?"

"I sold $60.00 worth."

"Who did you sell them to?"

I was reluctant to answer, sensing where he was going.

"I sold Bibles to Aunt Jennie and to Ken and Verna Martin."

"What are you going to do when you run out of relatives and friends?"

What indeed?

But Gwen was there to smile and encourage me. She had no doubts about how we would manage.

One day a few weeks later, I saw an old home made house trailer for sale. $135.00. Wow, just the ticket. It did not look too fancy on the outside, but it was great on the inside and had everything but a bathroom. We could work that one out. We had been there before. Gwen and the kids were excited. My little sedan delivery truck already had a trailer hitch, so we were all set.

Gwen had been working as a waitress at Robert's Restaurant, the best in Hamilton, but she gladly quit and traveled with me. It was fabulous. For the rest of the summer we were together as a family. I worked hard day and evening calling from house-to-house. By now I was working in the Fenelon Falls area. We parked at the beach there for several weeks and it was wonderful. Paul learned how to swim – Marilyn Bell, the first woman to swim Lake Ontario taught him.

At the end of the first month my Bible sales totalled $420.00. I prayed about each day's work, then pray continually as I called door-to-door. In my report to the Bible Society, I stated, "I have worked hard in the areas you requested, I have sold $420.00 worth of Bibles. I do not know whether this is good or bad, but I hope it is satisfactory."

Mr. Stevens, the business manager, replied quickly, I opened the letter with trembling hands. Would I be fired? I hoped not. To our surprise he wrote,

"Congratulations, Brother Crookall. You have sold more Bibles than has ever been sold by the Bible Society in your area in one month before."

I later found out that my territory was considered the most difficult in Ontario.

From that point on, I was either first or second in sales amongst all eight colporteurs for the next six years. I do not take credit for this. God did it in answer to prayer. The Bible speaks for itself. Getting as many Bibles as possible into the hands of those who need them was one of our main objectives.

LINDSAY FAIR

At Lindsay Fair, Ontario's fourth largest, people purchased $1,000.00 of Bibles. Wow! It was awesome! I became the fair-haired boy of the Bible Society. I had never been the fair-haired boy anywhere until now. When a new colporteur began they sent him to me to train, or sent me to him. I was thirty-one years old. One year they sent me to be the speaker at an Anglican Church in Toronto. When they realized it was our birthday, they sent Gwen, too. The Church people were so kind. They had a very special birthday cake made for us, a delicious fruitcake, like a Christmas cake only better! Gwen and I had fun that day.

Gwen and I enjoyed ministry for the Lord and were always happy when we could minister as a team together. When we had free time we enjoyed that, too. The Lord rewarded every sacrifice of time apart and gave us great joy when we were together.

Although our little home-made trailer was not much to look at, it was fun. During the summer we were able to park it often beside the water at Fenelon Falls, Bobcaygeon, Coboconk, Norland, Minden and many other places. It was like a dream come true for our little family. It was quite a change from the rigors of other places. I would call door-to-door from morning until 4 p.m., come back to the family, and have supper and a swim, and then go back working from 7 till 9.

In our first year there were a lot of new opportunities for ministry. One of which was the Ontario Plowing Match. Ralph Rumball, a veteran colporteur whose territory bordered mine, was my closest source of information about the unknown. Ralph explained that the Plowing Match included what they called the "Tented City" of displays. Thousands would attend each day.

But it was October, and getting cool. As I prayed about how to handle this situation, the Lord gave me a plan. I would build a portable plywood Bible House. It would resemble a Bible with a red roof. My brother, Roy, was the chief architect. I helped in the construction. My Dad did the lettering. It stood eight feet high. An opening at the front gave opportunity to show a rack of Bibles and for me to stand behind them to serve customers. It could also be locked up at night. It was an innovative idea and it worked well. It was pre-fab with six sections and was bolted together with carriage bolts. The whole thing could be carried on roof racks on the top of my van. My Dad was a professional sign writer, handyman, and inventor. Our son Tim said, "Poppa can make anything." So this sort of thing was in my genes.

Gwen could go with me for the three days of the match. We took our house trailer and parked it on the site. We prayed and we hoped we were ready. It was great. We met hundreds of people each day, sold Bibles, plus got orders for Christmas.

Gwen and I manned the display together during crowded times and alternately during less busy times. It was good to get warm in the trailer. Gwen was always in strong support of everything I did. She never thought any of my ideas were crazy. She encouraged me in everything. She was just what I needed. I am sure she wondered sometimes just what I would come up with next. Life was never boring. It was always exciting. There was always a new adventure in "Drawing Souls to Christ."

We were able to get $1,000.00 worth of Bibles into the hands of the people. You could buy a Bible for 55 cents in those days. We probably sold more than 1,000 Bibles at the Plowing Match. To God Be the Glory! We prayed about each one and the blessed hope that many would find Christ. We also witnessed to many and gave out hundreds of tracts. The Bible House stood out as a reminder of our need to honour God and "seek first His kingdom."

At the Peterborough Fair, Alex Bapti stopped and chatted. He asked where I lived. I told him in Hamilton, but we would like to live in a good location for my Eastern Ontario district.

"Would you like to live in Peterborough?" he asked. "If you would, I can tell you about a house for rent for $40.00 per month." Wow!

I got the particulars and Gwen came up by train to see the house. I did not see it. She said it was okay and described it to me by phone at wherever I was by then. It was not until moving day that I saw the house. It came as a shock. You could not get much of a house for $40.00 per month. Houses were renting then for $100.00 or $125.00. The price was what we could afford, and in our time with the Salvation Army we had lived in worse. The address was 181 Edinborough Street, so with a sense of irony, we called it "Edinburgh Castle." It was wonderful to be together, and my travel was reduced.

I think Edinborough Castle had a lot to do with my aversion to, and dread of winter. The house was old, made of yellow brick, with no insulation, no basement, just a root cellar you accessed through a trap door in the kitchen floor. It was a two-story brick barn with no furnace. We tried to heat it with an oil space heater with stovepipes extending up through a hole in the ceiling. When it was 25 below zero outside our bedroom would be just at freezing. I wore a toque (wool cap) to bed. We added a Quebec heater in the kitchen. How we survived I really did not know. We lived there for three years.

Then we found out about a Veteran's Land Act subdivision at

the five-mile turn south of Peterborough. That is another story and another "Adventure in Christ".

LINDSAY FAIR

Third largest fair in Ontario we would sell $1,000 worth of Bibles in a week

OTTAWA FAIR

The Ottawa Auxiliary of the British Foreign Bible Society had heard reports about our work at the Fall Fairs. They asked if I could help them for a week at the Ottawa Fair. We were to have the use of an aluminium tent. I had never seen an aluminium tent – and I still haven't. It wasn't there. Nor was anyone from the Ottawa Bible Society. The person who had contacted me had gone away for the week.

After searching for more than an hour, I found "The Church in Action" location. It seemed more like "the Church Out of Action." It was tucked away in an almost inaccessible corner behind some buildings. The gateway was narrow and uninviting. No one from any of the churches involved had yet appeared.

In the midst of this chaos, suddenly there appeared a bubbly, jolly, smiling young man named Bill Spinks. He was a missionary to Cuba. Bill announced, "I'm here to help you. Mr. Walden hired me to be your assistant for the week." That was good news.

Bill had a crippled arm as the result of a bad break that did not heal properly when he was a child. But the other arm was powerful.

Together we found a horrible, dirty, old, tattered tent (absolutely no exaggeration). It was huge, with two main supports the size of telephone poles. After a few hours of blood, sweat and tears the huge tent stood there in utter disgrace. We both agreed this would never work. If only I had known I would have brought my Bible House, but it was too late now.

What to do? The first thing was to take down that monstrosity. Then we decided to move to the end of the lane nearer the crowds. We constructed a makeshift lean-to out of bits and pieces of tent and studs. We set up our Bible display and we were in business. We did a lot of praying.

Bill Spinks and I were made for each other. We worked as a team just great. We understood each other. We could almost read each other's thoughts, perhaps because we both had expressive faces.

Together we witnessed to thousands, gave out tracts, and sold about $1,000.00 worth of Bibles. In the heat of the action with people swarming around our display, Bill talked with a Roman Catholic priest who wanted a Bible. Bill came to me and said, "He wanted a Bible, but did not have any money."

"You can give him that Bible free," I shouted.

The priest had gone. Undaunted, Bill went running after him to give him a precious gift, the Book of Books, the incomparable Word of God.

The Spinks family that grew to nine children became lifelong friends of the Crookalls. We ministered together many times through the years to follow.

MISSED BY A BULL DOZER circa 1955

One morning as I was driving south of Peterborough on Highway 28 , I noticed a big flatbed truck approaching at high speed. It had an extra large bulldozer bouncing up and down on the back. As it went over some train tracks the bulldozer came lose. It bounced off the truck, the blade hitting the pavement digging in three feet, and then hurdled sixty feet through the air in my direction. It passed within six inches of my truck, head high as I sat there amazed.

The driver jumped out of his truck, his face ashen and body trembling. He could not speak. I hung around until the bulldozer was reloaded. Then I went to a coffee shop to compose myself before continuing. But as I drank my coffee and thanked the Lord, I decided to go back home instead and take the day off. Thank you, Lord, for your protection. Who was praying this time? Gwen was glad to see me and thankful that the Lord had protected me. The Lord knew I needed constant prayer-support and He gave me that in Gwen who was the greatest prayer warrior I have ever known.

Our purpose as colporteurs was to make the Bible available to people at a price they could afford, to get Bibles to those who didn't have them, to encourage daily Bible reading, and to lead people to Christ if they were strangers to His Grace.

We had permission to cut the price or give them to those in need.

It was not a matter of who could sell the most; it was the urgency to get the Bible into the hands of the people.

Over time, I learned that in areas where there was an Evangelical Church, there was a much greater interest in the Bible among both those who did not attend church, and those who attended a liberal church. Salt and light does its work.

We gave out scripture tracts and a great variety of excellent booklets on how to read the Bible through in a year, etc.

At least three young men, who bought their very first Bible from me, later became Evangelical preachers. It was my privilege to see them grow and be faithful in ministry.

I called house-to-house on Indian reservations. At Deseronto I stayed with a Pentecostal preacher and his wife. I enjoyed learning to eat cornmeal for breakfast.

At Curve Lake Reservation,, I remember making my way down a long narrow path to an isolated home. As I got near to the house, I saw a big ferocious black dog, growling and salivating, running at full speed toward me. There was nowhere to hide. I just prayed. Suddenly an Indian lady appeared and whacked the dog on the top of his head with a big stick, using all the power she could muster. There were two thuds – when she hit the dog, and when the dog hit the dirt, unconscious. As I talked with the lady, the dog staggered to his feet and wobbled off, bewildered. I gave that lady a Bible. Another adventure in

Drawing Souls To Christ

"Drawing Souls to Christ."

As I talked to people at the door or in their homes, I found many had attended church all their lives, yet did not understand the Way of Salvation. Some sang in the choir or taught Sunday school. Some were ministers. I told them of my experience attending churches and Sunday schools where God was honoured, and I was taught many things about the Bible, but not how to be saved. What joy it was to see some come from darkness to light and truly enter into a saving knowledge of Jesus Christ.

I called to see each minister in the community. Some were glad to see me and some were not. Some ridiculed me because I believed the Bible. One older minister, who was close to retirement, asked me about my church denomination. When I told him I was a Baptist, he said, "Oh, you are very evangelical then?"

"Yes," I replied. "Don't you think everyone ought to be evangelical?"

"Oh, yes, I used to think that way. I hit the sawdust trail in one of Billy Sunday's meetings. I used to preach as you do, but I don't any more," he said.

Whereupon I asked, "What do you preach then?"

He went on to say, "Oh, I preach to build people up in the faith."

"But what if they are unsaved and not in the faith? What if someone comes to your church for the first time and is not saved, and never goes to church again, you don't tell them how to be saved? Isn't that an awful chance you take?"

"That's just the chance I have to take," he said.

A year or so later, I called to see the same preacher. This time he told me that he was about to retire and he felt his life was a failure. How sad. He would not have felt that way had he been faithful to "preach the Word."

One preacher told me that he was preparing a message for a father and son banquet at a large church in Peterborough. He went on to say, "I'm thinking about speaking about Sputnik (the Russian space craft). What would you speak about?"

I told him that I would preach, "Ye must be born again". He laughed. We talked for some time about the issues. He told me that some time ago a young man like me had come to see him and witnessed as I did. As the young man was leaving, the minister said, "Oh, well, you and I do not agree, but we are going the same way."

"Oh, no," the young man replied. "We are not in agreement on the greatest issue in life. You are either saved or lost for all eternity."

Some time later, I met a man who had attended that father-and-son banquet. He said, "Rev. H. told us all about you and your talk together. He told us about how to be born again." How wonderful. Bless the Lord! To God Be the Glory!

During 1958, my last year as a colporteur, I canvassed door-to-door in the Orono area. It was the most spiritually dead community I had experienced in six years.

In three weeks, I sold less than a dozen Bibles. I lead one person to Christ in their home. I became burdened for the people and prayed that the Lord would send someone to Orono to make a difference.

Sixteen years later, we purchased "Cedarcove," a home in Newcastle. We started a Bible study prayer meeting in our home. Within a few months, the numbers coming were more than our house could hold. Some of the people who came lived in Orono, five miles away. They arranged for us to meet in the Orono United Church on Tuesday evenings. That prayer meeting continued in Orono for fifteen years. It was awesome what God did. During a three-year period, we baptized sixty people. And God continued week after week to confirm His Word with signs following. I had asked God to send someone to Orono and did not expect Him to send me, but I am glad He did

WE PRAYED FOR EVERY BIBLE WE WERE ABLE TO DISTRIBUTE THAT IT WOULD BE READ AND BRING ABOUT A TRANSFORMED LIFE. THIS MADE DISTRIBUTING BIBLES AN EXCITING ADVEMNTURE IN DRAWING SOULS TO CHRIST.

One of the great tragedies of religion in North America and Britain, the bastion of missionary activity throughout the world, is the large number of ministers who are strangers to God's Grace and not saved themselves.

At seventeen when I was converted, I did not understand why several ministers I had listened to faithfully had not made the Way of Salvation clear to me.

Later in the Navy I met several chaplains, none of whom gave evidence of being born again themselves.

Drawing Souls To Christ

As a Salvation Army Officer I learned none of the theology professors at Mount Allison University was born again. As a Bible salesman, I was openly ridiculed and laughed at by many liberal ministers of several large churches. They ridiculed me because I believed the Bible to be true. Many of them did not believe in Hell or Heaven. They did not believe in the virgin birth of Christ. They did not believe that Jesus Christ was the Son of God. They believed in the Golden Rule, "Do unto others as you would have them do unto you." They were trusting in good works to get them to heaven (Ephesians 2:8, 9). I attempted to give a clear-cut testimony at every home regarding the Way of Salvation. I was able to lead some into a saving knowledge of Jesus Christ. How many that bought a Bible and read it and became converted I had no idea.

The greatest apparent success came with people who, when I asked their church background and experience, told me about teaching Sunday school, singing in the choir, being an usher or church treasurer, etc. Then I would ask, "Has there ever been a time when you realized that you were a sinner, that Christ died on the cross so that your sins could be forgiven? Did you ever pray and ask God to forgive your sins and help you to turn from them and invite the Lord Jesus Christ to come into your heart and life?"

I can recall a dear lady who purchased Bibles for her church each year. The first time I called to see her, she admitted that she had worked in her church all her life, but really did not know Jesus as Saviour and Lord. That day the truth dawned on her at last. Her heart was opened and she prayed, inviting Jesus to be Lord and Saviour of her life.

There was such a change in her appearance that when her husband came home for lunch he was startled. He asked, "What has happened to you? You look so happy and free."

Each year, after I called with Bibles for the church, her husband would look at her and say, "That Bible man must have been here again today." To God Be the Glory!

TWINS BORN

Early December 1954 I had gone to the Kingston area to work. I was staying at the home of my good friend and mentor, Dr. Merle P. Estabrooks. On the tenth, I suddenly felt so ill at ease and uneasy. I just felt I should go home. I told my friend Merle about it and he said one word, "Go." Gwen was expecting our third child. When I got home, she was ready to go to the hospital. I arrived just in time to take her. It would be a heartbreaker.

Twins, Peter and Ruth, were born prematurely. One was stillborn and the other lived one day. We asked all our friends to pray. The doctor said to me, "Your wife is going to need all the help you can give her." It was good advice. I did all I could.

Each year for 46 years our calendar was always marked on December 10. Gwen always remembered. It was hard for me too. It took more than a year before I could look at a baby without crying.

Difficult as the experience was, we learned how God can heal the wounds of sorrow and grief. We learned how to help others in their grief.

At Gwen's memorial service January 27, 2001, a couple who had lost their baby, came to me and said, "Your letter helped us more than anything other than the Lord in our time of deepest grief. We want to thank you."

HAVELOCK

Calling door-to-door with Bibles and a personal witness for our Lord was indeed spiritual warfare.

In January 1955 we began what I called "The Battle of Havelock". Reverend Bill Pieper, a dear Baptist brother, was with me to be trained. January is the worst time of the year to sell anything.

Bill was shy and timid. We would have to pray much about this, and we did. I prayed that the Lord would enable us to sell more Bibles than we had ever sold before as an encouragement to Bill. I sure prayed for Bill, too.

After three days working together side by side at each house, I announced, "Bill, tomorrow you will work one side of the street and I will work the other." I could see Bill begin to shake already.

I don't know whether or not Bill slept that night, but the next day the Lord gave him victory and he began to witness and sell Bibles. He got to like it and became good at it. Bless the Lord.

When "The Battle of Havelock" was over we had sold more Bibles per capita than anywhere else. My estimate was that we sold a Bible at every sixth house. It was an awesome adventure in "Drawing Souls To Christ."

Bill remained a colporteur until the Bible Society discontinued that ministry in about 1960. Then he went back into the pastorate at the Locks Baptist Church in Huntsville.

WHAT GWEN DID WHILE I WAS AWAY

While I was away from home, often a week at a time, Gwen looked after whatever Bible Society business there was to do. She also cared for our two children, Marge and Paul, taught Sunday School class, was Peterborough area director for Child Evangelism, and conducted a weekly children's Bible Club, often more than one.

Each summer she was director of Vacation Bible School at the Church of the Open Bible in Peterborough. It was two-weeks long. There were so many students they used the YMCA building next door as well as the church. Scheduling was a huge task, but Gwen did it without ever being flustered. She was what my mother called a 'brick,' solid. We have a scripture plaque we got as a wedding present in 1942. It reads:

"Be ye steadfast, unmovable, always abounding in the work of the Lord, for you know that your labor is not in vain in the Lord." (1Corinthians 15:58)

Gwen did not just read that text, she lived it. She was thirty, mother of a daughter, eleven, and a son, seven. Yet, she was a leader and a real soul winner

1956 OUR FIRST HOUSE

The Department of Veteran's Affairs had purchased 44 acres of land at the five-mile turn south of Peterborough. By the time we found out about it there were only two two-acre lots left.

In an interview with Murray Humphries and Bill Theobald, we found out that a $500.00 deposit was required. The deadline was September. They asked me what my salary was. When I told them that I made $30.00 a week and 15% commission on the Bibles I sold, they laughed.

"How about money in the bank?"

When I told them we had no money in the bank they laughed again, louder.

"But we will have $500.00 by September," I promised.

"Where are you going to get it?" they wanted to know.

When I said, "The Lord will provide the money," they laughed so hard one of them almost fell off his chair.

The Reverend Gilbert Smith, minister of St. Giles Presbyterian Church, came to see us at Edinborough Castle once and Gwen served her famous lemon tarts with tea. The chandeliers at the castle were long electric wires hanging three feet down from very high cracked ceilings with flimsy, inexpensive lamps with pull chains. The stylish Venetian blinds were cast offs from Zellers Department Store, cut down to fit. The drapes were plastic. Most of the furniture had been previously owned. The stovepipes extended across the room and up through a hole in the ceiling were a relic from 50 years earlier.

The good Rev. Gilbert asked if I would like to fill in at area churches when they needed a pulpit supply. It would pay an honorarium of $10.00 or $15.00 per service. I took my chalk drawing equipment, and the people loved the unusual presentation of the Word

The three-point charge of Norwood, Westwood, and Havelock had called the Rev. Munce Drennan from Ireland to be their minister. I was asked to fill in until he could come. The honorarium was $40.00 each Sunday, for three months: $520.00.

When I took the money in to the Department of Veteran's Affairs they asked, "Where on earth did you get the money?"

I just looked at them and told them I had promised that the Lord would provide and He did. They were not laughing now. They were visibly shaken.

Gwen and I wanted our house to have a touch of class. We picked out a split-level with Douglas fir beams and two-inch cedar deck as you see in the photo. They did not think we could do it, building it ourselves. Gwen and I had to talk with V.L.A. top brass in Toronto for hours, and just when they had almost convinced us to build a house that looked like a box, we managed to convince them to let us build our plan. God again answered prayer.

Two of our closest friends in Peterborough, Tom Schauff and George DuMoulin, were building contractors. They had assured us we could do it, and both helped us when we needed it.

The roof was a low 1/12 pitch and required tar-and-gravel. As the two-inch red cedar roof deck was exposed inside, we required one inch ten-test insulation on the outside between the roof deck and the tar and gravel roof. The insulation must be kept dry and we could not afford the size of tarp required, so we prayed and set a date with the roofer.

When the time came, I spent all day and until after midnight putting the ten-test insulation on. I was praying as I did it and on the way home, too. We went to bed and slept until 6:30 a.m. When we awakened the sun was shining. It was a glorious day. Then, all of a sudden, 'KABOOM', thunder and lightening and rain like you would not believe. When I looked out the window of Edinborough Castle, the water was filling the ditches three feet wide. It was raining a gully washer and a trash mover. I just could not believe it. I was sure the Lord would look after our roof and keep it dry.

I drove immediately to the house and the roofers were busy applying the tar and gravel. When they saw me coming, they laughed so hard one almost fell off the roof.

"Look!" they shouted. "For 15 feet around this house everything is perfectly dry, but beyond that everything is soaking wet."

One of them pointed up and said, "You must have good connections."

It was another awesome adventure in "Drawing Souls to Christ".

When the V.L.A. building inspector, came to inspect our basement, he walked around the house twice, then sat down and laughed. It was a little alarming until he said, "I have never in my life seen a tar line that straight on a basement foundation. What else would an artist do?" (I had used a chalk line to get it even).

COMING IN UNDER BUDGET

We were the only family on the subdivision to come in under budget. It was built for $10,000.00, and we had $1,250.00 left over. I bought a one-year-old Volkswagen Bug with the extra money. We had a nice house at last. All we had to pay was $40.00 a month until it was paid off. It had been a great lesson in God's provision in answers to prayer.

MEETING GREAT CHRISTIANS LIKE
OSWALD J. SMITH

Gwen and I entertained the Lord's servants whenever possible. We wanted our children to meet great Christians and learn from them. We also wanted to make visiting preachers feel at home away from home. We knew what loneliness is like.

Sometimes it would be for a meal, at other times it would be overnight or longer. One guest was Dr. I.D.E. Thomas, a Baptist preacher from Wales. I asked if I could take him to see people or places he was interested in seeing. Immediately he replied, "I would like to do two things. One, meet Dr. Oswald J. Smith, and two, visit Joseph Scriven's monument."

I arranged both for the same day. Joseph Scriven's monument is at Bewdley. We stopped there on our way to Toronto to meet Dr. Oswald J. Smith.

Joseph Scriven wrote "What a Friend We Have in Jesus", a hymn sung around the world and one of the best known and best loved.

When I introduced Dr. Thomas to Dr. Smith, I expected to step back and fade into the woodwork. Not so. As I backed away, Dr. Smith took me by the arm and said, "And who are you my lad, and what do you do?"

"Oh, I am a colporteur for the Bible Society."

"Are you now? I was a colporteur years ago."

A sparkle came into Dr. Smith's eyes, and he talked about colportage experiences in the Canadian west when he graduated from Bible College.

We talked for twenty minutes. Then he put his arms around me and prayed for me. What an unexpected blessing! How wonderful to meet one of the world's leading missionary statesman and to receive his blessing and encouragement. Dr. Smith said, "Go into our book room and choose any three books and I will autograph them for you." The verse he inscribed is Ruth 2:12, "The Lord recompense thy work, and a full reward be given thee of the Lord God of Israel, under whose wings thou art come to trust."

While I was in the book room, Dr. Smith chatted with Dr. Thomas. It was the pastor of the largest church in Canada talking with the pastor of the largest church in Wales. And it was my honour and privilege to introduce them to each other. How great is our God! He delights to bless His children in ways like this.

PORT HOPE – A POLICE ESCORT OUT OF TOWN
"The Chief wants to see you. You had better come along with me," advised the policeman.

I had been selling Bibles door-to-door in Port Hope, Ontario. The wife of a policeman had bought a Bible, so when I saw the policeman calling me, I thought he wanted another. Not so.

I had been getting a lot of doors slammed in my face and I knew some of these homes were Roman Catholic. Apparently one had called the local priest. The priest called the Chief of

Police. The Chief told me to get out of town or go to jail. He cited a local by-law that a license was required to canvas door-to-door. He would not listen to any explanation on my part. As a rookie colporteur, I did not know which alternative to choose, so I asked permission to call the Bible Society manager, Mr. Stevens. He advised me to leave town. I did not feel good about that. It was only a few years previously that I was discharged from the Navy after serving four years fighting for freedom. It seemed to me that this was one of those freedoms I worked so hard to maintain. I really expected Mr. Stevens to demand our freedom to call door-to-door. I really did not expect him to say "Leave."

I really wished I had made my own decision and gone to jail, but now it was too late. Baptist pastors were being imprisoned in Quebec in those days for preaching the Gospel on the streets, and I felt this persecution should be dealt with.

Years later with Bible Art Ministries I would have the privilege to speak at every elementary school in Port Hope, reaching every student with the Gospel. One Port Hope school principal said, "What my students saw and heard today will be the only Art Gallery some will ever see and the only Sunday school they will ever attend."

A LESSON IN DISCERNMENT
Spiritual discernment, simply put, is knowing when it is God speaking to you. Lack of spiritual discernment is one of the greatest problems we face today.

One morning I was travelling along Highway 7 through Marmora. I had prayed for guidance as I always did each morning and evening. I noticed a house set back some distance from the road. There were several school buses parked there. Suddenly I felt an urging or prompting to go to that house. The Lord often just gives you leading one step at a time. He seldom tells you what to do next before you obey the first step. Should I obey this feeling? Look at those school buses. It was mid-morning. Probably three or four bus drivers were in that house talking. They could give me quite a roasting,. I tried to reason it out. The buses were intimidating. That is when the enemy tells you it was your imagination, not the prompting of the Lord. I slowed down, hesitated, and then kept going down the highway.

Some time later I learned that a school bus driver from Marmora had taken a busload of people to a Billy Graham Crusade in Toronto and got saved himself. My heart sank.

Had the Lord wanted me to lead that man to Christ that day? When I failed, did the Lord use Billy Graham? Or was it after the Crusade and the bus driver needed a Bible or needed encouragement in The Way. Perhaps the other fellows were giving the new convert a hard time. Or perhaps they wanted to know Christ, too. I felt I had missed the Lord that day and I was sorry. But I was learning an important lesson. DON'T TRY TO FIGURE IT OUT. GOD'S WAYS ARE PAST FINDING OUT. I was learning to obey. I was learning to take that first step of obedience.

"Behold, to obey is better than sacrifice and to harken than the fat of rams."

Prayer: "Lord, help me to listen and obey."

AIRMAN

Getting home to see Gwen and the family was something I had looked forward to all week. I always counted the days when we were apart. Getting there as quickly as possible without breaking the law was what I was about.

I had selected the shorter of the two possible routes home, but suddenly there was a feeling that I should go back to a junction I had just passed, and take the longer route home. I did not understand why. I only knew that for some reason I was being apprehended of the Lord and it is vitally important to obey His leading. I remembered times when I had failed to discern God's leading and I did not want to fail again! So I wheeled my van around and headed back a mile or so to the junction.

There was a man in an air force uniform hitchhiking. I didn't usually pick up hitchhikers. Gwen had asked me not to. Was this Airman my assignment from the Lord? It seemed so.

I let him in. He saw my cargo, and asked, "What are all these Bibles about?" What a question! What an opening! What an opportunity!

We talked about God's wonderful plan of redemption. He absorbed the truth like that church building in Geraldton absorbed the paint. I told him how the Lord had helped me to stand for Him in the Navy and of His marvellous leading in my life.

The Airman's farm home loomed into view. He said, "This has

been a very special day in my life. This journey has changed my life and my direction."

It had been for both of us an awesome adventure in "Drawing Souls to Christ."

Gwen and the children were the first to hear this story. This is one of the stories she wanted you to know.

During the six years of ministry as a Colporteur with the Bible Society in addition to selling Bibles door-to-door, I called to see all of the ministers in the areas where I worked. I would ask them to announce that I would be working in their area so that the church people would know who I was when they saw me at their door. There were about twenty Fall Fairs I attended with a Bible display and some seventeen Christian Summer Camps. At the camps I would fit into their services and draw a stick man Bible story.

My Chalk Art became a special ministry and soon I was preaching nearly every Sunday somewhere. How many decisions for Christ were registered in Heaven I do not know. Even today people tell me the title of my Bible stories they saw and heard some 50 years ago. To God be the glory!

Loading the Chalk Art equipment in our 1954 Chev sedan delivery wagon at Utterson. Preparing to minister in a summer Bible camp. Margie and Paul looking on.

Drawing Souls To Christ

I particularly enjoyed the three Pioneer Camps and Camp Mineowe. Some campers made decisions for Christ. That was what we were about and that was always exciting. These summer camps were the very best with an alive program and enthusiastic campers. Their leaders were dedicated and capable. It was great to work with them.

While in the tourist areas, I would often take my stick men and wherever possible share the Gospel. Our Salvation Army experience in Open Air Meetings enabled us to adjust to many outdoor settings. People were attracted to the drawings and crowds came closer to get a good look. Chalk Drawing is one of the greatest ways to communicate anywhere. Somehow it does not seem as though you are being preached at and those who are strangers to God's Grace feel more comfortable with this method of preaching.

Wherever possible I would set up a small display of Bibles and New Testaments. As children, and people of every age, talked with me at the display there were wonderful opportunities to pray with them about a variety of needs.

Once while selling Bibles near Utterson, Ontario, I drove into the ditch on a narrow country road. When the tow truck arrived, the driver and I seemed to know each other. We finally realized that we were both in the Navy and served on the same ship HMCS Sussexvale. John owned a Texaco Service Station at Utterson and had half a dozen tourist cabins there. The photo was taken there.

Each summer we were welcome as a family to stay at John's cabins and work the Huntsville and Muskoka area from there. Gwen also had relatives in Huntsville and we had wonderful times staying with them. We did not have much money but we sure had a lot of fun. The Bible Society provided us with a brand new car every four years. That was a big plus. It was the first time we had ever had a new car. Sometimes I would receive an honorarium of $10.00 to $15.00 for preaching on a Sunday. That was a real bonus. We never thought about money; we only thought about ministry. To this day I am always surprised when someone gives me an honorarium after ministry. I just had not thought about that. The opportunity to minister and the importance of those needs were all I had thought about. Most of our preaching opportunities gave no financial honorarium.

Chapter 6

Evangel
Baptist church

At Fair Havens Bible Conference in 1958, I met Mr. and Mrs. Tom Worrod from Hamilton. Tom was chairman of the deacon's board of Evangel Baptist Church. Later the church extended a call to me to become their pastor. Evangel had just sponsored Elliot Heights Baptist, a new church in another part of Hamilton. Evangel's Pastor and several families moved to the new church. Keeping Evangel going represented quite a challenge.

Gwen and I had been feeling the call to go back to the pastorate and after praying for several weeks accepted the call to Evangel in December 1958. It became another chapter in "Drawing Souls To Christ."

Hamilton was home to both Gwen and me. Our families were glad to have us move back.

Percy Ward was Evangel's song leader. Percy had been our iceman during the great depression when I was a boy. The Sunday I had decided to let them know, Percy met me as I arrived and eagerly asked, "Well, Pastor, have you made your decision?"

Looking directly into his eyes, I answered, "Yes." Percy's eyes filled with tears. It was the confirmation I needed. Percy would prove to be the most faithful friend I had.

Evangel did not have a parsonage. When we accepted the call they could only offer us $35.00 per week as the church had a heavy missionary budget with two in Africa, and one in France. We had to move in with Gwen's Mom for a while. We rented the Peterborough house not knowing we would need it again sooner than we expected.

Drawing Souls To Christ

While at Evangel, a fellow pastor, Don Wheaton, told me that he would be attending Toronto Baptist Seminary five days a week. Don invited me to drive with him and take the same course. Our church approved and it was a wonderful opportunity. Don became a wonderful friend and mentor. We each owned a Volkswagen Bug. He drove one day and I drove the next. We discussed our courses en route. Don taught me how to study and remember what I had learned. I shall be forever grateful to him for helping me.

We had traveled together for some weeks before Don had an opportunity to meet Gwen. There was a special meeting at the Seminary and our wives were invited. I remember the double take that registered on his face when he met her. She really was all I had told him. She was like that always just sweet, wonderful, wholesome, beautiful Gwen. He let me know that he was impressed and that I had not exaggerated one bit. Her beauty was never a snare. Her spirit and manner left no doubt about her commitment to Christ and her husband and family. Gwen impressed everyone she met. She was like Nathaniel. Someone in whose spirit there was no guile. She was that same sweet wonderful girl I met at the picnic, all her life.

Once while we were at the Salvation Army Training College, a Toronto Star photographer came to take photographs for a newspaper article. He wanted to photograph the youngest, prettiest girl there. He chose Gwen. She said, "Oh no, I am not the one you want. I am married. I have a child. You want one of those others."

"Oh, no," he said. "You are the one I want."

GWEN WAS SPECIAL

Vacation Bible School can be a great outreach to the community. It is a great opportunity to reach people of every age who may be a little hesitant about coming to your church for any other type of meeting.

While conducting VBS one summer at Evangel, Joan M., a young married woman living in Ohio, was back home in Hamilton, visiting her parents. She was passing our church and took note of the VBS activities going on. She came in to make inquiries – she met Gwen first. Then Gwen brought her to me. Joan was a born-again Christian. She had been praying for her family who were Roman Catholics, but unsaved. She asked, "If I bring my family here to church, will you look after them spiritually and make sure they become established Christians?"

My answer was, "You had better believe we will. I promise"

True to her word, she came to our church on Sunday and brought her youngest sister whose husband was in prison. The sister got saved that morning. She told us that her husband was about to be released from prison, and she would bring him with her next Sunday.

The husband came and he, too, got saved. Later he told me that he had not intended to stay with his wife and baby, but the Lord changed all that when they both became Christians. He saw that my car needed body-work and painting, and offered to do it for free if I could pay for the materials. He learned auto-body repair while in prison.

Joan went back to Ohio, but her mom, dad and the whole family came to church, and over a period of the next three weeks, everyone in the family had made a commitment to Christ. Wow! It was revival time. And they kept coming to church. What a delight! What a precious family! What a joy to disciple them! Later when I was forced to leave Evangel due to illness, the greatest heartache to me was leaving precious people like these who needed to continue growing in grace. I prayed that the Lord would look after them.

TOO OLD TO WIN SOULS?

Mrs. Bogie was a senior and a widow. She would call me on the phone and say, "I have another lady ready to receive Christ as Saviour. Can you call to see her and lead her to the Lord?"

When Mrs. Bogie said they were ready - they were ready. After making sure of their salvation I would ask them to come to church next Sunday. I told them I would give them an opportunity at the close of the service to come forward to the front of the church to publicly confess her faith in Jesus Christ as Lord and Saviour. I found that this was no problem for these new converts when they understood what was expected, and they did it joyfully. At the same time, the church welcomed them as new believers in God's Family.

NEEDING A NEW YOUNG PEOPLE'S LEADER

Doug Dakin was a tremendous young people's leader. I was so happy to have him in that position. He was so good in helping young people to grow in maturity as Christians. I used to pick his brains as to how he did it, and I learned much from him. One day, he announced that he would be leaving to go to Bible school. There was no one in the church who could replace him. For weeks, I prayed, and just about the time Doug was to leave, a fine looking young man came to our Sunday morning service. It was easy to see that he absorbed every word that was preached. At the conclusion of the service, as he and I talked together, he said, "I enjoyed the service. I plan to come back." Wow!

Lloyd Much was an electrical engineer. He had moved to Hamilton to oversee installation of large industrial machinery in the various steel mills of the city. He became our youth leader and he was God's special gift to us. Our God is a God of the impossible. When things look hopeless, there is always hope in God. It was a lesson for me to learn. Oh, how great is our God and greatly to be praised!

Lloyd also helped me with my new special chalk-drawing easel. It included black light and various coloured lights with rheostats and switches that could be operated from a distance to enhance the drawings and make them come alive. The Lord does exceedingly abundantly above all that we can ask or think.

THINGS THAT HAPPENED AT EVANGEL

When I was twelve, my brother and I went to an art teacher's home to be tutored. We were awe- struck by his beautifully de-tailed paintings. One was "The Violin Recital." The violin being played in the painting was small, but every string was perfect. It was a challenge to us to "Do likewise." Our teacher, Tom Bod-fish, was also an accomplished violinist. Sometimes when we arrived we could hear him playing, so we would wait a few minutes on the porch to listen. We were proud of his accomplishments and felt fortunate we had the great privilege of studying under him. I wanted to be able to paint like him. This was 1934 at the depth of the great depression.

Twenty five years later, while I was pastor of Evangel Church, my Dad informed me that my former art teacher's Dad was seriously ill, and not expected to recover. So I went to see him. He was living in one tiny room at the head of a long stairway in a boarding house. I learned that Tom, the artist, lived in Vancouver, more than 3,000 miles away, but his Dad didn't know just where. His son had been too busy to write. It was plain to see that the father missed his son and longed to see him. The father was a born again Christian. I was glad about that. So when we prayed, I asked the Lord to apprehend Tom and cause him to contact his dear father.

The following day, Tom was in Toronto, just 50 miles away. Suddenly he got the greatest urge to go and see his father. What a glad reunion they had. And guess what – the father regained the will to live and recovered. To God be the Glory! Mission accomplished! Hallelujah! "Before you call, I will answer." (Isaiah 65:24) My Dad was pretty happy about it, too.

The time that Tom became concerned about going to see his Dad, instead of returning to Vancouver as planned, was the same time his Dad and I were praying the Lord would cause him to do this. Coincidence? No! And God did more than re-unite father and son. He brought a double healing, in restoring the father's health. "Call unto Me, and I will answer you, and show you great and mighty things that you know not..." (Jeremiah 33:3) "He is able to do exceeding abundantly above all we can ask or think..." (Ephesians 3:20) Even as I write these words 48 years later, I can see that little attic room and feel the presence of the Lord as we prayed that day so long ago. I am sure the Dad had prayed many times about his son. God heard each of those prayers. Does not His perfect timing in creating His answer truly cause us to stand in awe of Him?

THE POWER OF PRAYER

The purpose of this book is to honour God as we recall His manifold abundant answers to prayer in seemingly impossible situations, so that fellow pilgrims may be encouraged to pray as I was encouraged to pray by others I met along this same journey who had learned to pray without ceasing.

There are conditions to be met in prayer. One is forgiveness. "If I regard (allow) iniquity in my heart the Lord will not hear me." "And when you stand praying, forgive, if you ought against any...." We must seek out God's conditions in His Word, the Holy Bible, and remember them when we pray. So we must be forgiven, and we must forgive others in order to be forgiven.

Job said, "Man is born to trouble as the sparks fly upward." As I write now, I am going through the biggest problem I have ever faced in 86 years, but I am encouraged that God has not changed, and that He hears my present prayers, and that out of my present problem He will answer in His own inimitable way that which is best. I remember, too, that it was when Job prayed for his enemies that God blessed him and restored twice as much as he had lost.

GRANDPA WILLIAM "BILL" ASPDEN

My father-in-law, Grandpa Aspden, was a chief petty officer motor mechanic in the Canadian Navy during World War II. He was in charge of the engine room on the Navy Tug Ellsworth operating in Halifax, Nova Scotia.

At one time, he had been an active Christian in the Salvation Army. But now he was what they called a "backslider." While I was pastor of Evangel he was a patient in Sunnybrook Military Hospital in Toronto. I visited each week. He recommitted his life to Christ. That was a real answer to prayer. A month or so later, Bill Aspden quietly went to be with the Lord. His roommates told me that just before he died, he said, "All ashore that's going ashore!" They wanted to know what that meant. It is a Navy command given to those who have permission to leave the ship and go ashore. For Grandpa Aspden, it meant that he saw the doors of heaven open to him. To God be the Glory!

DEALING WITH DISAPPOINTMENT

While at Evangel, I was guest preaching and was invited to dinner with a parishioner. They didn't tell me the wife had hepatitis – the infectious kind. I caught it. I became seriously ill.

I had been bedridden for over a month – and some of my deacons felt I wasn't really that sick. So I went back – and suffered a critical relapse. Dr. Ron Elliott, an exceptional Christian, told me the only hope was to resign and move to a quiet setting. Our house in Peterborough would be ideal – but we had rented it out with a long-term lease.

We prayed about what to do. The next morning, our neighbour in Peterborough phoned to tell us "I have some bad news – I saw a moving truck at your tenant's last night – they've moved out without telling anyone." Bad news – not to us. We were able to move back home.

After a month, I tried to work part-time. I couldn't. "You are not going back" Gwen said, and she took over my job, at the Christian bookstore.

Gwen placed a calendar at my bedside with Jeremiah 30:17 "I will restore health unto you, and I will heal you of your wounds, sayeth the Lord." That was my ray of hope. I prayed it every day. Psalm 37 also became precious.

In recovery following a life threatening and debilitating disease, you are finally ready to get back into action in ministry, but churches needing a pastor look askance at you. What do you do? You pray.

In 1962, I was invited to apply for the position of pastor at Trenton Baptist Church. I had preached there several times and was respected and loved by the congregation. Now as I was given an opportunity to "preach for a call" (as Baptists do when selecting a pastor), I was excited about the possibilities.

The congregation was warm and seemed excited about the possibility of me becoming their pastor. Meeting with the Deacons Board, I told them candidly about my illness and recovery. Basil Ritter, chairman of the Board asked, "Brother Crookall, what is the state of your health now?" I said I felt fine and ready to resume a pastorate, but added, "Who can tell what a day may bring for anyone of us? Do you know the state of your health?"

My good friend and mentor, the Rev. Tom Delaney, had been their pastor. Under his capable leadership, Trenton Baptist had grown, flourished, and built a new church.

After he left, they had called another pastor, who had been with them only a few months when he died of a heart attack. You could understand their concern.

I did not get the job. I was very disappointed. It was a defeat to my hopes and dreams What now? Pray! God had something better for me, and His "No" answer was a blessing in disguise.

Gwen was always the great encourager. "With the Lord's help, we will make it." When the Lord closes a door, He always opens a window of hope. We need to stay close to Him and not allow discouragement to tarnish Faith. We read Psalm 37 again, and again, and again.

Due to my work as a Bible Society Colporteur, I was well known and had been continually on call as a supply preacher. My ability as a Chalk Artist was an added attraction for special meetings and Evangelistic Crusades. But often there was no honorarium and now we needed a steady income. Since my illness, calls were much less frequent.

Drawing Souls To Christ

When I recovered from a year's illness with hepatitis, my doctor said, "You may never be able to work full time again." I was forty years old. What kind of work could I do?

My doctor said, "You may have to get a job where you work for a week and then take a week off."

"Do you know where I can get a job like that?" I asked.

The doctor chuckled, "No, I don't."

But I was not laughing. It was serious. Somehow I believed God for more than that.

Chapter 7

Gospel Light

How could I do something for the Lord, and what could I do? Gwen and I prayed about it each day. As we prayed, I remembered my work with the Bible Society. They had discontinued colportage work, but perhaps I could be a Bible salesman on my own. If I could obtain Bibles and Christian supplies like wall mottoes and books at wholesale prices similar to the Christian bookstores, maybe it would work. It was worth a try.

Bill Lawson had been song leader at Philpott Memorial Church in Hamilton, and now worked for Home Evangel Books, Canada's largest wholesale Christian Book Store supplier. I called him, and he gladly arranged an interview with his boss, Gordon. That lead to another adventure in "Drawing Souls To Christ."

As I told Gordon what I wanted to do, he asked me a bunch of questions that didn't seem too relevant to buying Bibles wholesale, such as what I knew about Gospel Light Sunday School curriculum. I told him what I knew, that we had used it in Vacation Bible School, and I thought it was excellent. Turns out this was a job interview – unbeknownst to me, Gordon was looking for a sales rep for Gospel Light.

He asked if I would be interested in working for him coast-to-coast out of Toronto. Wow! He gave me a complete sample set of Gospel Light Sunday school curriculum, and asked me to take it home, analyze it, and write a report recommending a plan to promote it across the country. I was excited. I could hardly wait to get home to tell Gwen about it. We were both excited. Gwen was always my biggest supporter. She knew me as no one else did, and she believed in me. She did not say one discouraging word. We prayed about the opportunity and asked God to give us wisdom and enable us to analyze the material.

The next day we sat down on the couch with the Gospel Light material between us and we read it. We discussed what it was about. I jotted down what we learned. Gordon wanted the

Drawing Souls To Christ

report in two weeks. I got it to him in three days. He sent my report to Gospel Light headquarters in California. They phoned back – "hire that man on the spot; he analyzed our material better than we could ourselves. He told us things we did not know." I was ready for action. From the start, God gave me health, energy, and joy.

Why me? How was I chosen for this great job? Now I could see God's Hand in closing the door at Trenton.

My car was an eight-year-old '54 Meteor. I got it repainted two-tone green and it served the purpose to begin with.

It has been said that sometimes the job makes the man and sometimes the man makes the job. Gospel Light became an "Awesome Adventure" that placed me with the best Sunday school writers, leaders and speakers. It was like being assigned to play right wing on a line with hockey's greatest player, Wayne Gretzky at centre. These "giants of faith" accepted me immediately. They had been reading my field reports of God's awesome answers to unusual problems and they were as interested in learning from me as I was in learning from them.

Names of great men I had come to respect were now my personal friends and co-workers. How thrilling to learn from them. No one at Gospel Light ever made me feel inferior. They were encouragers without exception.

My '54 Meteor wasn't up to the job. We prayed about a good car at a price we could afford to pay. Norm Grierson worked for Ciba Drug Company. He told me about his manager's car, a leased 1960 Chevrelot Belair hardtop, white with a copper coloured roof – sharp as a tack! It was two years old with low mileage. Price $1850.00. Wow! Just the ticket. It proved to be one of the best cars we ever had. Tom Schauff drove our son, Paul, and me, to Montreal to pick up the car. I had purchased it sight-unseen, depending on Norm's recommendation. Two days later, Gwen, Tim (then three years-old), and I started for Glendale, California – a 3,000 mile journey, for an extensive training at head office, and to participate in Gospel Light's Annual Conference.

In those days, White's Hamburgers were five for a dollar. We ate them coast-to-coast on our journey along Route 66 through Illinois, Missouri, Oklahoma, Texas, Arizona, Nevada, and California. We saw the Painted Desert, the Grand Canyon, the redwood trees, Boulder Dam, and had a marvellous trip. Glory to God!

In Texas we bought Tim cowboy boots, hat, and the whole kit. At Forest Home Conference they sang "Happy Birthday" to Tim and called him the Canadian Cowboy.

Canadian Cowboy Tim

The breathtaking beauty of America, was an unforgettable experience, and it was all part of my job. Wow! We were filled with awe and thrilled by the grandeur of God's creation – continually changing from state to state. We fell in love with America. We were seeing all the wonderful places we had learned about in school, but they were more exciting than the best photographs. It became the honeymoon we could not afford when we were married...

By the time we reached Arizona we were getting fed up with Whites Hamburgers. We saw great billboards advertising Rod's Steak House. We decided to splurge on a steak dinner.

The menu was pricier than we could afford – except for one item with an exotic name that I can't remember. When it arrived, we had a good laugh. It was hamburger molded in the shape of a steer. But it was good – ground sirloin.

We bought petrified wood from the Indians at fifteen cents per pound. I can see a ten-pound chunk in our living room as I write.

Gospel Light people from the top down treated us royally. They were real people, sincere, dedicated, committed, and anxious to help in every possible way. No one was holier-than-thou. Each showed respect for the others.

Looking back now, on visits to thousands of schools in four countries, I see how the principal can have a great influence on

Drawing Souls To Christ

the character of the school. It's the same with companies. Dr. Henrietta Mears and the William T. Grieg Sr. family were leaders who helped make Gospel Light what it is. I wanted to learn from them, and to my great surprise they wanted to learn from me.

Gwen and I were honoured at a special dinner in Glendale. As we picked up our knives and forks to eat, we were suddenly aware that everyone was watching. They said, "We wanted to see if you would use your cutlery the English way. We are delighted to see you do."

I had always been embarrassed about using my fork upside down in my left hand until then, but not anymore. From that day on, I have felt at ease wherever I eat because of their warm response. It was not something to be ashamed of, but rather to be proud of.

In promoting Gospel Light Sunday School Curriculum, I felt it was necessary to teach booksellers its particular features and values. It was necessary to contact pastors, their Sunday School Superintendents, and the teaching staff. It was important to tell the Gospel Light success story to students in Bible Schools across the country. I was sold on the curriculum myself, and looked upon promoting it as a ministry.

Gospel Light began with Dr. Henrietta Mears (the Mother Theresa of the Sunday School movement) at First Presbyterian Church in Hollywood, California. When Dr. Mears, a Baptist, became Christian Education Director of Hollywood Presbyterian, she could not find just what she wanted in Sunday School Lesson materials. So she designed her own.

When the Sunday school grew from four hundred to four thousand in just four years, people took notice. They asked for the curriculum. At first it was mimeographed, but the demand became so great that William T. Grieg Sr., a printer and close relative, began Gospel Light Publications in Glendale, California, right next to Hollywood.

It was our privilege to visit the Sunday School in action at Hollywood Presbyterian. It was a truly unforgettable experience. The church complex covers an entire city block at Hollywood and Vine Streets.

The Primary and Junior Departments were very special, with a theatre-type auditorium all their own. You could follow the journey of Abraham on an illuminated map that lit up in colour as he proceeded. We checked Tim in, at his department, and received a ticket identifying him. When we went to pick him up, we had to produce the ticket.

The college and careers group led by Dr. Mears herself produced a number of world leaders like Bill Bright, Bob Pierce, Dawson Trotman, and many others. It was without doubt the finest and largest Sunday School we had ever seen.

During the 1960s Sunday Schools of one thousand were not unusual. Dr. Charles Blair's Assemblies of God Church in Denver used Gospel Light and grew steadily to several thousand. What a thrill to meet Dr. Blair and get his enthusiastic recommendations. As I met these great leaders across the continent I learned and learned. Now I could share with churches small and large the secrets to success. What a delight. To God Be the Glory!

The next summer, 1963 I was on the road coast-to-coast across Canada and the U.S.A. for the entire summer. The company rented a house trailer so I could take Gwen, Margie, Paul and Tim along. We stopped for several days each at Thunder Bay, Winnipeg, Regina, Saskatoon, Edmonton, Calgary, Pentiction, Vancouver, Salem Oregon, Portland, and San Francisco. I set up Sunday School Conferences and Conventions for the following year.

Later I joined a team from Glendale working from the East Coast to the Midwest. When that team returned home exhausted, I joined another team to tour Western conferences. Everything was bathed in prayer. It must be that way. We need God's leading guidance, favour, and anointing every moment of every day.

We visited the great Bible Colleges and schools across the land. At Prairie Bible Institute it was my turn to be the main speaker to four thousand students. In setting up the service, the service leader said, "Now, don't be funny." When I asked, "What do you mean, don't be funny?"

He replied, "You know you Americans always have to tell a lot of jokes."

"But I am not American. I am Canadian."

"Oh, that is great. You will be O.K. then."

We had to get a large plywood sheet and rig it up for my chalk drawing message, "The Three Hebrew Boys in the Fiery Furnace."

Stick men Bible stories have humour. That is just part of it. The students were almost rolling in the aisles with laughter. But you can move from laughter to tears in a moment with

Drawing Souls To Christ

the Lord's anointing. The students were learning great lessons from the Word and a unique way of preaching "Drawing Souls to Christ".

Several days later I received a warm and wonderful letter from Dr. Maxwell, Dean of the school, in which he stated, "Our students will not soon forget the story of the Three Hebrew Boys in the Fiery Furnace."

The Jabez-type prayer I had prayed as a Pastor at Evangel Baptist Church in Hamilton was being answered. The Lord had indeed "enlarged my coast from drawing for hundreds to drawing for thousands." To God be the glory! One of the big things about praying is believing God for the answer.

Getting opportunities to speak with busy Pastors was a lot easier if you invited them to lunch at the best steak house in town. Having been a Pastor, I knew what they would want to know and could share with them from the vast wealth of information working with what Gospel Light had taught me, plus our personal experience in churches, both large and small. Suddenly I was considered an expert in the Sunday School field and Pastors of great churches were asking my advice. When I got a question I could not answer I would check it out with my Gospel Light specialist and pass the information on immediately.

Invitations to speak to the entire Sunday school staff at great churches amazed me. Gospel Light sales skyrocketed in Canada. What Gwen and I had learned in our evaluation of the curriculum, gave Sunday School workers an understanding of Gospel Light's complete Bible teaching program, individually designed for each age and learning level. When they learned how the special interests of the Primary and Junior level students were being met, they became more enthusiastic teachers.

I kept in touch with Fritz Ridenour, editor of TEACH magazine, and shared with him the questions I received. It was exciting. I was giving him questions asked across the continent, in churches of every size in every denomination. It made his job more exciting and provided the information people needed.

Having a heart for Pastors of small struggling churches, I sought them out and shared methods that worked for me and for others. I took them and their wives to a great dinner. I remember a Pastor in the Midwest who wept in the middle of dinner. He said, "I have never had a dinner like this in my life before. And to think you did all this for me." I felt my eyes moistening as well. Encouragement to pastors and church workers was a given - and praying with them became a delight.

BORN TO TROUBLE

Job said, "Man is born to trouble as the sparks fly upward." We faced problems continually, but God had the answer.

In my first visit to Glendale, I was warned about problems I would have with 'Joe,' a distributor of Sunday School curriculum in one of Canada's largest cities. He was opposed to Gospel Light, would not carry it in his stores, and counselled churches not to buy it.

Even so, I wasn't ready for what I faced at the first Sunday School Conference I was at in Joe's city -- he had people at every entrance handing out anti-Gospel Light leaflets. That was beyond what I would have expected from the Christian competition.

I prayed, "Lord, what should I do about this?" The answer came quickly. "If thine enemy hunger, feed him..." Great idea. Thank you, Lord. Help us to become friends.

My display was about one hundred feet from Joe's display. When everyone had gone into the next general session, Joe and I were alone in the display area. I went over with hand extended. "Hi, I am Stan Crookall."

"I know who you are," was the less-than-gracious reply.

Ignoring the tone, I continued with my plan: "Do you know a great Steak House near here?"

"Why, there is one just up the street six blocks," he replied.

"Joe, I would like you to be my guest for dinner tonight. What would be a good time?"

Joe was amazed. "I'd like that," he said.

At dinner I asked about his conversion and about his family. Toward the end of the meal, Joe said "I really don't know much about Gospel Light."

"Well, Joe, it isn't my purpose to talk about it now, but next time I'm in town let's have dinner again and then we can go back to your store and talk about Gospel Light. But I will just tell you this much -- it has been my privilege to meet and work with Gospel Light editors and writers. They are some of the finest people I have ever met. They are committed and dedicated to winning souls and teaching the Word. I have learned so much from them."

Drawing Souls To Christ

Two weeks later Joe and I met again. I had done a lot more praying. I explained that I knew some of his customers were going to switch to Gospel Light and we did not want him to loose their business. There were churches we would like him to supply, but we could only send them his way if he sold Gospel Light. When he got the picture of Gospel Light's overall curriculum plan to meet the needs of each student at every age and learning level, he got excited and stocked up on our material. We became good friends, and had some good fellowship together.

Gospel Light Glendale was amazed when they read my monthly report telling this story. God does amazing things when we pray. Expecting God to answer is energizing and exciting...

UNSAINTLY SAINTS

Some times the saints don't act very saintly. At Winnipeg, in the Canadian Midwest, we had made arrangements for a Sunday School Conference sponsored by Gospel Light. We partnered with the local Bible Bookseller. The Conference was to be held at Calvary Temple.

When I arrived in Winnipeg some weeks before the Conference, I found that a local pastor, who was a part-time worker for another major publisher, had threatened the local Bible Bookseller. If they sponsored the Gospel Light Conference as scheduled, he, the Pastor, would ask his congregation to boycott the Bible Bookstore and refuse to make purchases there.

In addition to this, the Pastor had arranged for his publisher's Sunday School Conference to be held two weeks ahead of ours at Calvary Temple.

The Senior Pastor at Calvary Temple did not want another conference in his church two weeks later. What to do? Pray!

As I prayed about it, I felt led of the Lord to look up the pastor of a large Baptist Church, Rev. Don Jost, and talk to him about it. Don Jost was a wonderful man of God, and he was willing to help a fellow Baptist in distress.

He said, "You can conduct your conference here at our church and we will sponsor you." We did, and it was great.

Many years later, the Pastor, who messed things up for us, established a Bible College of some renown. An American T.V. Evangelist recommended the school highly and vouched for the integrity of the faculty. When I heard it, I hoped what he said was true. I hope the Pastor had repented of his questionable ways and had become indeed a person of integrity.

When one of the saints acts unsaintly like this, it is best to just pray and seek God's guidance. Then do exactly what God leads you to do step-by-step. God will look after the problem without you making a bigger mess of it.

Some of the great men of faith in the Bible failed and later repented, and were restored. We are admonished to "pray for those who despitefully use you."

It is important not to allow someone else's sins to contaminate you with bitterness and unforgiveness. No one can afford such a self-inflicted injury.

Gospel Light had been a great learning experience.

WHAT I LEARNED FROM GOSPEL LIGHT

Gospel Light had the best editors and writers in the business. They also had many of the finest teachers conducting workshops at Sunday School Conventions.

Ethel Barrett was known as America's Story Teller. To meet her in person and to hear her tell her stories was an education in itself. I also read everything she wrote about public speaking and gaining and maintaining children's interest.

Leslie Millar, a former missionary to Africa and editor, spoke from his heart and every message was challenging. He told us about a teen age girl in California who committed her life to Christ and took great interest in church and Sunday School, but then began to miss a few Sundays.

Millar wondered why. When asked about it, the girl rolled up her long sleeves to reveal terrible bruises. "I have bruises like this all over my body. This is what my father does to me each time he finds out that I have attended church or Sunday school. I still want to come, but I can't always make it."

Millar told us about the African farmers who carried their produce to market on their heads. A boatload of these farmers was crowded on deck with the bundles on their heads. Suddenly a woman lost her footing and tumbled into the water. She screamed for help, but no one moved to help her. The woman drowned. When asked why no one offered to help her, they said, "But we would loose our produce if we did."

Millar asked the audience, "What are you willing to risk in

order to win the lost, or will you be content to allow them to die in their sins?"

Dean Dalton, a department editor, has been a long time friend. He now lives in Largo, Florida, just down the road. We get together occasionally.

Gospel Light lessons are designed to win students to Christ and teach them how to grow as believers. Dr. Henrietta Mears had a favourite acrostic: GROW:

GO TO GOD IN PRAYER EVERY DAY
READ THE WORD OF GOD EVERY DAY
OBEY THE LORD EVERY DAY
WITNESS FOR CHRIST EVERY DAY

In every ministry I have worked with, it has been first and foremost my desire to serve the Lord in helping people, first in evangelism and second in Christian growth and development. The sales aspect was a natural outcome -- a by-product of the accomplishment of the former. When I visited a pastor, I wanted to help him more than sell him something. I wanted to help him to help others. If I did not have a sense of ministry, there was no reason good enough for me to spend my time away from home. Only a conviction that I was doing what the Lord wanted me to do could keep me away from my home where I longed to be more than anywhere else. Wherever possible I took Gwen and the family with me.

Once in Vancouver, when I had taken my family with me via house trailer, the plan was to leave them in Vancouver while I flew to California. While I was talking with the bookseller who sold the most Gospel Light lessons in Canada, she asked me about my itinerary and my family. I told her I was flying to Glendale, California and leaving the family in Vancouver until I returned. She asked why I did not want to take my family with me. I told her it was my boss's idea. She picked up the phone and called my boss. "G-," she said, "why don't you give Stan the opportunity to take his family with him to Los Angeles?" They talked for a few minutes and I got permission to hook up the trailer and take my family with me.

When Glendale learned that I was driving down, they asked me to take in a Mennonite Conference in Salem, Oregon on the way. What a delight that was! We parked the trailer at the farm of a Mennonite family. Paul got a chance to pitch hay and work on the farm. Gwen, Margie, and Tim enjoyed the farm, too.

The farther away you are from home the more you are respected. The Mennonite People were so good to me. How I enjoyed being with them and sharing what I could with them.

I sure appreciated that Vancouver bookseller, too. What a treat it was to take the family from Vancouver to Los Angeles and see San Francisco, the Redwoods at Eureka, California and so much more. And how much more effective I could be with the family in tow.

THE CRUCIFIXION

Adjacent to Gospel Light Publications building is the famous Forest Lawn Cemetery. One day, Bill Grieg, Jr., Vice President of Gospel Light, suggested I see the painting of "The Crucifixion" at the Cemetery. All he told me was that a missionary who saw it a week previously said it was the greatest painting he had ever seen. I went, and was amazed that the painting was 190 feet long and 45 feet high.

It is shown in a purpose-built theatre. Beautiful gold curtains are drawn back slowly accompanied by the majestic music of a symphony orchestra. It is a breathtaking experience. It is like being there at Calvary.

Jan Styka's Masterpiece, "The Crucixion"

Drawing Souls To Christ

There is a twenty-minute explanation of the painting just like Bible Art Ministries' presentation. At the conclusion we all stood in silence and awe.

I bowed my head. "LORD, WHATEVER TALENT YOU HAVE GIVEN ME, I GIVE BACK TO YOU. I PRAY YOU WILL BE PLEASED TO BLESS IT AND MULTIPLY IT AND USE IT SO THAT I CAN PAINT ART FROM THE BIBLE AND TELL THE GREATEST STORY EVER TOLD."

For the first time in my life, I became aware how Fine Art could be used to "Draw Souls To Christ." My chalk art "stick men" were effective in a sermon, but a fine art painting kept on "speaking" for years and years.

That painting changed my life. It became the seed that God planted in my heart, which grew into BIBLE ART MINISTRIES fourteen years later.

When we got back to Toronto, I immediately enrolled in evening classes at the Ontario College of Art, to become a Fine Art Illustrator so that I could be a Fine Art Biblical Illustrator. I also enrolled in the Famous Artists Correspondence Course which would take three years to complete.

At Ontario College of Art, I was blessed to have Professor Eric Friefeld as my drawing instructor and Jerry Sevier as my instructor in illustration. When I used Bible stories in all my assignments, Jerry asked "Are you some kind of a Religious Nut?" But he helped me with interest nevertheless.

When I was on the road away from home I worked day and evening. I gave it everything I had. I was getting to the point of burn out. At times, stress pain was so bad I could not move. The doctor recommended two Tylenol 3 whenever this happened.

I first knew I was in trouble physically while working one day in the Niagara Falls area. No, I was not thinking of going over the falls – with or without a barrel. As I sat in my car trying to relax and pray before my next appointment, I realized that tears were rolling down my cheeks. I knew this was serious. The only time I did this before was when I was absolutely exhausted while suffering from hepatitis. I had not yet learned that all work and no play made makes one a sick person.

My doctor said, "Why don't you quit this job?" When he read my face, he said, "Oh, you don't think anyone else can do it as well as you do?" That was it. I laughed with him. The doctor asked, "What would you really like to do?"

"I would really like to be a Biblical Illustrator."

"Are you good enough?" "I think so."

"Then why don't you do it?"

I began to pray about it. Larry Remple, the associate Pastor at Calvary Temple in Winnipeg, had talked with me about wanting to do what I was doing. He could take my place. It was early December, and I told my employer (I worked for a distribution company in Toronto that had the contract with Gospel Light) I was thinking of making the transition at the end of March.

My boss did not want me to quit. He wanted me to see his doctor. I didn't.

I was in my office in Toronto the morning of Christmas Eve, working on correspondence and looking forward to returning home to Christmas with my family. My boss walked in. After a few pleasantries, he asked, "Well, Stan, what have you decided to do, stay with us or leave?" I had in mind leaving in three to six months time, to give him time to replace me, make a good transition both for them and for me into a new phase of ministry.

I began to explain this when he abruptly commanded, "Give me your car keys and clean out your desk. You are through as of this moment." Wow! I had not expected anything like that. I was shocked. Fired on Christmas Eve. It was a bit overwhelming.

I had been driving a company car. I would have to go home by train. I phoned Gwen and told her I had just been sacked. Always ready for the unexpected, she said: "Don't worry, we will manage. The Lord has always met our need." Sweet, wonderful, understanding Gwen. She was one in a million.

There was a small party at the office and we were each given a Christmas turkey. Mine was easy to carry because it was the scrawniest. Some received a Christmas bonus, but not I. There was no holiday pay either.

Riding home on the train with that emaciated bird on my lap I felt like a turkey myself. It could have been a great time for a pity party, but it was more a state-of-shock. I thought of Scrooge and poor Bob Cratchet. I understood the story better now. I had never heard of anyone being fired Christmas Eve. I knew Gwen would be waiting at the station for me. We would have a nice Christmas together as a family.

Gwen and I had a sense of vision and destiny. We knew that Biblical Art was a future priority. Perhaps it was just coming sooner than expected.

Chapter 8

The transition

Bill Gothard in his Basic Youth Seminars talks about THREE STEPS TO FULFILMENT OF A VISION. First there is the BIRTH OF A VISION, then the DEATH OF A VISION, and finally the FULFILLMENT of that vision. My ministry as a Biblical Illustrator would go through those steps.

Within the week my ex-boss, Scrooge (er, Gordon) was on the phone to me. No, it was not an apology. A large group of churches I had been working with was considering purchasing Gospel Light curriculum for all of their churches. They had asked for me to come to their upcoming convention and speak about the curriculum and the possibility of Gospel Light printing it with their church logo on it..

At the time I was busy with planning Evangelistic Crusades featuring Art from the Bible and Stick Men Chalk Drawing Bible Stories.

Getting fired was pretty decisive and I really did not want to go back to the office again. I offered to write a letter that Gordon could take and read at the convention. I was no longer an employee and I did not want to misrepresent my status to the Moderator who was a personal friend, or to the denomination, who could feel taken advantage of if they were expecting that I would be at their service in the future.

Had my departure been more pleasant I may have felt more like going back to do this one favor. As it was, I spent more than a day to prepare a good comprehensive statement. At the time, I felt I had gone the extra mile.

Two weeks later, Gordon phoned again. He had hired Larry Remple to take my place. Larry was overwhelmed by the complexities of the job and said he needed my help. I agreed to go back for three weeks to coach him – he was my friend and I wanted him to do well. When I was satisfied that Larry could make it on his own I felt free to leave, with the provision he could call me any time.

Another bridge had been burned behind me. I wish it had been a happier ending. In every difficult situation, we had found the answers to our need in God's Word and prayer.

My Gospel Light friends are still my friends today. Some who act as friends are fair weather friends who feign friendship to gain their purpose and use you to gain what they want. When you are no longer useful to them, you are discarded. It is the people who seem too good to be true who usually prove not to be true. It makes you feel cheated and taken in – but more wary the next time. It also helps you to appreciate those who are indeed true friends. I was always, before, during and after treated well by Gospel Light. But the independent Canadian distributor, HE Books, who was my employer – well, that was different.

The scriptural way to work for any employer is to work as unto the Lord. When we put the Lord first in all we do no matter what happens, we shall have been a success in His sight and that will bring its own rewards.

The Bible tells the whole story about the saints good and bad. My purpose is to show that everyone, without exception, will face unkind things we must deal with in a Scriptural way. You don't give in or give up - you look up and pray about it and go on.

Again it may have been part of burning bridges behind us. If I had not been treated the way I was, I may have stayed on doing what I was doing and missed the next step towards what the Lord's Plan for my life involved.

The world says, "Don't get mad. Get even!" God's Word says FORGIVE and FORGET and GO FORWARD.

A famous football coach had a sign in the locker room, "WHEN THE GOING GETS TOUGH, THE TOUGH GET GO-ING." Even better, I found, is when the going gets tough, get into the Word and be reminded of God's PROMISES. CHALK DRAWING EVANGELISM

Drawing Souls To Christ

Chalk Drawing showing God's Handiwork

Immediately I went into Chalk Drawing Evangelism. I had a wealth of Pastor friends who were delighted to have me conduct Crusades in their churches. It was a lot easier than what I had been doing, and I was getting rested and my health restored.

Our Stickman Bible Stories chalk drawing sermon titles were listed for the week:

A WHALE OF A PROBLEM
THE ROMANCE OF A MOABITISH ROSE
SEVEN DUCKS IN THE RIVER
A PURPOSE TRUE
BOW DOWN OR BURN
BEWARE A SULKING KING
SINGING IN THE DUNGEON
LIONS WITH LOCK JAW

Stick-men stories are fun. They pack a real spiritual punch and are remembered for a lifetime.

An evangelistic service should have good music meaning full praise and worship and the right combination of humour and serious challenge to commitment.

In order to help people to invite others to the crusade, we offered a framed painting to the person who brought the most visitors.

This enabled children and adults to invite all their relatives and friends and proved a real incentive. It made it easier for visitors to attend if they were helping someone especially a child to win a good Biblical painting. Those paintings are a lasting treasure and reminder of a mission accomplished.

When it came sermon time I gave the sermon title, i.e. SEVEN DUCKS IN THE RIVER. The first person to give the name of the Bible character involved was entitled to take home a drawing as a reward.

A Baptist congregation in a small railway town in central Ontario had struggled in storefront locations for years. Now they had completed a fine church building, and wanted to increase attendance. They were interested in a Chalk Drawing Evangelism Crusade Sunday to Sunday.

I asked the pastor if they could arrange to have a P.A. System set up in the church basement to hold an overflow crowd. The pastor was a little shocked by my request, but said,"I will discuss it with the Deacons."

At the next meeting with the Pastor I asked about the P.A. System for the basement. The Pastor told me that the Deacons said, "Why should we do that-we have never had the church full before-and we don't expect to get it full for this crusade."

The first night of the Crusade, the church was not packed, but there were more people than the Deacons expected. I could see them looking a little surprised, but confident that they were right. The next night there were more people. They were beginning to get uneasy. By the end of the Crusade they were bringing in extra chairs and some were sitting on the floor with others standing. Oh, ye of little faith.

One boy registered 65 visitors. Another boy had registered thirty.

If you have ever tried to invite people to attend an Evangelistic Service, you know how difficult it is to get them to come. I felt they both deserved a prize so I gave two framed paintings instead of one. That cut down on my honorarium, but it increased my joy.

When asked about expenses for a crusade I would say, "Pray about it and give me what the Lord leads you to give." That is not the best way. I found out that sometimes I would receive $70 or $75 for a Sunday to Sunday crusade, which meant I could not work the next week as everyone wanted a Sunday to Sunday Crusade. When I took travel expenses and a picture frame or two out of the $75, it did not provide what I needed to raise a family with three children. I just could not bring myself to state a fair cost of the Crusade, and it was my fault perhaps, as much as theirs, that I did not do so well financially. I just kept thinking, we will make it up on the next crusade.

We always sang,

"There's a welcome here,

There's a welcome here,

There's a Christian welcome here,

Hallelujah!' (and repeat)

We wanted to build each congregation and hoped many visitors would keep coming after the Crusade was over.

There were decisions for Christ in these Crusades, but not as many as we hoped for. Sometimes no one had walked the aisle to the front in years and souls being saved were a welcome sight.

Something happened in November of 1973 that changed the fruit of our labours and made Drawing Souls to Christ far different than ever before.

DANIEL

One of our evangelistic crusades was conducted at Ville Emard, a suburb of Montreal, Quebec. Our good friend, Bill Spinks, was home from missionary work in Cuba and had become pastor of a Baptist church in Ville Emard. I was overjoyed at the prospect of working with Bill again.

One of the problems we encountered was a gang of teens who were out to have some fun by disrupting our meetings. They would make a noise and throw stink bombs into the church in the middle of a service. Naturally, we were praying for those boys.

On Saturday afternoon, we had decided to go where the people are in a park and conduct an outdoor service. I drew a stickman Bible story of Daniel and also explained a fine art painting of Daniel in the Lions Den. When you go to any outdoor location to minister, drawing draws a crowd – and much more so when you pray about it.

I recognized the gang of boys in the crowd listening intently. Then at the conclusion, the gang ring leader came up to me all excited in his French Canadian way of pronouncing English shouting, "Daniel, Daniel, that is me. I am a Daniel!"

"Oh," I said, "you may be Daniel, but you are not like that Daniel. That Daniel honoured God and served the Lord with all his heart – you are one who threw stink bombs into the church. This Daniel would not do anything like that!"

The boy was shocked that I recognized him – he told me he was sorry. He asked if he could come to church Sunday, and bring his gang with him. I told him that he and the gang could come if they would promise to behave. He assured me that they would be good.

Sunday morning there they were. They filled one complete row right across the church. They took in the message. Later on, when the crusade was over, they came back to the church, and I believe some made a decision for Christ. To God be the Glory! God answered prayer. God loves each one of those boys. Christ died for them. When we learn to love sinners the way God loves them, and pray for their salvation, it is awesome the way God brings about his solution. His ways are past finding out.

We had not reached the gang of boys by just ministering in the church. It was when we went to the park on neutral ground that they responded.

There were converts in those crusades, but not as many as I saw after November, 1973. We were praying about what we should do. One night I looked in the Peterborough Examiner job wanted ads – amazing – two jobs for artists were listed. We prayed about it and I applied for both jobs. I got both jobs! Now – which one should I take?

Chapter 9

Becoming
an art teacher

I had two job offers: one was local, in Peterborough designing bottle tops, packages, etc. The other was 50 miles away in Bowmanville as an art teacher at the Ontario Correctional School for Boys.

I went to the employer in Peterborough and told him my dilemma. "I can tell you which one to take," he said, "Take the teaching job. This job would drive you up the wall. The other job is a great opportunity for you. Take it with my blessing." Take it I did. It would be a ten-year Adventure in Christ and one of the happiest times of our lives. It would provide opportunity for ministry we never dreamed possible.

BEGINNING BOWMANVILLE TRAINING SCHOOL
The principal started me with a minimum number of students. Some classes had only half a dozen students. In getting to know them there were a few surprises.

Gerry was 15 or 16 years old, red hair, good looking. Gerry was with us for automobile theft. He blamed the judge and called him a creep. Gerry told his story. "First I stole a car and got caught. Then I came up before the judge and I was scared. The judge looked at me and said, 'I should send you to Bowmanville – but I am going to give you another chance. But if I ever see you here again I will send you to Bowmanville.' The next time I got caught stealing a car I was really scared and I came up before the same judge. I was sure I was going to Bowmanville. The judge looked at me and said, 'I should send you to Bowmanville, but I am going to give you another chance.' The fifth time I came up before the same judge – the creep sent me here!" Oh, to be consistent.

Gerry learned his lesson at our school and did not return.

The 300 or so boys at the Correctional School were a mixed bag. Many of them were head-and-shoulders taller than I and outweighed me quite a bit. I did a lot of praying. You were given a bonus of $300 called danger pay. That was scary enough.

The boys were always trying to escape from the school. If they escaped from your custody, you were on the carpet. I sure did not want to be there again. I'd had enough of that.

After only a couple of days on the job, I was on my way home from school when, a couple miles from my home, I saw two of our boys hitching a ride. I recognized the Khaki shirts and trousers – the big boots and the special coloured belts. They were both huge. What I did not know was that they were the school Rock and his first Lieutenant. The two toughest guys in the school. Each correctional institution has a prison inmate who fights his way to a position of leadership amongst his peers. All the inmates knew who he was, but it takes the staff some time to find out. I did some quick praying. "Lord, help me."

I pulled my little red Volkswagen over and let them in. They did not recognize me. One sat in the back, behind me, and the other in the front. The police station was five miles away. I headed in that direction which is also the way to Ottawa, where they were headed. I put the accelerator to the floor, and whatever that little beetle could do, it did it. I was hoping I would get stopped for speeding.

I had one eye on my rear view mirror and the guy behind me, the other eye watched the road and mostly the guy in front. We wheeled up to the O.P.P. station in minutes that seemed like hours. Parking was about 100 feet from the door – there was an open field every which way. I was praying and swallowing hard. Finally I mustered up the most commanding tone of voice I was capable of, and said, "Okay fellows, this is it. Let's go!"

They looked at me and then at each other – then they marched in to the police station. Only God could make that happen. "What have we here?" asked the officer. "Two escapees from Bowmanville," was my reply. The boys refused to talk and were taken to a cell. Wow! What did Gwen think? She was glad

Drawing Souls To Christ

I was safe. We thanked the Lord.

The next day at the school I arrived to a hero's welcome. The new art teacher had single- handed captured the Rock and Assistant Rock. I had respect! God did it. There is no other way. It was an Awesome Adventure in Christ.

The Superintendent was impressed. The school principal and vice principal were impressed. My fellow teachers thought it was hilarious. I just thanked the Lord for His Divine protection and help.

To my great surprise the other boys at the school admired what I had done and showed me great respect. What a beginning. God is so good. He gave me favour.

Some new teachers did not last a day. Some did not last an hour. I would be there ten years with the Lord's enabling. I prayed each day continually.

Some students made it into the Kingdom. That was the most important.

Our school campus covered one hundred acres. There was no fence. In ten years I never lost a single boy in my custody. That must be a record of some sort. Only God could give me that favour. My art shop was the easiest to escape from as it was surrounded on three sides by open fields. Then a new shop was built close to the main offices.

At first I listened to other teachers and staff personnel about how to handle the boys, but soon learned to look to the Lord about each individual need – and that worked.

I worked on Biblical paintings in my shop after school. Next day, students would comment on what they liked and offer suggestions. Some began to paint Bible scenes and that was exciting.

One time when the Grand Jury came from education headquarters to inspect our school they were surprised to see paintings in progress of David and Goliath, Daniel, and Noah's Ark -- especially in a correctional school.

Each lunch break, I would read my Bible and then pray in the Spirit. My good friend, the Rev. John Wesley Oake, who was one of Billy Graham's associate evangelists and minister of Trinity United Church (Bowmanville), visited me once a week. He would walk into the shop, pause, lift his hands up and exclaim, "Oh, I feel the presence of the Lord here." Others felt it, too, but most did not know what it was.

There is a sense of God's presence where people pray. As you take time to pray in tongues each day, the Lord is able to pray a perfect prayer though you by the enabling of God the Holy Spirit. Again you are enabled to pray about needs you are unaware of.

Gwen designed what she called her Prayer Circle. She would use it each day as a guide as she prayed for families.

Gwen and I had times of prayer together each day, but we also prayed alone each day. Getting alone with God each day is a vital part of growing in the Lord and maintaining a right relationship with Him, our spouses, our families, and with everyone else.

Gwen told me about special things the Lord said to her, and I did the same. The last thing the Lord said to Gwen before she went to be with Him, December 27, 2000, was "Well done!" Gwen was so happy about that, and so was I. In the midst of her illness, the Lord said, "Rejoice!" Gwen fastened the word RE-JOICE on our fridge and it remains as a daily reminder to me.

One boy, Al, who was really interested in art, returned several times. Later I found out that he did some simple thing to be sent back so that he could study art at school. He later went on to study at the Ontario College of Art, won a Disney scholarship, and became a staff artist at Disney Studios in Hollywood.

Some of my art classes had twenty or more students. Just think of taking the worst boy from twenty different schools and putting them together in one class totalling twenty bad, rebellious boys. It was not easy. You had to be either a great teacher or a great policeman. I felt it was easier to be the former. You know I had to be praying continually. Each day when the bell rang at 3:30 it was like the bell at the end of the 15th round at a prize fight. What a relief!

Centennial Mural of Canada painted by a dozen of our art students at the Correctional School. Painting was featured in the government building at the Canadian National Exhibition, Toronto, for several years.

A typical day in the art shop at Bowmanville Training School

ACCOSTED BY SATAN'S CHOICE GANG MEMBERS

During the mid-sixties, Satan's Choice Motorcycle gang from Toronto moved into Peterborough and were tolerated by the police.

I had purchased a used Porsche for the daily commute – an inexpensive one I had fixed up. One day as Tim, aged nine, and I were driving down Lansdowne Street , we encountered four huge Satan's Choice bikers flexing their muscles. They were riding two-to-a-bike. Appearing from nowhere they began to ride in circles around our car as we drove forward. After they had made a few such circles, I watched for an opening and floored it out of there, leaving Satan's Choice far behind. They had their fun and I had enough. I thought that was it. Wrong!

When I turned down a lonely stretch of road near the lift locks, I looked in my rear view mirror and was disturbed to see the bikers were after me. They had taken my action as an affront to them and they had retribution in mind.

One bike cut in ahead of me and the other was on my rear bumper. We were trapped. If I did not stop I had to hit one or both of the bikes and somehow that did not seem a good choice. I was praying, "Lord, help!"

When we stopped the four big bikers got off their bikes and strode menacingly around the little Porsche to deal with me. When they were just inches away and grasping for the doors of my car, suddenly we heard a voice, "Is there a problem there?"

All heads swung back to behold Ontario's finest – an Ontario Provincial Policeman in his cruiser. Thank you, Lord. Immediately the bikers in unison said, "No problem at all." They got back on their bikes and took off pronto.

Tim and I just sat there for a moment thanking the Lord. Then it occurred to me that we should thank the policeman, but he had disappeared as quickly as he had appeared. Was it a real policeman or an angelic being? How could six people fail to see his approach? How did he get there at the split second he was needed? How did he drive off and disappear when we tried to catch up with him in a fast sports car?

Any way you look at it, it was an awesome answer to prayer. To God be the glory!

What did Gwen say when we told her the story? She just smiled and shook her head. I can imagine my guardian angel said, "This guy is a real assignment."

Chapter 10

The beginning of interests in miracle services

Gwen had attended a miracle service conducted by A.A. Allen. She had taken a friend who needed a miracle. When they came home disappointed that her friend was not healed, I wrote the thing off. I thought that if it was real, her friend should have been healed.

Gwen had also listened to Kathryn Kuhlman on radio each night while we were in Geraldton. She was praying that I would join her in her quest to find out what the Full Gospel was about.

After working at the correctional school at Bowmanville for four years, Gwen and I and our daughter Marjorie attended a Kathryn Kuhlman Miracle Service in Toronto and our lives would never be the same again.

BACK ON THE HOME FRONT

K-Mart opened a new store in Peterborough – just four miles from our home. Gwen got a temporary job stocking shelves before the store opening. Shortly before opening day the boss was going to assign permanent jobs to some of the workers. Gwen hoped she would get a job as a cashier. We prayed about it.

When the Boss came to Gwen he said, "You are my Credit Manager!" Wow! Gwen told the boss that she did not know anything about being a Credit Manager. He said, "You can learn." Learn she did. God is so good. Gwen became a great Credit Manager. I was so proud of her. God always does the exceeding abundantly.

CARS

When you are a child of the great depression of the 1930s, you learn to see life differently. As young children my brother Roy and I admired automobiles. Cars were scarce in those days. We did not have one. In our neighbourhood in Hamilton, Ontario, there would be two or three cars per city block. The Model T Ford always painted black was the most popular, but we liked Chevrolets, Cord, Auburn and Buicks. Pud Murphy, who played hockey for New York Americans, had an Auburn. He lived across the street from us. We prayed for the day we would have a car.

We could not afford toy cars so we made our own, using photos of cars we clipped from magazines. We played cars often. We would rig up our Morris Chair with a china platter as the steering wheel. Roy being two years older always had to be the driver. I wanted to be the driver in the worst way.

When I was 16, Roy bought his first car. It was a 1927 McLaughlin Buick. It cost $17.50. It was literally tied together with baling wire. But it ran. Graciously my brother taught me to drive that car, and I drove it fast, especially when he was not with me.

My first car was a 1932 Buick straight 8. I paid my brother $150 for it. Through the years I have driven many cars. A car to a preacher is like a horse was to a saddle bag preacher year ago in the days of John and Charles Wesley. You need a good set of wheels. Most of mine have been good used cars. Sometimes you have to wait a while to get one, but it is worth the wait. This, too, is something to pray about.

When I saw a 59 Porsche on Hans Faller's used car lot for $275 I did a double take. That is could be driven off the lot with only three of its four cylinders working was a bonus. Wow! A Porsche. I talked him down to $250. How could I go wrong?

My good friend, John McGuire, our auto servicing teacher at the Correctional School where I worked at the time, was excited, too. He said, "We can fix it. We can get it going for you." Our welding teacher and sheet metal teacher were also game to let their students have a go at it. The painting and decorating teacher, Ray Swan, had worked painting railway passenger cars, and he told me how to paint it and loaned me a $75 brush.

Russell King granted me use of his garage for painting the

car. I did not realize that he would not allow his family to use the living room over the garage for two days while the paint dried. I took his son John (now a Wycliffe International leader) for a ride and that was exciting for both of us.

PORSCHE #2

Before I could get my first Porsche on the road, it needed a rebuilt engine. John McGuire advised me to see Ludwig Heimrath, a Porsche mechanic in Toronto who raced Porsches.. Ludwig rebuilt an engine for me and we became friends.

When I went to pick up my Porsche after the new engine was installed, Ludwig was excited about it. He said "It makes your car go like STINK! It's a Super 90. It was true, that car was special and fast. It cost me about $1000 and lots of donated labour to get the car on the road.

Ludwig and his staff must have had a few chuckles about me and my old junker Porsche. Once the car began to heat up and smoke poured from the dash, but I got things under control before the car caught fire. When I phoned Ludwig, he asked, "You got insurance?"

"Well, yes."

"Why did you not let it burn?"

Most of Ludwig's clients had good incomes. One time when I took my car in for service, Ludwig showed me a beautiful four year old 1962 Porsche he had for sale. It was a doctor's car. He took me for a ride. What a ride, with Canada's leading sports car racing driver!

The doctor would sell to the highest bidder. I prayed about it and offered $1,975. More than a month went by, and then I got a call from the doctor. My bid was $25 higher than anyone else. Wow! Originally the car was $6000. It was a sophisticated dark grey – gorgeous! It had only 35,000 miles on it. Unbelievable.

But when I drove it home there was something drastically wrong. I went right to see John McGuire. John took the car for a test drive and said, "Nothing to worry about. You have a tire out of round. We changed the tire and Wow! To help sell the car, the good doctor had brand new tires put on it, after my test drive. One was defective. I guess all the others who had driven it were worried about what was causing the problem, and made lower bids.

It is really interesting when you are a visiting preacher to see the church reaction when you drive up in a Porsche that cost exactly what a brand new Volkswagen Beetle cost, but looks like it cost a mint.

Every drive was fun. It was fun to drive to work. It was fun driving home. It added zest to driving. Your eye sight improved, too, as you kept a wary eye watching for radar traps.

Suddenly I had four cars, two of them Porsches. I sold the 59 Porsche quickly and the 65 Volkswagen to the first customer.

After a few near accidents, I realized that people could not see my dark grey car. I had it painted Bahama yellow, a real Porsche colour, and no more problems. But it did add a little more interest.

Being an artist and an art teacher, as well as a part time preacher, gave me the right to be a little different in the eyes of some.

AN OFFER TO PONDER

I commuted from Peterborough to Perth each week for several months to preach at a Baptist Church. They asked me to become their pastor. Gwen did not feel it was God's place for me or for us. This was the one time she said, "No." She was right. I felt the same, but I wanted to be sure. I did not want to miss God in this.

I had told Gwen about the beautiful church with its great organ and about the people – and the not-so-great barn of a parsonage. I wanted her to see it all to get her feeling and reaction.

So we boarded the little Yellow Porsche and Gwen went with me to Perth the following Sunday.

After the morning service, we were driving back to our motel, and there was Colonel Hartland Sanders in his white suit standing outside the brand new Kentucky Fried Chicken restaurant. We hopped out and greeted the friendly Colonel. He gave Gwen an autographed copy of his recipe book that we cherished.

I told him that we had looked for K.F.C. in Kentucky, but could not find it. Whereupon the Colonel said, "A prophet is not without honour save in his own country."

He assured us that Corbin, KY would open a store next year. That was about 1968. Later Gwen and I would stay overnight at Corbin and eat dinners at the original KFC Restaurant there.

It was quite an experience.

The Colonel was a born-again Christian, and he was glad to talk about it.

When the new highway bypassed his restaurant years ago, he packed his bags and frying pans and set out for Canada. In Canada he became a great success as he travelled opening franchises everywhere. Much later he developed KFC in the U.S.Al

I believe he was 65 years of age when he started in Canada. A great example of trusting God and finding success in answer to prayer.

Guess what we had for dinner that day? It was so much better then when the Colonel made sure his chicken was right.

As for the offer – the decision was taken out of my hands when the Baptist Committee in Toronto decided I was too evangelical for the Perth church. I was relieved, as I felt better working at the school and being free to preach in many places and not just one location. It just was not God's place for me.

Stan's first car in 1929

FLORIDA OR BUST

Gwen standing in front of our first Porsche at St. Petersburg, Florida

Gwen and I drove that old Porsche to Florida for our 25th Wedding Anniversary. It was great. There were a few scary moments when it did not want to start, but a little prayer and sandpaper on the points got it going. You just never knew what would happen when you turned the ignition key. Speed limits were 70 mph then and traffic to Florida drove 80. You sat so low in a Porsche that you could see under the fog. The "I 75" was not complete in '67 and 25 was full of hills and turns. It ran right through Hill Billy country. We could not believe the shacks with the fridge on the porch, etc. I stopped to take a photo, but leaned on the horn by mistake, and a bunch of hillbillies in bare feet came running for us. We were glad the car started that time. We took off like a scalded dog.

25 years later at our
50 wedding anniversary, this
is the original wedding party,
only Len Goddard, Sr. missing.

Stan and Gwen's 50th
Wedding Anniversary
1992

Gwen was a great driver. It was in her genes. Her brothers Ken and Roy were champion stock car drivers. That trip was an adventure. When we arrived in Florida, we stopped at Ocala and had a swim at the motel along with free donuts and coffee. It was wonderful.

Florida birds fascinated us, especially the Pelicans zooming at you as you drove over waterways.

We got sand in our shoes on that first trip to Florida and forgot all about California. Florida was green. California was brown. Green was better.

We stopped at St. Petersburg, Florida and attended church. The pastor was Ross Moyer whom I had succeeded at Evangel Baptist in Hamilton. Ross lined me up to preach that night and we stayed overnight with them.

MEETING FAMOUS ARTIST BEN STAHL

The next day, heading south to Fort Lauderdale, we were driving through Sarasota on the Tamiami Trail when Gwen read, "Museum of the Cross." Wow! That would be Ben Stahl's exhibit of the 15 Stations of the Cross. The gala opening with 4,000 guests had been the night before. We were the first paying visitors.

While I was having a closer look, Gwen talked with the Curator. She told him that I had taken the Famous Artists Course of which Ben Stahl was one of the founding members. "Would you like to meet Mr. Stahl?" he asked. Would we! It was almost too good to be true.

The meeting was arranged for Thursday on our way back. On Thursday I called to confirm. His wife said, "He won't be back till 4, but he wants to see you." It was now 2 p.m. Mrs. Stahl suggested we go to Siesta Beach for a swim and then drop over. She said, "If you all bide your time I am sure it will be worth your while." It sure was.

Ben and his wife were so intrigued by our Porsche and the fact that I was an Art Teacher at a Correctional School. Ben had written and illustrated the book "Black Beard's Ghost" that Walt Disney purchased for the movie. He autographed several copies and gave them to me for the boys at the school.

I had prepared four full sheets of questions for Ben. He was delighted to answer them. As he showed us through his studio there was a large canvas on his easel. It was painted dark brown. I chuckled, "My Painting Teacher in Toronto told me I could not do that." Ben said, "I begin almost all my paintings that way." A lesson from the master.

Blackbeard the pirate lived at Siesta Key. Siesta Beach is my favourite beach in Florida. I never would have found it without Ben Stahl.

Ben told me that he was about to paint the Resurrection on that canvas. Then in all seriousness he asked me, "How would you paint it?" I had told Ben that I was a preacher and wanted to paint Art from the Bible. My answer was, "I don't know – I would have to pray about it to find out."

A year or so later someone stole all of the Museum of the Cross paintings. They were never traced or found. It was a blow from which he never fully recovered.

Twelve years later I painted a mural of the Resurrection. It was Gwen's favourite. Somehow it becomes special to all who see it. To God be the Glory!

As I prepared for the painting I made many sketches of different scenes of the Resurrection. Which scene to paint was a hard decision to make. It was on a Tuesday prayer meeting night. I was in my studio in Oshawa. Gwen called up to me, "Are you going to prayer meeting?" "No," I responded. "I am trying to plan my painting. I am too busy." The words rang in my ears. "Too busy." I decided to go with Gwen to the prayer meeting.

At the prayer meeting as we were praying, the Lord revealed to me just how I should combine all my sketches into one large mural of the "Resurrection." And that makes it extra special.

As I was writing just now, the Lord gave me another idea for a great painting – again a mural of the 16 Stations of the Cross. That is what Mel Gibson's film is about. I can hardly wait to get started. Thank you Lord!

As you keep the consciousness of the presence of the Lord in all you do, the Lord is pleased from time-to-time to communicate special messages and assignments to you including, in my case, sermons and paintings. I have found it wise to jot them all down immediately when that happens. When it is God's idea it is better than anything we are capable of coming up with. Just do it!

If you want excitement in your life, just allow the Lord to lead you. Be sure to obey His leading one step at a time.

BAPTISM IN THE HOLY SPIRIT

In my Salvation Army days I read everything Commissioner Samuel Logan Brengal wrote about holiness, but somehow it did not seem to work for me. There seemed to be one part of the puzzle missing.

Later I met Pentecostals who seemed more interested in speaking in tongues than they did in Christ-like living. One said to me, "I just wish you had what I have." He had cheated me in business, and whatever he had did not appeal to me. Some even laid hands on me and prayed for me, but did not teach me what I needed to know and understand.

It was not until 1970 when I attended a Kathryn Kuhlman meeting that I realized that the baptism in the Holy Spirit was far more important than I had imagined.

I found that most of the Pentecostals I met were vague about the baptism in the Holy Spirit and more concerned about speaking in tongues.

Soon I realized that many believers who were not Pentecostal wanted to understand and receive the baptism in the Holy Spirit. Then when the Full Gospel Business Men's Fellowship International came on the scene the Holy Spirit baptism was taught in terms clear enough to be understood and received.

John Sherill's book, "They Speak With Other Tongues," became an eye-opener to me. After reading it, I agreed with John Sherill that the experience was NOT OPTIONAL.

CEDARCOVE

Stan Crookall's painting Cedarcove at Bond Head, New Castle on the north shore of Lake Ontario – gorgeous!

Drawing Souls To Christ

Commuting 80 miles a day from Peterborough to Bowman-ville to teach, was great fun in my little yellow Porsche. But I got a little tired of driving it sideways on icy spots. We loved the house we had built, but a house on the lakeshore nearer work would be a great replacement.

We had been praying about it and watching at Bowman-ville and Newcastle for some time. One day, Fred Yates, a fellow worker at the Correctional School, invited me to his home for lunch. Fred lived at the beach at Newcastle in a wonderful little community known as Bond Head. As we sat outside enjoying Lake Ontario, I took note of the house next door. It was a one-and-a-half story Cape Cod style. Its location and bearing intrigued me. The house took full advantage of the magnificent view of Lake Ontario, with large windows overlooking the water. It had a two-car garage, an old-fashioned huge natural stone fireplace, a living room 24 by 14 feet facing the lake. Fred told me that Conn Smyth, the owner of the Toronto Maple Leafs N.H.L. hockey team, rented it as summer home in past years. If it was good enough for him, it was sure good enough for us.

"Fred," I said, "if that house ever comes up for sale, please let me know."

"It will never come up for sale, Stan. You are wasting your time thinking about that one."

"Well, if it ever comes up for sale, please let me know immediately."

The following year, I got a phone call from Fred. "Guess what? The house you like is coming up for sale."

We did not waste a moment. We got on the phone to the owners and lined up a showing by the owner for the coming Saturday.

Gwen's enthusiasm for the house was evident. I was trying to get her to cool it a little, but too late. The owner Mr. Rushton asked, "How do you like it?" Gwen exclaimed, "I love it!" I was sunk, there could be no price negotiating after that. But it may have been Gwen's attitude that influenced the owner to sell to us. There was no guile in Gwen. There was nothing artificial or put on. She was just warm, loving, beautiful, wonderful Gwen. We bought the house then and there. We were ecstatic. It was another amazing answer to prayer. We had no idea that in a few years time fifty or more people would come here each Tuesday evening for prayer and Bible Study.

Gwen named the property "Cedarcove" Because it was lined on three sides with cedar trees. I painted a sign that we attached to the garage at the road.

Cedarcove was a story-and-a-half Cape Cod style summer cottage, with the upstairs not finished. I was 46 years old in 1968, and was up to the renovations. For the first time in our lives, we had a bit of cash, the cottage cost $10,000 and we sold the house for $17,500. When I deposited $13,000 in the bank at Newcastle, the manager, Del Moore, called me into his office to express appreciation. Gwen and Alva, Del's wife, worked together in Bible Clubs, V.B.S. and Pioneer Girls. Del and Alva became lifelong friends.

While we lived at Newcastle, Gwen's interest in Kathryn Kuhlman was renewed. She had originally become interested when we lived in Geraldton. She told me about this amazing lady preacher who came on the radio at 6 p.m. I finally agreed to forgo my daily trip to the Post Office at 6 p.m. to listen. What I heard in a slow, drawn-out speech was, "Hello there – have you been waiting for me?" It wasn't just what she said. It was the way she said it. I was not too fond of lady preachers, but this one was too much. I was out the door and on my way to the Post Office.

Now, twenty years later, Gwen wanted to take our daughter Marjorie to Kathryn Kuhlman's meeting hoping she would be healed of epilepsy. That got my interest.

At the same time, my little yellow Porsche needed extensive repairs. I was lined up to buy a second-hand Porsche from the Doctor again, but the price of new Porsches had skyrocketed He said, "I can't afford a Porsche anymore. I don't know how you can. I am going to hold on to the one I have, and would advise you to buy a Chev." I bought a big, black 1965 Cadillac, in 1971, for $1,750. It looked like a Mafia car. We got a lot of respect. The first time I drove the car to work, the road crew were filling huge pot holes. Having dodged these pot holes for some years, I was delighted to see them being filled. I rolled my window down and thanked the workmen. I really meant it. They scrambled to attention. "Yes, sir," they said. "We are glad we could do this for you." Wow! I was shaken. Road crew "Yes-Sirring" me – how come? Then as I drove away the light dawned. I was considered a big shot Mafia or Government person.

It took some getting used to. Parking lot attendants gave

me special treatment. I did not like it. I was the same guy I had always been.

Well, when we drove up to the O'Keefe Centre in Toronto for the Katherine Kuhlman service, people were lined up for blocks waiting to get in. I stopped, ran around to Gwen's side of the car to open her door to let her and Marge out, and the crowd parted to give them the right-of-way inside. We were flabbergasted. Gwen and Margie went right in. I went to park the car about eight blocks away. When I got back, the doors were closed and locked. The building was packed, with thousands waiting outside. I did not have to take in the service. I was overjoyed!

Along with many who were unable to get in, I sat down on the cement curb and waited for three hours. Suddenly the doors opened and people began to come out of the building. I quickly found Gwen and Margie. Gwen said, "They are going to have a second service. You should attend."

"But what would you do?" I countered.

"We will be glad to attend another service." They had already attended a three hour service and wanted to take in another? This must be worth seeing and hearing. I decided to give it a whirl.

We were not disappointed. The presence of the Lord was stronger and more wonderful than I had ever experienced in a service before. The only thing I could compare it with was what I felt as I knelt in prayer and the elders laid hands on me at my ordination service in Philpott Memorial Church in 1952.

The Lord was confirming His Word with signs following. Miracles of healing were taking place. The worship was so beautiful. I had the witness of the Holy Spirit that this was real and that it was of God. My mind was in a whirl. They had taught me at the Seminary that the Gifts of the Spirit ceased 2,000 years ago. But what I was seeing was proof that the Pentecostal Power and the Gifts of the Spirit are for today as well as for Christ's time. The revelation was overwhelming. I could never be the same again.

GEORGE AND LUCIEN DUMOULIN

After attending the Kathryn Kuhlman meeting in Toronto, we called in to see Lucien and George DuMoulin, who were brothers, and Baptist Deacons. When I told them about the Kathryn Kuhlman meeting we attended, George said, "That's the devil!"

I had purchased a case of Kathryn Kuhlman's book I Believe In Miracles. I told George and Lucien about the book and offered them a copy if they would promise to read it. They promised to read it – and they both received the Baptism in the Holy Spirit ahead of me. Bless the Lord!

George and Lucien had helped us building our first house. George had gone with me one day to sell Bibles door-to-door.

When Gwen and I attended a Miracle Service in Peterborough, George came over to me and said, "I want to thank you for that book. It changed my life."

GWEN'S HEALING – WHEN THE LUMP DISAPPEARED

In the fall of 1973, Gwen and I drove to Hamilton to attend special Miracle Service conducted by Bill Prankard at the People's Church. He began with "If anything happens to you while I am preaching – come up and tell me right away."

Part way through his service, I noticed Gwen looking at her leg, rubbing it, and seeming surprised. She whispered loudly to me, "Can you see the lump? I can't see or feel the lump."

Gwen had injured the calf of her leg severely when the chain broke on a metal swing. The weight of three people who fell with it, gouged a chunk out of Gwen's calf and caused a lump the size of an egg. It was rock solid. The doctor was perplexed and did not know what to do. He had suggested waiting to see what may happen. It was a great idea. Little did he realize that Dr. Jesus would heal it.

No, I could not see the lump and could not feel it either. Wow! Was I excited! We had seen a miracle and it was ours.

After rejoicing for a few minutes, I said, "He said you were to go up and tell him if anything happened." Gwen was hesitant. She said, "But he's preaching." Rev. and Mrs. Jack Chamberlain were sitting right behind us, and Mrs. Chamberlain leaned forward and said, "I'll go with you." So together they went to the front and stood looking up at the preacher.

"What is this?" Bill asked.

Gwen told him about her leg being healed – then added, "But I have another problem. I also have a sore shoulder." "Well," Bill said, "if God can heal a lump, he can heal a shoulder as well." He reached out and touched Gwen. She immediately fell under the power of the Holy Spirit.

When Gwen was able to stand up about ten minutes later,

she had been healed of about four or five problems. One was a chronic bladder problem. She did not know this until the next day. Then she said, "The Lord gave me a complete overhaul." Bless the Lord!

Gwen was excited and I was just as excited as she was. Maybe more so. I had felt badly about her accident and the deformity. Now it was made whole. I just felt so good about the Lord doing that for Gwen and for me because a husband and wife truly are one.

You can never be the same again after a healing like that. We were energized spiritually and physically. Things were happening so fast. Gwen and I both received the Baptism in the Holy Spirit and Gwen was healed within days. You could not hold us back. We drove to every Miracle Service we knew about within 100 miles of where we lived.

Just prior to this, we had both been turned off by a meeting Bill Prankard conducted at the Pentecostal Church in Cobourg, Ontario. We had gone to Miracle Services for almost two years. As an ordained Baptist Minister, I took a lot of convincing that the Baptism in the Holy Spirit and speaking in tongues was for today. It was at a Sunday morning service when the sermon was about the Baptism in the Holy Spirit that we got turned off, me, in particular, but Gwen seemed to agree. When the invitation to come forward to pray to receive the baptism in the Holy Spirit was given, there was such a commotion and so much noise I was disturbed. I said to Gwen, "Let's go home – I don't like this." On the way home, I said, "That's enough. I am through with this Miracle Service thing and the Baptism in the Holy Spirit." Gwen was very quiet, but she went along with me – or so I thought at the time.

Gwen in her wisdom may have been led of the Lord to say very little and just pray.

But within a week or so, I had an accident and tore the cartilage in my left knee. I was in constant pain and I could hardly walk or stand. Being an art teacher at the time it was extremely difficult for me to walk about my art shop to teach. It was had for me to walk from my car to the school building and I parked just a few feet away.

Phil Esposito, the NHL hockey star, had just undergone surgery to repair torn knee cartilage, and I could see that it was either surgery – OR – a miracle I needed. I began to wonder if the Lord was speaking to me. When Dr. Ewart pinched the spot on my knee I almost hit the ceiling. But he allowed me to think about it, just as he allowed Gwen to think about her injured leg.

Dr. Ewart was our neighbour. He had a cottage just three houses down from us at Bond Head, Newcastle on Lake Ontario. He always had a cigar clamped between his teeth, chewing on the one end, when he talked. The nurse would take it out of his mouth when he walked into the operating room. It was Dr. Ewart who would later say three times to Gwen, "It's a miracle that you are alive." after examining the unbelievable bruise that the seatbelt had made when she was in a head on collision. Dr. Ewart must have wondered about us.

Well, it was Saturday. I looked in the "Toronto Star" and sure enough Bill Prankard was scheduled to conduct a Miracle Service in Toronto the next day. I was there.

Bill asked those with physical needs to come forward. I went. That's why I was there. Bill laid hands on me and prayed. The pain did not leave for three days, but I knew I was healed. I just knew it. And I was. Now, I had to rethink about Baptism in the Holy Spirit. I went to the book display at the back of the church and prayed, "Lord, when I open my eyes, I want to be looking at a book that will explain to me what the baptism in the Holy Spirit is all about." When I opened my eyes, I was looking at a book by John Sherill, They Speak with Other Tongues.

I could not put that book down. I read half the night. John Sherill was editor of Guideposts. He was asked by Fleming Revel Publishers to write the book objectively as a person who did not know the experience. As he wrote the book he said, "I came to realize that for the true believer, the experience of the Baptism in the Holy Spirit was not optional." As I read the book, I came to the same conclusion.

BAPTISM IN THE HOLY SPIRIT - GENERAL RALPH HAINES

From 1972 to November 1973 I had been seeking to understand and know the Baptsim in the Holy Spirit. I believed in Miracles, but I was not sure that speaking in tongues was for me.

We had learned about Full Gospel Businessmen and we went to Toronto to attend one of their meetings. It was held at St. Paul's Cathedral on Jarvis Street. The speaker was Jerry B.

Drawing Souls To Christ

Walker. We went to receive the Baptism in the Holy Spirit. Both Gwen and I were ready.

As I looked around that great congregation of 1500 or more, I wondered: How many people here know me? What will friends think of me, a Baptist minister, rolling on the floor speaking in tongues? But as the moments went by, I did not care if the whole congregation knew me. All I wanted was to know the Baptism in the Holy Spirit.

When the invitation for prayer was given, both Gwen and I went forward immediately. We were led to a special room where we could pray. Stew Berlett, who was Canadian Director for FG-BMFI, quoted, "What man of you if his son asks bread will give him a stone. And if he asks for a fish will He give him a serpent. If ye then being evil know how to give good gifts to your children, how much rather will your Heavenly Father give the Holy Spirit to those that ask Him?"

I immediately thought, "That's it." God won't give me something that is not good. As Stew Berlett laid hands on me and said, "Receive Ye the Holy Spirit," a burst of Joy welled up within me. I felt the Joy bubbling up just like in the chorus:

It's bubbling, It's bubbling It's bubbling in my Soul,

There's laughing and singing since Jesus made me whole.

Folks don't understand it, nor can I keep it quiet.

It's bubbling, bubbling, bubbling, bubbling, bubbling day and night.

I had often wondered what the writer of the chorus was talking about. Now I knew – and it was Glorious indeed.

But I did not speak in another tongue. Stew Berlett said, "You are a Baptist. It may take you a little longer. It may happen in an hour a day or a week or more."

Gwen was disappointed she did not receive the Baptism that night. While she was looking at the book table, I went out to the car and there alone I prayed and spoke a few words as in a new language. It was exciting. God again answered prayer!

When Gwen arrived at the car, I was shouting "Hallelujah, Praise the Lord!" Gwen sat back and looked at me. As we drove home I told her what had happened and she just sat in silence. She had wanted to receive the Baptism in the Holy Spirit for several years, but she was waiting for me. Now she wondered if she had missed it. Her concern would turn to Joy within a few weeks.

Life could never be the same again. Hallelujah!

John Sherill's book showed all of the ramifications of the Baptism in the Holy Spirit. Power for service was the emphasis Jesus made.

I had been reluctant to seek the Holy Spirit Baptism because it might interfere with my plans for early retirement. I had a feeling that it would mean full time service for the Lord again and I did not know if I was ready for that commitment. I wanted to move to Florida permanently and become a Beach Bum. Somehow I felt that was not going to happen now.

A few weeks later, we were attending a prayer meeting at the Pentecostal Church. Early in the meeting the pastor said, "There are some here tonight who want to receive the baptism in the Holy Spirit. If you come to the front row now, I will lay hands on you and you will receive." Gwen wasted no time. Four or five others joined her.

When Pastor Rodgers laid hands on Gwen's head, she said it was like FIRE went through her and she began to LAUGH. She began to say He Ho Ho and when she came back to her seat alongside of me she was still laughing. She kept on laughing when we got home. In fact she laughed all night long. At last her long quest was realized and she was glad.

Life CHANGED DRAMATICALLY for both of us now that we were united in the Baptism of the Holy Spirit. Personally, I would often pray in the Spirit all night long and arise in the morning as fresh or more energized than if I had slept all night.

We began praying in faith for people and we began to see the Lord meet needs, often miraculously.

Bill Prankard asked me to fill in for him in Ottawa and conduct a Miracle Service on a Sunday afternoon at Highland Park High School. Gwen and I arrived at the Ottawa Motel at about 4 p.m. Saturday, I was scared. I felt so helpless. I prayed until midnight and read the Word. Finally as I read the first three chapters of Acts about the healing of the lame man, I saw it was "IN JESUS NAME." The Lord directed me to pray that way. It was settled and I was at peace.

The next day in the service when the invitation was given, several hundred people came forward for prayer. As I prayed with the first person, the adversary said, "Nothing is going to happen." Just then the second person fell down – slain in the Spirit. Bless God! As I prayed for a man's back and placed my hand on the small of his back, I could feel the bones snap back into place – and hear them, too! I don't know all of what happened, but I'm sure the Lord met many needs.

After this experience I was ready to pray about anything with anybody. The Lord leads us step-by-step. Just as David fought the lion and the bear before he faced Goliath. When you fully realize that it is God alone who heals and you don't have anything to do with it but ask, it takes the pressure off you and prayer with people becomes a joyous experience.

My next big meeting was at Thunder Bay FGBMFI Convention. Again Bill Prankard was the main speaker Monday to Saturday, but I filled in on Thursday while Bill was back in Ottawa for his Thursday meeting there.

I had taken for granted that Bill's Monday, Tuesday and Wednesday meetings were like all of his other meetings, so I just went ahead and expected the same to follow, and it did. I recruited two husky FGBM to act as "catchers" and taught them how to help people as they fell, literally and figuratively, under the Holy Spirit.

We had a great service. Several nuns were there without their "habit" and they were receiving from the Lord and being slain in the Spirit all over the place. The catchers worked so hard that the next night they both asked me to get someone else to do it, as they were exhausted.

When Bill came back, he asked me how things went. I said, "Great!" and related what had happened. He seemed surprised and told us that Monday, Tuesday and Wednesday nothing like that happened. I sure was glad I did not know. But Friday and Saturday were great as Bill and I worked together. On the Saturday night, I think we prayed with 400 or more people. Bill prayed with about 10 or 12, then switched with me and we took turn about praying and catching. I remember a very large lady Bill prayed with and it was my turn to catch. I did not make it. She sent me flying and the people roared with laughter. At least I broke her fall.

At the time I was struggling with the reality of the Baptism in the Holy Spirit, I was staying overnight with the Musclows in Belleville, Ontario. Child Evangelism workers had asked me to do some stick-men chalk drawings at the Belleville Fair. By radio I heard General Ralph Haines, an American four-star General, give his testimony about receiving the Baptism in the Holy Spirit on the platform at FGMBFI Convention in Buffalo,

N.Y. He was seated beside Harold Bredesen. That was a clincher for me.

General Haines said, "Prior to that time I really did not know whether or not I was headed for Heaven or Hell, but wherever I was going, I was going in a dignified manner."

Later it was my privilege to meet the General in Hamilton, Ontario and in Bradenten, Florida. He saw my paintings and thought Bible Art Ministries was a great idea. I was able to share with him how his testimony helped me.

Up to this time I did a lot of supply preaching in churches of many different denominations, but now I focused on Pentecostal churches to find out more about the baptism in the Holy Spirit.

It is no secret that the Evangelical churches are divided on the issue of whether or not the gifts of the Holy Spirit are operating today or whether they ceased two thousand years ago. For the first 33 years of our lives and ministry together, Gwen and I believed as we had been taught. But when we attended Kathryn Kuhlman's service in Toronto in 1970, we realized that what happened in the book of Acts was still possible today.

Gwen and I attended Full Gospel services for two years watching carefully everything that happened before we received the baptism in the Holy Spirit. When this happened our lives and ministry changed dramatically as the following pages of this book will show.

Immediately we wanted everyone to know about the new joy and peace we had found and the power for witnessing. Wow!

In November 1973 Gwen and I both received the Baptism in the Holy Spirit along with the ability to speak or pray in a tongue unknown to us. The years of ministry following show a dramatic increase in results. I remember my prayer one Saturday night in my study at Evangel Baptist. God was answering my prayer.

LEFT FOOT

When I was ordained by my Baptist brethren, they offered me the right hand of fellowship. When I shared with them my acceptance of the gifts of the Holy Spirit being operative today, they extended to me the left foot of fellowship. I understood that. I had been there – done that. I understand their sincerity and stand for what they believed to be the truth.

Drawing Souls To Christ

Evangelical Christians who are true believers are clearly divided into two different categories or groups:

1. Those who believe and teach the gifts of the Holy Spirit ceased to exist 2000 years ago,
2. Those who believe and teach that the gifts of the Holy Spirit are for today as well as 2000 years ago.

This book is an honest report of the awesome things God did. It can only be honest and true if the whole story is told. Whether or not you agree theologically with us, we cannot compromise our testimony.

For the first 34 years we held the former position. Gwen and I graduated from the William Booth Memorial College and were commissioned as Salvation Army Officers. Later I was ordained by the Associated Gospel Churches, and after accepting a call to a Baptist Church, was ordained by them as well. I took by correspondence the Scofield Bible Correspondence Course from Moody Bible Institute and studied also at Toronto Baptist Seminary one year.

The transition from position #1 to #2 did not come easily for Gwen and myself. The book tells the story. We feel it must be told in total honesty, without compromise, and to the glory of God. We make no apology for what we believe and have experienced. It has been on both sides of our experience an Awesome Adventure in Christ.

Kathryn Kuhlman said, "Once you have seen the power of God you can never be the same again." It was in a service she conducted in Toronto in 1971 that my theological position was challenged, and our ministry forever changed.

> THIS ABOVE ALL ELSE
> TO THINE OWN SELF BE TRUE
> THOU CANST NOT THEN BE FALSE
> TO ANY MAN

CHECKERS ANYONE?.

One of the greatest evidences of the change the baptism in the Holy Spirit made in my life was the change in my attitude toward the boys and the dramatic change in the atmosphere in my art shop at the Correctional School.

Now, when a boy began to act up, I would pray, "Lord, show

me what is wrong with this boy and please show me what I can do to help him."

Almost overnight the boys became their own policemen for me. When a new boy would begin to act up, two of the other students would converge on him and whisper in his ear, "We don't do it here." The new student would say. "Why don't we do it here?" "Because Mr. Crookall does not like it." And I had not a single major problem from that day on.

I set up my checkerboard in my shop. When I saw a boy getting a little frustrated I would invite him to play a game of checkers with me – and let him win if possible. This also gave me an opportunity to talk with him about his problem. Then he would go back to his assignment content.

Before the baptism in the Holy Spirit, Gwen knew how hard some days were for me, and she did a lot of praying for me at home. Sometimes she hated to see me go to work, knowing what I had to face.

Soon I was telling the boys about Miracle Services that Gwen and I were attending at Evangel Temple right in the heart of Cabbage Town in Toronto, where many of them lived. They wanted to go too.

It all started when a boy brought his art work to my desk for evaluation and help. Knowing he was from Cabbagetown, I said, "My wife and I were in Cabbagetown last night."

"What were you doing there?" was his question.

"We went to a church service at Evangel Temple – and we saw a miracle happen – a lady who had one leg shorter than the other by about four inches limped to the front for prayer – and ran back perfectly healed with both legs the same length."

Wow! The boy seemed awe struck. He went to his desk, but came back in a few minutes. "Can I go with you next time?" he pleaded.

"In order for you to go, you would have to obtain permission from the chaplain, the superintendent, and your housemaster."

"If I get permission, can I go?" he asked.

"You sure can."

"I'll get it," and somehow I knew he would.

Soon the chaplain called me. "Great idea, Stan. I'll recommend this to the Superintendent." In no time they offered me a mini bus with driver and permission to take 12 boys. That was the beginning of a real ministry and a number of transformed lives.

Larry had epilepsy; he could have a grand mal seizure at any time. Staff made him wear a football helmet for protection when he fell. Gwen and I knew all about epilepsy with our daughter Marge. Larry committed his life to Christ. At Evangel Temple Larry would be slain in the Spirit in every service. I would have to check whether he was having a seizure or was slain in the Spirit. He never had a seizure there. Larry was so changed, everyone knew it.

One day, Larry's housemaster came to see me. He said, "Don't you think it is time you took Larry to another meeting?"

My replay was, "Why?" I thought I knew the answer, but wanted to hear it.

"Well, when Larry comes back from a meeting he is so good, and it lasts for several days. Then with all the other boys bugging him, it begins to wear off. I think he needs to go again." We were glad to oblige.

At one meeting, Larry was kneeling at the front praying when a boy, handicapped in a similar way, knelt beside him, put his arm around him and prayed with Larry. He took the crude home-made metal cross and chain from around his own neck and placed it around Larry's. It was a dramatic, heart-warming moment.

Larry loved that cross and wore it continuously. Then, at a meeting, Larry saw a handicapped boy kneeling in prayer. Larry knelt beside him, prayed with him, then took his treasured cross and placed it about the boy's neck. What a gift.

Once eleven of the twelve boys we took went forward to pray the sinner's prayer.

Those were awesome experiences in Christ. Gwen always took homemade cookies and lemon tarts to enjoy on the ride home. How could you not love Gwen? She was like a mother to those boys.

One evening when we were planning a trip to Toronto, one of the housemasters came to me and demanded that I take a boy named David with us. I was reluctant. I didn't have a good feeling about David. "You're discriminating against David" he pressured. So the team decided David would go..

As the crowd was leaving the church, David made a break for it. He got away from us. The other boys were upset. Gwen took the eleven other boys to the mini bus and waited there while I used the phone in the Pastor's study to report the escape to the Correctional School.

Rev. Ken Beasley came in and asked what was wrong. I told him. He put his arm around my shoulder and prayed, "Lord, we pray that you will help us to find David and take him back to the school. If he is still in the building help us to find him. If he is outside help us to find him and take him back to Bowmanville." I really felt better after we prayed and just relaxed.

Within minutes, Gwen came running into the office and exclaimed, "We got David." She and the other eleven boys were waiting in the mini bus when one spotted David half a block away. He shouted, "There's David!" Gwen said, "Go get him!" And they did. The other boys were upset about David's behaviour. They recognized these trips were very special, that an escape might result in the trips being cancelled, and were loyal to us in response to our love for them. All twelve could have gone. But they didn't.

When Pastor Beasley's prayer was answered so quickly, it was literally awesome to me. It did something very special to my faith. I have never been the same since. I learned to pray and expect in a new way.

I later learned that the housemaster knew that David was planning to escape from the school that night, and he did not want it to go against his record. He was not concerned about our situation or David.

DANNY B.

Danny B. was full of beans – the Mexican jumping kind. He had a mischievous grin and a personality to match it. Danny earned a bad behaviour report almost every day – but had never had one from me.

One day at our art shop, when Danny came to my desk with a question, I told him that on Sunday I was going to preach in the city where he lived.

"Where?" he questioned with keen interest.

When I told him it was at Highland Park High School, Danny got excited.

"That is my school," he said. "My parents go to those meetings and I have a week end pass and I will be there – right in the front row." He was there, right where he said he would be

– with both arms waving and the biggest smile you ever saw.

After that Danny wanted to go on our mini bus adventures to Evangel Temple.

One night, just as we were leaving a service, suddenly a car came screaming around the corner and screeched to a halt. Both doors flew open and two men jumped out running in opposite directions. The police were right behind them.

"Stop that man!" shouted one of the policemen. Whereupon little Danny ran and tackled the fugitive. In a moment the policeman was right there and the criminal was handcuffed and taken away.

I was pretty proud of Danny. That took courage. So I wrote a "Good behaviour report" and dropped it in the assistant superintendent's box when we arrived back at the school.

The following morning, Walt Hall, the assistant superintendent was waiting for me. He was smiling and shaking his head. He held the report in his hand. "Do you mean to tell me that this is for real? A good behaviour report for Danny B.? I never thought I would ever see this." He walked away still shaking his head.

From that time on, Danny B. had a struggle. He wanted to be good, but it sure was a battle. We found that giving him special assignments of his own choice became a safety valve for all that energy. One of those assignments was painting "The Flame Room," where we had the kiln for firing ceramics. He painted it to look like Hell – literally. He painted massive flames on the walls. His handling of this assignment was priceless.

CONVERSION

Had you asked me who would be the most unlikely convert at Bowmanville Training School., I would without hesitation say William. His lifestyle was far from Christian. The men who worked under him disliked him. He had an attitude that got under your skin.

One Saturday morning, I was on my way from home to Oshawa. As I neared Bowmanville, I felt this prompting, "Go to your shop." It was Saturday – no one would be there – but if this was the Lord it was important to obey His leading. Sometimes you are not sure. Sometimes you wonder if it is your own thought and not the Lord. It's always a good thing to check it out.

So I changed course and went directly to the school. My art shop was a portable adjacent to the main administration building. It was locked. There was no one in sight. As I tried the door, I heard a voice, "Silly duffer." I knew that voice, too, so I realized that God was in this. I unlocked the door and stepped into my shop. Within seconds William appeared from nowhere. His first words were, "I'm sorry I have not gone to any of those meetings you invited me to." "That's ok, William," I said. "We have another meeting coming up next Saturday. I will be glad to take you with me." Then I began to share what the Lord had been doing to our meeting and in the lives of people including our own.

As I told William about the way of salvation, great beads of perspiration came out on his forehead. His knees buckled and he fell back against the wall. He said, "Stan, I don't know what's wrong with me – I cannot stand up." I said, "That is the power of God – you need to trust Jesus as your own personal Saviour." "I will, I will," and he did. We held hands and prayed the sinner's prayer.

It was one of the most dramatic conversions I had ever witnessed. And the change in William's life was just as dramatic.

Now William asked for a special prayer. "There is a woman named C- I really like and I want her to like me. I would like to marry her." "But what about your wife, William?" "We have been divorced for five years. She's living with another man." As I began to pray, I prayed, "Lord, bring the one of your choosing into William's life." William interrupted, "C..., C..." I had not forgotten her name. I explained to William that God's choice is the very best.

William said, "Can you come to see me at my house tonight?" I was really busy and had much to do, but if you are seeking first the Kingdom, you find time to do what is most important. Here was a brand new convert asking for help. You do it. Ministry involves sacrifice, but the rewards are out of this world. William became a real witness for the Lord. He shared his faith with everyone. In less than a year, he and his wife were remarried.

A DREAM OR A VISION

Gwen was the one who eagerly sought the gifts of the Spirit first.

Kathryn Kuhlman said, "You can never be the same again after attending a great Miracle Service." That certainly held true for us.

Drawing Souls To Christ

In 1972 Bill Prankard, who caught the spark from Kathryn Kuhlman meetings, began conducting miracle services. Gwen and I attended every one we could over a period of about two years. I was looking, checking, wanting to be sure that all this was for real. Wanting to step out in faith for miracles, but a little afraid of the commitment required, and how it could change my personal plans for early retirement and an easy lifestyle.

Marie Brydges and Gwen Prankard had written a hymn together. They sang it as a duet and the Lord used it to bring me to a point of decision and full surrender to the Lord's plan for my life.

You've A Place In God's Plan

You've Place In God's Plan
By your side He will stand,
And He'll guide you each step
Of the rough, narrow way,
If you make Him your King
You will have peace within,
You've a place, you've a place in God's Plan.

He has plans for your life
That will calm all the strife,
His sweet Peace He will give any man,
He will give you His Love
And a home up above,
You've a place, you've a place in God's Plan.

I think it was written just for me. A few days after that surrender, I was speaking a new language and life would never be the same again.

My wife Gwen and I became known to Bill and Gwen Prankard through a healing she received in one of his meetings. Bill was scheduled to speak at a FGBMGI breakfast meeting in Belleville, and Gwen and I were planning to be there and praying for the Lord's blessing.

Three nights before the breakfast meeting I had a dream -- that Bill Prankard failed to show up, and they asked me to take his place. When I woke I was angry with myself for presuming to dream such a thing. Who did I think I was?

Stan and Gwen at the River Jordan in Israel

I told Gwen about the dream, then tried to put it out of my head. But the thought lingered – was God asking me to be ready?

When we arrived at the hotel, we were met by the FGBMFI president immediately as we set foot inside. What he said almost floored me: "Are you Stan Crookall? We have a place for you at the head table."

I looked at Gwen – we were speechless. Moreover, the room was just as I had seen it in my dream. And there was no sign of Bill Prankard. That was not unusual, because he usually entered late. But there was no Cliff Stevenson or any of the TEAM! The dream was coming to pass. Wow! I began to pray real hard.

The meeting chair did ask me to be the speaker. He simply announced to the audience that Bill's car had slid into the ditch and he could not make it, and that Stan Crookall would take his place. Apparently Bill had phoned and said, "Stan Crookall will be there. He will have something to say."

I had never conducted a miracle service before, but I was believing God and looking to Him. I gave my personal testimony and concluded with an invitation for prayer for spiritual and physical healing. About twenty people came forward with various needs. They were directed to a prayer room.

I expected that others more experienced would go to pray with them – but the chapter president directed me to go with them. He also asked a new convert, who had given his testimony that morning for the first time in his life, to accompany me.

No one else came to help. I said to my helper, "I think we should get the others to come along with us." He heartily agreed. So I started for the other room to get help. When I was within a few feet of the door, the Lord spoke to me and said, "I am here. You don't need anyone else." Wow! I stopped in my tracks, returned to the room, and told my helper, "You cannot help these people and I cannot help them, but the Lord is here and He can meet their needs." He agreed.

So we had the people form a circle and I said, "I cannot help you and my friend cannot help you. But the Lord is here and he can meet your need if we trust and ask Him." The two of us laid hands on one person at a time as we moved about the circle and prayed for each need. When we came to about the third person I felt this prompting "Have this lady sit down," but, I could not figure that out and felt it was my imagination. Then I laid hands on the lady and she fell to the floor – slain in the Spirit. I stood in amazement. This had never happened with me before. It was awesome.

Immediately my helper became catcher and stood behind each person we prayed for.

One man was six feet tall or more. He looked like a preacher – black suit, white shirt, black tie. When I laid hands on him he jumped back – resisting the power of the Holy Spirit. I told him to relax and receive what the Lord had for him. He did, and down he went under the power of the Holy Spirit. Several years later we met again when I was invited to preach at his church, and he confirmed that he received the baptism in the Holy Spirit that day. To God be the Glory!

As I stood before the last person to be prayed with, I felt a terrible pain in my chest. I realized that this was a word of knowledge, that the Lord was about to heal her. I asked if she had a heart problem – she did. This was exciting. I believe the Lord healed her that day. As we prayed the pain went away.

Now I understood the dream. God was answering prayer in ways far beyond our greatest expectations.

As Gwen and I drove home, we rejoiced together. That day was a new beginning in ministry for us. Gwen's prayers and mine, too, over many years, were being answered. Bless the Lord.

HELEN WRAGG'S SISTER

In 1974 while promoting Full Gospel Businessmen, Gwen and I visited my cousin Ron Wragg and his wife Helen to invite them to our upcoming meeting. We shared with them many wonderful things the Lord had been doing. As we were about to leave, Helen said, "You said that we can pray for people who are some distance away and the Lord will heal them. Could we pray for my sister?"

"Sure, what is wrong with your sister?"

"She is in hospital awaiting major surgery tomorrow morning."

I prayed, "Lord, please heal her without the operation."

Next morning Helen Wragg phoned. "My sister is home from the hospital. She doesn't need the surgery." When they checked her before surgery they found she had a cold and a fever and sent her home to recover and come back later. In the meantime, she found she was healed and did not need surgery. Bless God!

F.G.B.M. PRAYER MEETING OSHAWA – BENNY HINN

One evening in early 1974, several Full Gospel Business Men and their wives met for prayer at St. Andrews United Church Oshawa.

As we stood to pray, the power of God came upon us and several men fell to the floor slain in the Spirit. We locked arms around each other as many were unable to stand. So we decided to kneel or lay on the floor as we prayed. We were praying that God would move in miracle power in Canada and around the world. We were praying that God would raise up men to be leaders around the world, particularly in miracle ministry.

While we were praying, an awesome thing happened just one mile away at Trinity Pentecostal Church. A slim young man with dark skin and long wavy black shoulder length hair had come from Toronto to be the preacher that night. He had never preached in his life before, mainly because of a severe problem of stuttering. When he got up to speak the power of God came upon him and upon the congregation. Suddenly he could speak fluently without stuttering. The service became a miracle service with the gifts of the Spirit manifest. The first miracle was for the preacher himself, other miracles followed.

A short time later we met that young preacher -- Benny Hinn. Benny has been a servant of God across Canada, the United States and around the world.

Our paths crossed often after that. I assisted Benny in services in Toronto and Moncton, New Brunswick. In 1989 Benny recognized me ten rows back in a service in Toronto. He gave a prophesy that startled me. He said, "God is not finished with you yet, Stan. He has much more for you to do..." I was 67 years old. What was Benny talking about? Was he trying to be kind to an old friend or was this really a message from God?"

Time would prove it was a message from God – for the past thirty years I have been focused on Bible Art Ministries. We met Omar Rincon and Heman Rozo in Florida. Over three winters we would disciple Omar and mentor one year with Herman. God then called both of them to serve him in their native Colombia. In the past fourteen years, they have, with B.A.M., shared the gospel with thousands and thousands of school students, and so many have received Christ as Saviour.

Disciple-ing Omar at our Florida home

MIRACLE BREAKFAST 1975 F.G.B.M.F.I.

While I was president of FGBMFI Oshawa Chapter in 1975, we had a miracle service. It was a catered breakfast at Eastdale Collegiate. Our planning committee estimated 150 meals would be needed. But the man responsible for notifying the caterers dropped it to 125 without telling me.

The caterers were frantic, 175 had showed up. "All we can do is feed 125 and give the rest a cup of coffee. We cannot even give a second cup.'

As I made this announcement from the head table, suddenly in my mind I got a perfect picture of the hillside in Galilee where Jesus multiplied the boy's lunch and fed the 5000. I felt the Lord was saying, "Trust me." So in the middle of the announcement I stopped, paused, then said, "This is ridiculous. We planned this service expecting God for miracles and I am telling you we don't have enough food. How many of you will trust God for a miracle of multiplying the food?" About 13 people raised their hands. That was enough. We prayed, "Lord, please multiply the food so that everyone can eat."

Then I sat down and asked myself, "What have I done?" The M.D. from Collingwood, who was our speaker, whispered in my ear, "The Lord confirmed that to me." Two others came to me and said the same thing. I felt a lot better. Then I sat down and watched and waited. My appetite was not good. The enemy was taunting me. What if it did not happen – I kept praying.

Suddenly it was announced that everyone had been fed and there was food left over. They did not skimp, they served full platefuls. There was food left over we took to the local Rescue Mission. To God be the Glory.

Still, 25 years later, people meet me when I am in Oshawa, and say with a big chuckle – "I remember that time when the Lord multiplied the food."

It was awesome!

The key to this miracle is that God gave a word of knowledge. That word was acted upon in faith. It was not presumption. God initiated the response. Step-by-step obedience is what God wants.

HALLELUJAH BILL

Hallelujah Bill got his nickname while working on the assembly line at General Motors. He could really shout hallelujah and did not mind where he shouted. Bill lived at Newcastle, a small town east of Toronto. Bill and his wife Urna lived on a small farm about a mile east from where Gwen and I lived.

The main business section of Newcastle was about two blocks long. Its feature is a beautiful town hall, donated and built by the Massey family – of political and farm machinery renown. If Bill spotted me a block away, he would cup his hands to his mouth and shout an attention-getting "Hallelujah". In reply, I would shout, "Praise the Lord."

Bill and Urna had known tragedy. Their 15-year-old son died of a rare disease. I can still remember Bill and I embracing at the funeral as the tears flowed.

Hallelujah Bill would be used of the Lord to one day meet a great need for B.A.M.

We needed a van to carry our 3` by 4` paintings. We began to pray about it.

While ministering in Carleton Place, we learned about an old Cargo Van which was being auctioned to the highest bidder. It was a clunker, but it seemed to me it would fill the bill – and meet our budget. We prayed and I asked the Lord for a price to offer. I felt the Lord nudging me to offer $2000. I was sure we would get it. WRONG. I was disappointed and could not understand it.

Then a few months later in Florida, we saw an Airstream Trailer for sale for $4,500 unbelievable. We bought it.

When we went to have a trailer hitch attached to our 1976 Dodge Aspen wagon, the hitch man refused to do it. He told us that our wagon was only half the weight of the Airstream. He said, "I'll read your name in the obituary column if you pull this trailer with that car."

When I told the trailer salesman what the hitch man said, he offered to give us our money back. "No, I said, "We will pray about this – give us three days, and we will see what the Lord would have me to do." That evening Hallelujah Bill phoned us in Florida. "The Lord has laid it on my heart to give you a brand new $10,000 Van for B.A.M." Awesome!

The Electric Company had bought Bill's Farm to run a big power line through our area. There had been two routes surveyed. I was praying that they would select the one that by passed Newcastle – I did not want those power lines near our house. But God overruled my prayer and met my need in spite of my wrong praying. God's "No" was because He had a better plan, and a better van.

Bill had attended a Tuesday Night Prayer and Bible Study where we had prayed for a van. Bill was unemployed at the time, but he quietly told the Lord, "If I had the money, I'd give Stan the van." Bill was true to his promise.

When I told the trailer salesman that God had answered our prayers and we had been given a brand new van capable of pulling the trailer, he was visibly shaken. He was a believer, but not accustomed to that kind of answer.

When we got back to Canada, Bill took me to Nichols Motors and ordered a brand new Chev. Beauville top of the line Van. It cost $9,400. He gave me a cheque for $10,000 and said, "Use the extra $600 for gas."

In working up the order, the salesman (a Christian brother) asked, "Do you want captain chairs?" I said, "No, we don't need that. "Oh, yes, you do" said Bill. Give them the best. What about a trailer towing package? "Put it on", Bill urged. What a delight. That van pulled our Airstream across the continent for ten years. It enabled us to reach many thousands of students in Florida, North and South Carolina, Virginia, Maryland, Ohio, Ontario, New Brunswick, Prince Edward Island, and Quebec. With other vehicles we ministered in Texas, Oklahoma, British Columbia, Alberta, Manitoba, Nova Scotia, Georgia and Pennsylvania.

In Prince Edward Island, they called our Airstream "The Silver Bullet". We spent three weeks there visiting schools all over the island. That was fabulous. At Sommerset High School there was a bomb threat. The principal came to me in the middle of our presentation and whispered, "We have a bomb threat. We are going to clear the auditorium till this is settled."

I remember overhearing a student say, "That was some good" referring to Art from the Bible. "Some Good" is an eastern expression meaning TERRIFFIC.

MR. DAN

Our Tuesday evening charismatic meeting held at St. Andrews Church in Oshawa had concluded. Half the people had already left the building. Then someone said, "It's too bad about Mr. Dancy." "Oh, what's wrong with Mr. Dancy?" "He slipped on the ice and his head struck a large stone. He has a fractured skill and is in critical condition. They don't expect him to recover."

We asked the remaining people to join hands and form a large circle. Then we prayed and asked the Lord to heal Mr. Dan.

A day or so later, I phoned the Rev. Mr. Morris about the use of St. Andrews for a FGBMFI meeting. During our conversation I asked, "How is Mr. Dan?" There was a long pause, and then Mr. Morris said, "I guess you will have to call it a miracle. He had dramatic unexplained overnight recovery and is being released from hospital and allowed to go home. Bless the Lord! To God be the glory!

SUSAN M

We met Susan and Kathy M. at a conference in Winona Lake, Indiana (summer of 74). Susan was 21 years old. They were seeking the baptism in the Holy Spirit for Susan.

The conference was sponsored by Underground Evangelism. Gwen and I supported U.E. financially. When the brochure about the conference arrived, I felt strong prompting to attend. When I suggested going to Gwen, she was surprised and delighted. She said, "I wanted to go, but I did not think you would want to go."

We selected the best accommodation in their brand new motel. Something new for us. It only cost a few dollars more. We had very little in the way of luxuries in our early years of ministry. It was good to have enough and some to spare.

The whole effort of U.E. was to raise money. There was not a single opportunity for prayer for salvation or any other needs. We found that incredible.

Somehow people in need at the conference were drawn to us as by a magnet. We were busy ministering morning, noon, and night. It was awesome. In our free time, Gwen and I had gone to inspect the Billy Sunday Tabernacle and the Sunday's home which was now a museum.

The tabernacle was huge. I wanted to know how well my voice would carry in that building, knowing that Billy Sunday preached before microphones were invented. So I marched up to the pulpit and thundered "Hallelujah! Praise the Lord." Some time later we were sitting next to a U. E. director in a meeting. He asked me about my denomination. I told him we were Baptists. "Strange kind of Baptists" he said."I was in the Tabernacle yesterday when you were there."

At one of the evening sessions, Susan and Kathy M. sat directly in front of us. Almost immediately the Lord prompted me to invite them to have lunch with us the next day. I wrestled with whether or not this was the Lord prompting me to do this or whether it was a figment of my imagination. I had no peace about it during the entire service. Finally, I said to Gwen, "It seems to me that the Lord is telling me to invite those two young ladies in front of us to lunch tomorrow." Gwen was all for it. She said, "Why don't you go ahead and do it?"

Gwen and I were in our early 50s. We were old enough to be their parents. I felt uncomfortable asking, but their response was staggering. "Who told you that we had no food?" Immediately we realized that the Lord was in whatever was happening.

Susan and Cathy had given all of their money in the offerings. They had run out of food. Their parents would be coming the next evening, but until then they were broke. I gave them money to tide them over until then, and we arranged to meet for lunch the next day. After lunch, we prayed and laid hands on Susan, she was slain in the Spirit. As she lay on the floor, she sang in the Spirit so beautifully.

A few years later, the sisters visited us in Canada. The Lord used them to minister to our son Tim, then a teenager, and they were a major factor in helping Tim to surrender his life to the Lord.

How marvellous. It was Susan's sweet Christian life that spoke to Tim. The Lord had brought us together again from a great distance for a great purpose. His ways are past finding out.

THE NEWCASTLE HOME BIBLE PRAYER MEETING

One of the most exciting adventures Gwen and I ever had was when we began a Tuesday evening prayer and Bible study in our home.

Ted White kept bugging me to start a home meeting. I really did not want to. I was president of the Oshawa FGBMFI and already conducting two meetings each week

But when tragedy struck a neighbourhood family, we decided to start the meeting for their sakes. The first meeting four attended. The second meeting eight came to our home. Then it exploded. Soon there were fifty and more.

Our house at Newcastle was on the shore of Lake Ontario, a beautiful location. The living room was 24' by 14' wide, with a large natural stone fireplace. Two large windows gave a panoramic view of Lake Ontario. We loved it.

The living room had wall-to-wall people. Many sat on the floor. There was just room for the leader to stand at one end and face the sea of faces. A neighbour complained about the number of cars, and the police visited. We just prayed and asked the Lord to solve the problem.

Within days a real estate agent called to see Mrs. Hill, who had complained. "Have you ever considered listing your property for sale?" "No," but somehow by 10 am that day she had listed the house and by 4:00 pm it was sold.

God did so many wonderful things people didn't want to miss a meeting. Our main ministry was to people who had attended dead churches and had never made a commitment of their lives to Christ. In three years, sixty people were baptized in water. Many received the baptism in the Holy Spirit.

When the house could not contain all the people, we sought the Lord's solution. Some people who came were members of Orono United Church. Their minister was sympathetic. He was a born again Christian.

One Tuesday, as I was preaching, we were reading "Paul, planted, Apolos watered, but God gave the increase .... Just as I finished reading that out loud – the phone rang. Gwen answered it and called me. It must be important or Gwen would not do that.

It was Rev. Basil Long. He said, "We have just held a board meeting and approved allowing you to use our church for the Tuesday Bible studies." Then he said, "I have a verse for you. Paul planted, Appolos watered, but God gave the increase." Wow!

A cheer went up from our crowded meeting. Next week we met at Orono United Church and that meeting continued for 15 years. To God be the glory!

Amongst those who attended was William, from the Training School, who had been an unlikely convert. He brought his friend who said, "I understand that you pray for people's problems and God answers your prayers. I have a problem. My 15 year-old daughter ran away from home three months ago, and

I have heard nothing from her. I don't know where she is. Could you pray that she will phone home?" The girl had become involved with drugs. The mother told the police, and the girl decided to run away from home.

We prayed for the girl's safety and that the Lord would prompt her to call home.

Next week the mother told us, "My daughter called home the very night I was here. She's in Houston, Texas." The girl had been taken prisoner by a man and confined to his home. The night we prayed he had gone out, she had found a phone, called the police, who traced the call, rescued her, and then she called home. "Please pray that she will come home" the mother asked. Three weeks later they came to our meeting together.

One Tuesday Bob M came along with a carload of people from my cousin's church in Oshawa. Bob was in the choir, was a Sunday School Superintendent, etc. As he walked into our living room, he just fell backwards to the floor. People responded – but he didn't need CPR. Bob smiled and said, "Don't worry about me; you don't know what's leaving me."

Later Bob said, "When I went to that meeting I thought I was on my way to heaven. Ten minutes later I knew I was not, but fifteen minutes later I knew I was." When Gwen and I moved away, Bob became leader of the prayer meeting.

Marg West came one night. When she was leaving, I told her how glad we were to have her attend. "I'll be back" she said. Next week she and her husband, Lyle, came. They had recently returned from Florida at Christian Retreat in Bradenton where they got saved. They were looking for a place to go to church and saw our ad. They came and kept coming. Years later, they became pastors of a church in Port Hope.

One evening just before Christmas, I returned from a tough road trip, doing Bible Art presentations in schools. I went to bed, and told Gwen not to wake me, no matter what. A few minutes later, she woke me. Mansel Stacy, a retired school principal, and his wife attended our prayer meetings. He had suffered a severe stroke and was not expected to live. I was up and dressed and drove twenty miles to the hospital as quickly as I could.

Mansel was in a coma. Half of his head and face was purple from the bleeding under the skin. Family and minister were there. I asked them to join hands and form a circle around his bed. As we prayed, you could see the discolouration disappear and normal colour return. Then Mansel opened his eyes and smiled and talked. God had answered prayer. The minister said, "I have never seen anything like that before." Traces of the stroke remained, but Mansel lived seven more years before going to be with the Lord.

There were many more miracles and conversions at those meetings that I would like to tell you about, but my editor tells me I must move on.

IS SPEAKING IN TONGUES FOR REAL?

There are two stories that forever settled this question for me.

At a weekly charismatic Bible study in our daughter Marjorie's apartment in Peterborough, a lady whispered in my ear, "I brought my neighbour, Julie; she is a Jehovah's Witness."

"Wow!" I wondered what the Lord would do that night.

As we were singing "Hallelujah," Ron Emery began to give a message in tongues. I looked over at Julie to see how she would react. Her eyes and mouth were wide open. She exclaimed, "How does he know Ojibwa?"

When Ron finished speaking in Ojibwa, he paused for a moment, then immediately gave the interpretation in English.

We explained speaking in tongues and interpretation of tongues to Julie. Then I went through the way of salvation in the Bible. Julie just opened up like a flower and received Jesus Christ as her Lord and Saviour. That was indeed a memorable occasion.

The next week Julie brought her neighbour, who said, "Whatever Julie got last week, I want." A few weeks later Julie and her neighbour came in great concern: "Our husbands are drunk and are coming here to beat you up." We assured the women that the Lord could handle the situation – so we prayed and went ahead with the meeting. A half hour later, the two husbands arrived, drunk. We invited them in. Julie's husband came in and got saved. The other ran home.

Julie and her husband went to North Bay for a visit and while there were instrumental in leading several relatives to Christ. To God be all the Glory!

At Pentecost when Peter preached, three thousand were converted, but later after the healing of the lame man, five thousand were converted. God's signs and wonder draw people to faith in Christ.

The second story took place at Evangel Temple in Toronto. It was during a Ken Mann Miracle Service. Gwen and I took a few neighbours with us and during the service Ken Mann had a "word of knowledge" about a severe chest condition someone had. Charlie Albin, one of our guests, went forward to claim that healing. He was slain in the Spirit, and when he stood up, he lifted both hands in the air and he began to shout in another language. Immediately three or four ladies rushed to him and embraced him and began speaking to him in the same language.

Gwen and I were about ten rows back. I ran up to Charlie, and asked the ladies, "What was happening?"

They said, "He is speaking Russian and we understand him, but he doesn't understand us."

"What is he saying?" I asked.

"He is praying for forgiveness of sins, for the anointing of the Holy Spirit, and for the salvation of the people of Russia."

Hallelujah.

Charlie Albin is an Irishman. On the way home in the car we were singing, "Give Me the Old-time Religion." We made up a new verse: "It makes an Irishman speak Russian, and it's good enough for me." That was exciting. Bless the Lord.

Chapter 11

Bible Art Ministries Beginnings

It began with the call of God which came unexpectedly, dramatically, and unmistakably at a precise moment in time in 1976. But was that the beginning? Almighty God, who knows the end from before the beginning had been preparing us throughout our lives for this moment and what was to follow. The story of Bible Art Ministries does not begin with the first school presentation. It is a life story.

This book was written to show how important prayer, Bible meditation, and discernment of and obedience to God's leading are in the life of a believer. It is a revelation of the simplicity of praying without ceasing. That it is not a struggle to obtain, but a release in faith that allows God to do it. It is not just for the very special few who have great talent and ability, but it is for ordinary people like us who will allow God to show Himself strong through our weakness. 2 Chronicles 16:9 "For the eyes of the Lord search throughout the earth to strengthen those whose hearts are fully committed to Him."

In writing this book, I have seen, more clearly than ever, the hand of the Lord upon us in preparation for the very unique and powerful ministry He designed. Art is one of the most profound subjects in the curriculum and perhaps the least recognized for its great value and potential.

In 1976, conducting miracle services seemed to be what God wanted me to do, and I was delighted to do it. It was exciting to see the Gifts of the Spirit in action, I wanted every believer to know the blessing of baptism in the Holy Spirit. I wanted to see the sick made whole.

In September, 1976, the Lord spoke to me very definitely; it seemed in words which were audible: This is not what I want you to do. I have many doing this and for them it is right, but not for you. I want you to go to the schools and speak to the students." What an opportunity! What a responsibility!

Bob Jones University published a book some years ago about the effect of a good art program in school. The research showed that in schools with a good art program marks in all subjects were higher than in similar schools without art courses.

I was at a conference where the keynote speaker, the Director of Education for Hamilton-Wentworth Schools, said: "I consider the most important teacher in any school to be - the ART TEACHER." Frankly, I was surprised – but thrilled. My school principal looked at me in amazement. Prior to that, he hadn't taken art seriously.

Does the Lord prepare us in ministries which like stepping stones lead us into the main ministry of our lives? I think so.

I was a qualified high school art teacher, with ten years' experience in a difficult correctional setting. That gave me credibility with public school administrators. And with prisons (plus our son Paul was a senior executive with Correctional Services Canada).

Just how to do that would require an additional revelation. I set aside two weeks to pray and seek the Lord about how to fulfill His commission. I read the Word and prayed each day. I just sought the Lord. I did not panic. It was a time of sweet fellowship. I had the assurance the Lord would reveal what I was to do – in His time. After more than a week of just waiting on God, one night at about 11 o'clock the Lord began to reveal to me that I was to prepare a fine art lecture of art from the Bible. The Lord directed me to begin with Cain and Abel and follow God's great plan of salvation through Abraham and Isaac, the Passover, the temple and up to Calvary and the resurrection. As God led me I sketched and scribbled until daybreak. Art from the Bible was born.

I shared my decision with Marie Brydges, our pianist and John MacFarlane, my helper. They were delighted. Marie said "Your drawings and paintings have spoken to my heart more clearly than all the great sermons I have ever heard. I think this is wonderful that the Lord has called you to go to the schools with this message."

Drawing Souls To Christ

John said "This is great! I'm for it. And I will support you financially." John became our number one supporter for the first few years, until he entered a Bible College to study. But to launch the ministry, we would need more financial support, and a Charter as a Charitable Organization from the Government. I spent the next three months painting a series of paintings and doing the paperwork needed.

Art from the Bible in our Oshawa home 1984

I asked Enos Brubaker of Gospel Text Publishers how to obtain a charter. Enos told me a lawyer was required that it would take 15 months and cost $1,500. We did not have the time or the money for that. Gwen got on the phone to various government offices. They sent us a booklet outlining what was required. I wrote the charter and had it checked by a Christian lawyer who made no change and it was approved within three months. Gwen was a big part of that. She was great on the phone to government people. Something I did not relish. People sensed her heart and wanted to help.

It was no sweat; it was trusting the Lord, seeking first His kingdom and following His leading. We asked God for favour with the authorities and He granted our request.

Next, we needed permission to enter the schools. I approached the Northumberland, Newcastle School Board, which had 78 schools. Remembering the advice of Frank Betger in How I Raised Myself From Failure to Success in Selling, I always showed respect for the secretary of the person I had to deal with.

I had prepared an outline of what our Art from the Bible presentation was about. I took time to explain this to the Board Director's secretary, a mature, gracious lady. As I expressed our purpose her eyes filled with tears. God had given favour. I did not have to see the Director. His secretary conveyed all that was required. Permission granted. Hallelujah! Wow, now we could do it.

That just got us into the Board. We then had to approach each school principal individually. I first approached Courtice High School. The principal was a Christian – I thought that was a good place to start – Wrong! He asked where I had done this. I said, "I am just beginning and I would like to start here." "Oh, no. Not here. Do it somewhere else, and then come and see me again."

The first presentation was at Uxbridge, a school of 900. The temperature was 20 below zero outside and the heat had been off in the gym all weekend. It was Monday morning. We had three sessions of 300 students each. The principal wrote a good letter of recommendation. The gym heaters were suspended from the ceiling and had noisy fans. These had to be shut off during the presentation – so it was cold. Those students deserved a medal for bravery.

CONCEPT OF B.A.M.

The concept of Art from the Bible as a means to communicate the good news of the Bible in school is indeed unique.

A pastor in Lucan, near London, Ontario arranged for me to speak at six public schools in his area. He went with me to each. He was so impressed by the message and the student response, he said, "Stan, do you realize that you shared the Gospel with every school age child in this whole area? I don't know how it could have been done in any other way."

Our expenses were low: no advertising, no auditorium rental, and we had the audiences right there.

We spoke to students, teachers, school principals, even the

cleaning staff. The Christian way is to show respect for each individual. The value of a soul is not determined by the prestige or position of the individual. A custodian and a Director of Education stand equal at the foot of the cross.

WHAT IT IS LIKE TO MINISTER IN A SCHOOL

It is awesome!

Children love to draw. Children love the stories of the Bible. The combination of the two is unique and wonderful. It is a language children speak and understand. When you love and respect children they respond in kind. Kids are fantastic.

Art from the Bible teaches art and the Bible. It came into being to take the most important and vital message in the world to children. The Good News that God made us, that God loves us, that we need His forgiveness, that He reaches out at the Cross of Calvary saying I want to forgive you.

The presentation is designed to teach art as well. We believe we owe it to the school to provide the best educational presentation possible. It is designed to show that understanding how to draw can be exciting and enjoyable.

As the students come in, the younger students sit at the front, within a few feet of where I will stand. I talk softly to them and smile. I ask, "Do you like to draw?" "What is your name?" "What is your favourite colour?" etc.

After the introduction we begin with enthusiasm. On a blackboard or newsprint pad is the following:

Drawing can be.........!

What do you think drawing can be? I want a three letter word. Drawing can be- - - ! Immediately students respond FUN! That's right. Drawing can be fun, and I believe that everyone can draw. If you can print your own name, you can draw.

Drawing is made up of four basic shapes. Everything you draw is made up of one or more of these shapes.

OLIVE is a single five letter name. (I have used this name to illustrate how to draw for the past thirty years. Just this summer, my great-granddaughter was born and named Olive).

The letter "O" draws a sphere. "L" when put upside and backwards beside another "L" draws a cube. Combining "V" and "O" gives a cone shape. Two letter "I"s in parallel, with an "O" at each end is the cylinder. Those four shapes provide the basics for all drawing.

HOW GOD PROVIDED A CARRYING CASE FOR B.A.M.
PAINTINGS

Jack was superintendent of the Sunday School at Ebenezer United Church. As I was loading the paintings into my car after showing them to his Sunday School, Jack gave me a hand.

The paintings were on masonite 4'X 3' with an aluminum frame. They weighed ten pounds each. But it was the size and awkwardness that made transportation difficult. I just laid them in the back of our station wagon with a blanket in between each one for protection.

I could see the wheels going around in Jack's head as we loaded the paintings. There were seven. Finally, Jack said, "There must be a better way of doing this." "Yes, there is," was my reply. "Do you have a plan?" "Yes, but I have not got all the wrinkles worked out yet." Jack said, "Give me your plan and a sketch with measurements, and I will make it for you."

The carrying case he had built for me was a masterpiece. We used it for many years until traveling to other countries by air necessitated smaller, lighter, more portable equipment

One day in Florida Gwen and I came across an art display shown by the daughter of a famous illustrator who painted portraits of Hollywood stars in the 20's and 30's. His daughter showed us a painting of Shirley Temple. It was painted on canvas and rolled up on a rod. As she unrolled it, I got the idea I could paint on canvas and roll the paintings on window blind rollers. It would be just the thing for traveling. We have used the system with great success ever since.

JESUS FESTIVALS

During the late 1970s there were great Jesus Festivals at Mercer, PA, Mount Union, PA, Kitchener and Hamilton, Ontario. 50,000 or more would gather to praise and worship the Lord. Great servants of the Lord would be there to minister like Pat Robertson, Josh McDowell, Winkie Pratney, Andre Crouch, Winston Noones and Randy Stonehill.

There we met thousands who stopped at our Bible Art Ministries booth. Many signed up to receive our BAM Newsletter. We counseled and prayed with hundreds of teens and young people.

At one Jesus Festival a man spoke to me about my painting of Noah's Ark which was on display. He said, "The Lord told me that you are going to make a painting like that for me." I replied, "Well, the Lord has not told me about it yet." "Will you pray about it? I will come back tomorrow and talk about it.

I prayed and I asked the Lord to confirm this by giving me a price to charge for the painting and to give the man the exact same price to offer for the painting.

The Lord gave me a figure – it was low. $200. Then I sort of dismissed the whole thing and went about my work at the booth. After a while the man appeared with a big smile. "Did you pray about it?" he asked. "Yes", I said, "I prayed about it." My friend went on to say, "The Lord told me how much to give you." That got my attention. "The Lord told me to give you $200." That was awesome. He got the painting.

The Shepherding movement came into being at that time, causing confusion and division in the Charismatic renewal. We had opportunities to counsel young people who were being misled by some who were demanding that they do strange things. Some self -appointed shepherds were putting their group into bondage trying to control where and when they could go on trips or holidays – when they should marry, etc. Some great leaders were deceived like Bob Mumford and Derek Prince. Pat Robertson and others stood against the false teachings and eventually the leaders acknowledged their mistakes. It was a difficult period.

The Jesus Festivals were used of the Lord mightily. One evening at Mercer, PA, Bob Harrington preached to 50,000 – it was awesome. It was estimated that there were 15,000 decisions for Christ that night.

Some we met at Jesus Festivals would later invite us to their areas to minister in schools. Hundreds of schools were opened to us in this way. Jim Creaser, a school teacher, scheduled weeks of school appointments year-after-year for us in Northern Ontario. Jim and I ministered together for a week with a Korean College and Careers group. Jim is a great singer, guitarist, and song leader. We prayed with many. Those were unforgettable days.

We also ministered extensively in Baltimore, MD, Fairfax, VA and the Washington, DC areas at the invitation of friends we met at a Jesus Festival. It was at Lorton Prison in Fairfax, VA that Bertrand, the prisoner, received Christ. I also remember two great meetings in that prison.

We met Joni at a Jesus Festival, I believe at Mount Union,

PA. I stood in amazement as she drew with a pencil clenched between her teeth. In my opinion, Joni Erickson is the finest paraplegic artist in the world. Her work is distinctively beautiful and shows no sign of inferiority when compared with the work of leading artists. She is very special. Personally, I greatly admire her and her work. What an inspiration. Somewhere on that same missionary journey we met the mother of Eve Tornquist.

In Baltimore we stayed at a home across the road from Joni Erickson's home. We had a wonderful visit with Joni's parents. They were so surprised that we went to see them, and not Joni, who was away at the time. Her father was a a carpenter, and a former USA Olympic wrestler. You could tell which houses he had built. They stood out as better than the rest on the street. Her mom was an artist.

GEORGIO VINS

"Free Georgio Vins!" was our battle cry as we marched on the Russian Embassy in Ottawa, Canada one Saturday in the mid-seventies. About two hundred of us had turned up early one Saturday at Ottawa's Centennial Park to form our march to the Embassy under the auspices of Underground Evangelism International and its leader, Joe Bass.

Giorgio Vins was a Russian Baptist minister, twice imprisoned for preaching the Gospel. He was serving a ten-year prison sentence. The conditions of these prisons were such that surviving the sentence would be a miracle.

When we arrived at the designated assembly site, we were met by the Royal Canadian Mounted Police, who treated us more like criminals than liberators. They noted our auto license numbers and tried to intimidate us out of marching. We were informed that the Canadian Prime Minister, Pierre E. Trudeau's office, threatened UE that their charter to provide receipts for income tax purposes would be revoked if they participated in the march. This explained why there were no Underground Evangelism workers or the promised signs and banners we expected.

The RCMP was suggesting that we go home and forget about the whole thing. Most of the 200 who had assembled were pretty well resigned to doing just that. But what about Giorgio Vins? If he had the courage to face imprisonment for preaching the Gospel, shouldn't we be willing to face this situation on his behalf?

Gwen and I had more experience with this sort of thing than most who were there. We encouraged them to march on the Russian Embassy on our own – not representing Underground Evangelism.

"But who would lead us?" they questioned. "Will you lead us?"

We were elected more by default than popularity. But as President Ronald Reagan said, "It's amazing how much can be accomplished if you don't care who gets the credit." Sometimes when others fail, the Lord gives us opportunities to step in the gap and do what they should have done. At times like these, the Lord gives the strength and courage we need to do what He wants us to do.

The police told us that we could march two abreast on the sidewalk across the street from the Embassy, but we could not go any nearer the building. We could not make direct contact with any Russians inside.

First, we prayed. Navy marching experience made it easy to form double ranks and shout, "Forward, March" – which we did. When we arrived at the Russian Embassy under RCMP surveillance, we followed their orders and marched back and forth chanting, "Free Giorgio Vins. Free Giorgio Vins."

The Russian Embassy in Ottawa is a huge building covering an entire city block and three stories high. To our amazement, Russian embassy personnel pulled back the curtains and looked out the windows with shock and amazement on their faces. They were terrified. They got the message.

One of the Ottawa radio stations covered the march and interviewed some of us about what we were doing and why. The Lord enabled us to accomplish our purpose in spite of the strong Canadian government opposition. To God be the Glory!

After Giorgio Vins was released from prison, he came to Canada. Gwen and I went to hear him speak at a Baptist Church in Whitby, Ontario. He was a huge bear of a man with a ready smile and a good nature. He spoke English perfectly. He was delighted to learn of our efforts to free him. How great is our God, and how greatly to be praised!

Whether our protest had a bearing on his release, we do not know. But he was released shortly after that time.

WALTER ZIMMERMAN

It is so easy to miss God! Jonah did. We can, too.

In one of my favourite Stick Men Bible Stories, "A Whale of An Experience," I draw Jonah as God calls him to go to Ninevah. It did not make sense to Jonah, and he said, "No way, I don't agree with God." And he missed it. My title for scene one is "The Wonder of God's Call," How marvellous, how awesome, that Almighty God – ruler of the universe - should condescend to speak to mortal man. For reasons difficult for us to fathom, God has chosen to work or minister through us.

Often what God calls us to do does not make sense to us. We are finite. He is infinite. We must recognize that we are incapable of thinking on the same plane as God thinks. He knows all the facts. He knows the end from the beginning.

Jonah was not alone in forgetting that God does not make mistakes. Ananias felt the same and reacted the same way when God called him to go to the street called Straight to minister to Saul of Tarsus. The greatest foe of the early church, Saul the martyr-maker. Saul, the religious zealot. He literally said, "God, don't you know about this man? You are asking me to commit suicide."

When the Lord began speaking to me I felt the same. A day or so after I received the Baptism in the Holy Spirit the Lord said to me, "I want you to go and see Walter Zimmerman and share your experience of receiving the baptism in the Holy Spirit." Wow!

Walter Zimmerman was six feet four inches tall. He was a Baptist Baptist. That's a Baptist who knows what Baptists believe and won't budge from it. He's one who will earnestly contend for the faith and possibly be contentious about it. I did not want to go. I thought Brother Walter was not only capable of throwing me out of his house, but that he might do just that.

What I did not know was that God had prepared Walter's heart just as he had prepared the heart of Saul of Tarsus.

So I talked to Gwen about it. We prayed together, and then I went to see Walter.

"Big' Walter," as he was called, had been part of the Military Police in the Canadian Army in World War II. You don't mess with them.

Walter was home – I was kind of half wishing he had not been. Walter's wife Olive was in Africa with Walter's sister who was a missionary there. His brother Paul was also a missionary in Africa. We had known the Zimmerman family at the Lake-head since 1950. We know Walter's brother, Oscar. They were a family of giants in stature and giants in the faith. None of this made my assignment any easier. Walter was a graduate of Toronto Bible College. That made it harder still.

As we sat opposite each other in Walter's living room, I shared my experience with him about receiving the baptism in the Holy Spirit. Big Walter leaned forward – was this it – was he going to throw me out of his house? But Walter amazed me – he said, "Brother Stan, I want to know this experience myself." What a relief. Thank you Lord!

But now what was I supposed to do? I had never led anyone into this experience and what if it did not work? I suggested we go to a Pentecostal Church where they knew more about this. Walter was ready for that.

In a day or so Gwen and I took Big Walter to Evangel Temple in Toronto, but Walter did not receive the baptism. Then I suggested going to a FGBMFI in Peterborough and Walter was game for that. That's where it happened – what a relief. Big Walter was stretched out full length on the floor, slain in the Spirit, and speaking in tongues. Hallelujah! Mission accomplished

After the meeting I tookWalter to see, Tom Schauff, whom we both knew from the Lakehead. Walter just poured out his experience to Tom. Walter was naturally slow of speech, but not this time. Both Tom and I were amazed by his fluency. We both knew that Walter had met God in a new and wonderful way that day.

When Walter met his sister and his wife on their return from Africa, he shouted, "Hallelujah! Praise the Lord." Olive exclaimed, "Walter's flipped." She was scared. But soon she, too, would be speaking another language.

Walter and Olive became two of our very closest friends. We went to the Holy Land together. Walter went with me on many missionary journeys to schools.

Once in a Public School near Oshawa I was explaining the Painting of David vs. Goliath so I had Walter stand beside me. Walter at 6'4" beside me at 5'6" truly was quite a contrast. I wanted them to get the idea of how a giant looked. These were junior kids, so I asked, "Can you see a difference between Walter and I?" One little fellow could hardly wait to respond and blurted out "Yes, Walter is wearing glasses." That was not quite the answer I had hoped for, but it was fun and everyone had a good laugh.

If anyone deserved recognition for being a helper Walter Zimmerman sure does.

Walter worked in a foundry lifting fifty pound castings. His back was severely injured, and he was unable to work. So he went to a Miracle Service and the Lord healed him. He was able to go back to work lifting those huge fifty pound castings all day long, until he reached retirement.

Once Walter went with me to schools in the Athens, ON area. I stopped at Mr. Fishman's Store in Elgin to inquire about the way to a public school. Mr. Fishman, who was Jewish, wanted to know all about Art from the Bible. He told me he had watched Kathryn Kuhlman on T.V., but he did not believe those people were healed. Enter Walter Zimmerman. Big Walter told his story. Mr. Fishman was convinced.

Walter loved to help people and ministries. He was a general handy man and worked on buildings at Christian Camps and Mission. When I broke my hip just after buying a new house, he helped out for the first three months. .

When Walter went to be with the Lord while holidaying in Florida, Gwen and I were there and helped Olive all we could. Gwen went and stayed with Olive overnight, and we saw her aboard the flight home.

PAPPA CROOKALL

Our son Tim and I were on our way to a Jesus Festival in 1979 when the Lord said, "Go to see your Dad." "But Lord, I saw him just yesterday. Why today?"

How often do we forget that God does not make mistakes?

After wrestling with the situation for a few moments, I said, "Tim, the Lord seems to be telling me to go and see Pappa." Tim's reply was "Let's go, then!"

As we arrived at the nursing home, we could hear Pappa screaming, so we ran to where he was. We found him shouting, "I am dying! I am dying! I am going down! I am going down." He was clutching the railing of the bed as though he was about to drop through the floor. The nursing home chaplain was there with him, but seemed unable to help. I asked, "Where are you going down to Pappa?" Pappa's reply was, "I am going down to Satan."

"You don't have to go down to Satan, you can go up to be with Jesus," I said. "How?" he asked. "If you just tell God you are sorry for your sins and ask Jesus to save you, He will," I assured him. Then came the words I had prayed so long for. With deep emotion Pappa said, "I want to." We prayed the sinner's prayer together.

Then Pappa let go of the bed rails and gave a big smile. He said, "I am not going down to Satan, I am going up to be with Jesus."

I really didn't know whether or not my father was dying, so I phoned Gwen and asked her to come to the nursing home and stay with Pappa. She did.

As Tim and I left the nursing home to go to the Jesus Festival, I said, "Oh, Tim, the mercy of God. I have prayed for Pappa's salvation for forty years."

Gwen stayed with Pappa that day and the next morning. Then he quietly went to be with his Saviour and Lord. A brand snatched from the burning. He was 93. To God be the glory! God is faithful. What an awesome answer to prayer. If the vision is slow in developing, wait for it.

Gwen arrived at the Jesus Festival that evening. The minute I saw her I knew what had happened. Pappa had gone to be with the Lord. I wept, but rejoiced.

At the funeral and the committal at the grave I had the privilege of relating to the family how Pappa had committed his life to Christ the day before he died. His body was buried beside my Mom's. I noticed the tombstone next to their grave said, "TOGETHER FOREVER" and related how Pappa and Gramma were now together in a way in which they had never before been together – and that they were TOGETHER FOREVER.

How great is our faithful God! What an awesome answer to prayer. Never, never, give up. Keep praying.

GRAMMA CROOKALL
"No man is poor who had a Godly Mother." – Abraham Lincoln

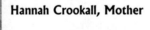

Hannah Crookall, Mother

Birthday 1940

Stan and Gwen 1943

Roy Crookall, Thomas R. Crookall, father, Stan Crookall

Drawing Souls To Christ

I remember well the things my mother taught me. My mother was converted a few months before I was born. I feel that had a profound effect upon my life.

My mother made the Bible stories live to me. I could picture the scene as she told the stories. She told me a Bible story each night when I went to bed. I could see David accept Goliath's challenge. I could see Goliath's head roll when David swung Goliath's huge sword.

When she told me the story of Samuel I was in awe as God spoke to him and called him by name. How I wished God would speak to me. I felt gypped. But there came a glorious day when God did speak to me.

My stick-man Bible stories and Biblical illustrations go way back to those early beginnings.

My concept of financing a ministry went back to the lessons she taught me about George Mueller asking God alone for the money and food required to feed thousands of orphan children. I could see the children sitting around the table as they gave thanks for the meal that had not yet appeared, but always did in answer to prayer. As a small boy I wondered how long they had to wait. I still wonder when I think about it.

My mother always had the most beautiful flower garden on our street. But I associated flowers with women and not men. When she asked me to take flowers to the teacher, I would only do so if they were wrapped in newsprint like fish-and-chips so that no one would know what I was carrying. I would sneak them in to the teacher's desk without anyone noticing.

Once while waiting for the school doors to be opened, I was leaning against the school yard fence. The flowers wrapped in newsprint clutched behind my back so that no one would see them. Why didn't I just throw them away? That would be dishonest. Another lesson well taught.

One of my classmates saw the package and asked what it was. He offered to give them to the teacher. What a break. I was elated.

When the teacher opened the package and saw the beautiful bouquet she asked, "Who brought the flowers?" I sat back at ease expecting my classmate to tell her he brought them, but he stood up and announced, "Stanley did!" The laughter was deafening, my whole world caved in. Taking flowers to the teacher was "sissy stuff" and the last thing I wanted was to be considered that.

Gramma Crookall organized a ladies sewing group. Our school had a large number of Army Cadet uniforms that were not being used. The ladies transformed them into windbreakers and trousers made to measure for needy boys during the depression years.

Gramma Crookall had a good influence on all who knew her. Gwen was very special to her. Gwen learned from my Mom and became so much like her in the process including the art of being a great cook. Gramma Crookall went to be with the Lord in her 87th year. Every memory of her is precious.

KEN ASPDEN

Gwen's brother, Ken, was one of those John Wayne kind-of-guys. He was a professional wrestler, a champion stock car racer. He owned a used car business and automotive garage. He was big and tough. Alcohol turned him into a tiger. When he was drinking, he was rough. When the police knew it was Ken Aspen they were going after, they responded with four officers.

Ken and a friend took on six of the Edmonton Eskimos football team in a bar in Hamilton and won. The football players took Ken and his friend to court. The judge listened to the case, and then said, "How many of you were there?"

"Two."

"And how many football players?"

"Six." Case dismissed.

At age 50 Ken was in hospital in Hamilton, awaiting surgery to remove a large tumor from his brain. One evening the Lord spoke to me and said, "Go and see Ken. It's now or never for him."

I told Gwen and she was ready to go in an instant. She phoned sister, Marge, to meet us there. It was a three hour drive, but when the Lord says "Go" you don't consider the distance or difficulties. "Behold, to obey is better than sacrifice."

We were praying and planning what to say. Ken was one of those tough cases who seemed so unlikely to come to Christ. Only the Lord could give the strength required for an encounter like this. When we arrived at the hospital Ken's wife and children were there, with Gwen's sisters, Marge and Betty. That made eight visitors. Things did not look promising with all those people there. Finally Betty said, "Stan, do you want to speak to Ken alone?" and moved everyone out except Gwen,

Drawing Souls To Christ

Marge, and myself.

I said, "Ken, you are facing major surgery tomorrow. The operation is serious. It could go one way or the other – you know that. We would like to pray the Lord will heal you but it is important to be on 'praying ground.' What I mean is to be in a right relationship with God. That means asking God to forgive our sin and inviting Jesus to come into our lives to be Saviour and Lord."

Then I told him about John Wayne's conversion. I said, "Ken did you hear about John Wayne receiving Jesus as Saviour in the hospital?"

Ken asked, "John Wayne got converted?" That made it easier.

"Yes, John Wayne watched Robert Schuler on T.V. then got out of his hospital bed and knelt on the floor and prayed, 'God forgive my sins....Jesus, come into my life and be my Saviour.' Later after being released from the hospital he took Robert Schuler a fine bronze statue of a cowboy on horseback as a special gift – and told his story."

Ken was ready to pray. I said :You must mean every word you pray," so Gwen and I sat on either side of him along with sister Marge. We held hands as we prayed. Ken had very large hands. He squeezed our hands with every word as he prayed. Wow! Gwen thought her fingers would break.

We prayed, "God be merciful to me and forgive my sins because Jesus took my place and died on the cross for me. Lord Jesus, I invite you to come into my life and be my Saviour and Lord of my life. Help me to live for you. Thank you Lord. In Jesus' Name. Amen."

Hallelujah! Thank you, Lord! Many had prayed for years for Ken's salvation. After surgery Ken lived for three weeks and then went to be with the Lord. Before he died, Ken witnessed to children from a former marriage and to other family members. He said he was sorry for the problems he had created for family due to his drinking, and promised that he would be a different person from now on.

We also prayed for Ken's healing, but that was not to be.

At Ken's funeral, Cayuga Race Track sent the pace car to drive in the funeral procession. Racing drivers and wrestling buddies were present in the service. Major Stan Burditt, Marge's husband, led the service. He asked me to tell about Ken's conversion. I knew that Ken's buddies knew all about his drinking problems and fights. This was common knowledge.

So I began by saying, "We all have our problems. If you knew Kenny, then you knew about his problems. But I want to tell you about what happened to Kenny in the hospital," and I went on to tell about his conversion. They were thrilled.

The driver of the pace car said, "Oh, I'm so glad for Kenny. This was a very special funeral service. I have never known a funeral like this before." To God be the Glory!

FRED

At a FGBMFI meeting in Oshawa and Fred was moved by the ministry of the Holy Spirit. When his 12 year old daughter was healed of a kidney problem that night, suddenly she couldn't see. She had been wearing thick glasses – when she took them off, she said, "Oh, now I can really SEE."

The Lord had healed her eyes as well as her kidneys.

A psychiatrist who was with me at the meeting said, "The eyes and the kidneys are related to each other and the eye healing is a confirmation that the kidneys are healed." He became an instant believer.

BOB BOBOLA

Bob Bobola was the Chief Project Engineer for the Space Shuttle Orbiter.

I first met him in Oshawa and later in Ottawa, where he autographed my N.A.S.A. painting. Bob asked me how many schools I visited in a week. He thought it might be two or three. When I told him often it was ten schools a week he was surprised. He reached in his pocket and took out an astronaut's crest. He said, "I don't have many of these, and I give them out sparingly, but I think you deserve one."

Later he sent me a large carton of books about the space program.

Bob told me that more than two hundred of NASA's staff became believers in Christ as Saviour after the successful return of Apollo 13 – in answer to prayer.

Drawing Souls To Christ

Dr. Bob Bobola, NASA Chief Orbitor Engineer for Space Shuttle

AN OSHAWA HIGH SCHOOL

Each school presentation is a series of challenges. First, permission must be obtained from the school board. Then each school principal must be contacted regarding his permission. Then you face the students. It is a spiritual battle and we go forward on our knees. If God is not in it; it does not work.

As I faced a tough worldly school principal I was praying, "Please open the door for a presentation in this school."

Several teachers I had worked with when I was an art teacher were now working at this school. That helped. The principal respected these teachers and immediately felt there was a common bond. But when I told him my presentation was "Art from the Bible," he began to squirm. I could see the wheels turning in his brain. "How do I get out of this one?"

Then I could see the light dawn. He had found the perfect solution. "We must run this by our art teacher. If he approves, O.K., but if not, NO DEAL."

I sensed that the principal was certain it would be "No." The art teacher had an "image" - a buckskin-fringed jacket, hair half-way to his waist, a long beard, beads and chains about his neck. His answer surprised us both: "That's a great idea. Let's do it next week." I learned later that he had become a Christian only days before.

The Lord indeed gave us favour with a touch of Holy humour added.

Sometimes getting approval for a presentation is like battling and landing a big fish. You just keep praying and believing for the miracle.

Howick School student

The painting at "Christ At Heart's Door" provoked a statement from this unnamed boy at Howick Public School who said, "I think that's really neat. Jesus does not force His way into our lives. He waits for us to open our heart's door to Him."

A HOSTILE SCHOOL PRINCIPAL

We prayed about each school, but some school principals were so antagonistic toward the Gospel they were rude and then some.

Drawing Souls To Christ

Some times it took a number of calls through the years to get permission. Often these men became our biggest promoters after they had seen and heard the presentation. One said, "I don't know why any principal would object to giving you permission or why they would hesitate." I just smiled. He had hesitated four times himself. Then he remembered, and he smiled too.

In Oshawa I met the principal of a large school in the hallway. I told him I was an artist and a former high school art teacher, and had given art presentations in hundreds of schools. Before I could explain the Biblical part of what we do, he told me how schools needed artists like me to visit and teach their students. He invited me into his office.

When I told him that I am a Biblical illustrator, his countenance changed dramatically. He jumped to his feet gesturing wildly, and shouted, "Don't say one more word. I don't want any Bible in my school." He pointed to the door, and in a loud voice said, "I want you to leave immediately."

I never did get into that school.

There were pleasant experiences as well, and they far outweighed the bad ones by about four to one. I remember a principal's secretary saying, "The principal is busy right now, but he saw the fish emblem on your calling card and said, 'This man is a Christian, and I want to see him if he can make it back at 4 pm'." You can bet I did. And we had a great time ministering in that school.

HARRY PANCHO

Early one morning the phone rang. Could I go to the Bowmanville Hospital to pray with Harry Pancho who had suffered a severe stroke and was not expected to live?

Eight year old Navin, who came from a Hindu background in Guyana, had been attending Sunday School at the church where I was interim pastor. When his grandpa suffered the stroke, he pleaded with his grandma to "call for the minister to pray with Grandpa and the Lord will heal him." I was on my way to Woodstock 200 miles away to minister in schools. It was possible to squeeze the visit in if I went immediately.

When I found Harry Panchoo in the hospital, he was not expected to live more than a few hours. His legs and arms were paralyzed, his face was twisted, but he could still talk with difficulty. He said, "I am dying. I need to have my sins forgiven."

Navin had been telling his grandpa about Jesus. I made sure he understood THE WAY and then we prayed the sinner's prayer and Harry invited Christ to come into his life.

Then I read from the Bible about Jesus healing people. I asked Harry if he would like me to pray that the Lord would heal him. Yes, he wanted that. So we laid hands on Harry and prayed, asking the Lord to heal him and raise him up to make him whole in Jesus Name. I had read Mark 13 and told Harry to hold on in faith until the answer came. I told him that sometimes the Lord heals instantly, sometimes in an hour, sometimes in a day. Then I went on to Woodstock.

Three days later when I returned I went direct to the hospital. I did not know what to expect, so I went to the information desk. Harry Panchoo is in room 114, not in intensive care. That sounded encouraging.

He was sitting up in bed. When he saw me he reached out both of his arms that had been paralyzed and said, "Oh, my priest, come here." As I ran to him he took both my hands and kissed them. Then he said, "Jesus is in me, and he has given me a miracle and healed me." Then he pulled back the covers and kicked up his legs around to show me that Jesus had made him whole. Hallelujah!

Knowing his Hindu background, I felt it important to seek to teach Harry in his new faith. I saws him daily for a few weeks. We read and studied the Word together then prayed.

A relative asked Harry, "Where are you getting the money to pay that priest to come and see you?" When he told them there was no money involved, they found it difficult to believe. The Hindu priest charged $100 a visit.

Harry and I became great friends. We called each other "Brother" and our warm friendship lasted for a number of years until Harry was called home to be with the Lord. The change in his life was so evident that his wife Eileen said "Harry you are such a good disciple of the Lord Jesus that I would like to stop calling you Harry and call you Peter instead." Harry's response was, "That's wonderful, call me Peter." That very night, the Lord called Harry (Peter) home.

Harry Panchoo was our first contact with South America. Later we learned that one of the first missionaries to Guyana was a man named Crookall.

FEEDBACK FROM STUDENTS

A letter from a teen age girl in Sackville, NB stated, "When I realized that your Art presentation was based upon Biblical Art, I was furious to think they had allowed you to speak in our school. But as the presentation went along my attitude changed and at the conclusion I was in an ecstasy of joy through knowing Christ as my Saviour."

After speaking at a Roman Catholic School in Peterborough I received a number of letters from students who said, "I received Jesus Christ as my Saviour today," or "I opened my heart to Jesus today."

QUOTES FROM SCHOOL PRINCIPALS

"You will never know how much our conversation meant to me today. You did what I wanted, you did what you wanted, and it was not offensive." (From a Middle School in Bradenton, Florida).

"There are some things that register in your mind forever, like the first time you enter a school classroom and see the letters of the alphabet illustrated on cards at the top of a blackboard. I believe that what our students saw and heard today will be indelibly etched upon their hearts and minds for a lifetime." (From Burks Falls, Ontario)

"What our students saw today will be the only art gallery some of them will ever see and the only Sunday School they will ever attend." (From Port Hope, Ontario)

THE AYLMER, QUEBEC STORY

The village of Aylmer, Quebec is situated across the river from the city of Ottawa.

Elwyn Reed was unable to work due to a lung condition caused by inhaling sawdust at work as a cabinet maker. He had already selected the tree he would drive into to end his life and provide his family with the insurance support. But somehow he went to a Sunday afternoon Miracle Service at the Highland Park High School in Ottawa where God touched his life and everything changed.

Bill Prankard had asked me to take his place that Sunday. At the conclusion of the meeting, I invited all who wanted to be prayed for to come forward. In most services at Highland Park, about 400 or more would respond so quickly that the front of the auditorium would be packed with people seeking salvation and healing. Elwyn Reed was part of that group.

There were so many people to be prayed for that there was not time to ask everyone what their specific need was. I didn't ask Elwyn anything, I just laid hands on him and prayed, "In Jesus' Name!" As I did, the power of God came upon him and he fell backward to the floor, slain in the Spirit.

When the service was over, Elwyn was so under the power of the Holy Spirit, he had to be carried to his car. It was some time before he was able to drive home. He said, "I just felt better and better and better every minute." He was completely healed and able to go back to work the next day. To God Be the Glory!

Later, when I got to know Elwyn, and found him to be extremely shy, I asked him how he ever got up enough courage to go forward for prayer in that meeting. Elwyn smiled his shy smile, and replied, "An angel took me by the arm and said, 'Come on, this is your day!' When we got up front, the angel disappeared"

The way I found out about this, and met Elwyn personally, was that one day sometime later, he phoned me to ask if I would pray for a neighbour who was sick with cancer. Somehow, I sensed that this request called for special attention. Arrangements were made to meet Elwyn in Aylmer, Quebec, not far from Ottawa and go with him to his friend's house.

Later, Elwyn called back and asked if others might come along, too. At least a dozen people came and we had a great visit and enthusiastic prayer time at the sick man's home.

One of Elwyn's closest friends was Bud Kerr. Sensing the earnestness of this group of neighbours, I asked if they had a regular Bible study prayer meeting.

"No."

"Why not?"

"We have no leader capable of doing this."

"What if you had?"

"Why, of course, but who?"

Feeling the prompting of the Lord, I asked, "What if I volunteered?" Tears of joy ran down their cheeks. The Aylmer once-a-month meetings began in the basement of Bud Kerr's farm home. For many years there was a very special meeting in Kerr's home. Even after Gwen and I moved back to Newcastle, we still travelled 300 miles to Aylmer once-a-month for the meeting.

Robbie Kerr, Bud and Shirley Kerr's youngest child, was six years old. Shirley suffered paralysis shortly after Robbie's birth, and neighbours, the Nesbits, had taken Robbie to their home to raise him.

One Friday as Gwen and I left Newcastle to drive to Aylmer for the meeting, Gwen was driving and I was sort of resting and praying as she drove. I had prepared a Bible study to share that night and was really excited about it. This was a really great message. I could hardly wait to teach it. But I was being disturbed by promptings from the Lord, "Not that message."

"If not that message, Lord, which message then?"

The Lord indicated that I was to do a simple chalk drawing of Noah's Ark. What a letdown. I was really disappointed. But the matter was settled. It would be Noah's Ark.

While I was drawing the stickman story of Noah, I found myself sort of standing back, listening to myself, saying, "This is so simple. This is too simple. This is sort of kid stuff and I wanted to share that deep teaching I had prepared. I hope someone is getting something out of this." Little did I realize what an important message that was and anointed of the Lord.

When I gave the invitation for prayer, little Robbie who had been standing at the back beside his mom and dad, broke loose from them, and ran to the front. His mother made a grab for him from her wheelchair but missed. His dad tried to grab him, but Robbie meant business. They didn't think he knew what he was doing. As I looked down at this beautiful little blonde-haired boy, I suddenly realized what this meeting was all about. It was about a little boy whose life would be forever changed that night.

"What do you want to pray about, Robbie?" I asked. His two arms shot up in the air and he said enthusiastically, "I want Jesus." There was not a dry eye in that crowd. As Robbie prayed the sinner's prayer, I laid my hands on his head and the power of God came upon him. He fell to the floor, slain in the Spirit. That was unforgettable.

The next day, Gwen and I went early to the Kerr's home. Little Robbie came bounding out into the living room and jumped in my lap. "Stan," he said, "Jesus is in my daddy's heart, right?"

"Right," I said.

"Jesus is in my mommy's heart, right?"

"Right."

"Jesus is in Gwen's heart, right?"

"Right."

"Jesus is in your heart, right?"

"Right."

"How can Jesus be in everyone's heart at the same time?"

"Well, Robbie, you see, Jesus is God as well as man. God is omnipresent, He can be everywhere at the same time, so Jesus can be in all of our hearts at the same time."

Robbie smiled, "That's great!" He jumped down and scurried away.

Later that day, Robbie went door-to-door down the road and told all the neighbours about Jesus and the story of Noah's Ark. Elwyn Reed was so impressed that he built a four-foot-long scale model of Noah's Ark with a special carrying case for our school ministry. Multiplied thousands of school children have seen and heard the story and seen the model of Noah's Ark. It inspired me to make a large painting for the school presentations.

When Robbie Kerr went to high school, five boys decided they would "Get Robbie Kerr. We will make him think like us." they agreed. "No more of this Christian stuff." A few months later, three of the five were like Robbie. He had won them to the Lord.

ROBERTA

Our Aylmer, Quebec Friday evening meeting at Bud and Shirley Kerr's farm house was really special. We didn't even have music (piano) at first. But people came expecting and they were not disappointed.

Roberta was about 50, a mother of two. Her husband came occasionally. His work may have interfered with our meeting time. When she came forward for prayer, it was for diabetes.

Wow! That's a tough one. You don't hear of many being healed of diabetes. So we laid hands on Roberta and prayed that the Lord would heal her.

The next meeting, I learned that Roberta was in the hospital. I kind of gulped when I found out, thinking that's not very good. But next meeting, she was back, and she was radiant.

She had been on two syringes of insulin daily. Suddenly her body began rejecting the insulin. She was hospitalized to find out what was wrong. The doctor put her through the same tests twice, then concluded, "Your body doesn't need the insulin anymore, it is reacting to too much insulin."

Roberta shouted, "Thank you, Jesus!"

The doctor asked, "Did you say something to someone?"

Roberta replied, "Yes, I sure did. I was thanking Jesus for healing me."

She grew in her experience and relationship with the Lord continually, week by week. Her testimony was always up-to-date, she was always aglow. If you ever needed a lift in the meeting – Roberta's testimony was the answer. Her testimony was always so fresh and exciting. She would tell me what she had learned from the Bible, and I would laugh. Roberta would say, "You are laughing at me again."

My reply would be, "No, Roberta, I am not laughing at you. I am laughing with you. It is so exciting to see how quickly you are growing as a believer. You are moving right by some who have been Christians for fifty years."

DUNCAN NESBIT

Duncan and his wife had looked after little Robbie Kerr for six years because his mom became paralyzed after he was born. Now Robbie was six years old, and the Kerrs could look after him, so he returned home.

With good reason, Duncan was a preacher-hater. I don't know the story, but I understood that two different preachers had been involved. But after Robbie got saved at one of the meetings, Duncan could see such a transformation in him that he became interested and attended a few meetings himself.

One weekend Bud and Shirley had invited me to go with them to their cottage. Duncan's cottage was right next door.

As we drove in, Duncan was just emerging from his outhouse. I stuck my head out of the car window and shouted, "Hey, Dunc, is that your cottage?" Immediately I was shocked by the words that came out of my mouth, and I just couldn't understand why I had said that. But Duncan laughed. He rather enjoyed the question.

I had gone to the cottage much in prayer for Duncan's salvation. I planned to really try to win him to Christ that day if possible. But Duncan was mixing cement and making a sidewalk. Three times I went over to talk with him and three times I just seemed tongue-tied, and couldn't witness to him. We talked about other things, but not about the Lord.

That evening, as we were leaving, Duncan came running out to us. He reached in to shake hands with me, and said, "When you are in the area, please come to see me at my home. I would like to talk with you!"

I assured him, "I will try."

As we drove on, I looked over at Bud, who was driving, and tears were streaming down his cheeks. "You don't know it, Stan, but that was a miracle. Duncan has been a preacher-hater for twenty years. You are the first preacher he has invited to his home in twenty years."

A few months later, Duncan was diagnosed with cancer. He was in the hospital. At the Friday meeting we all prayed a special prayer for Duncan's salvation. Bud and I went to see him Saturday morning at the hospital. Trying to lead Duncan to the Lord was like trying to land a great fish. Finally I said, "Do you ever to intend to receive Christ as your Saviour?"

Duncan's reply, "It's just as you wish."

"Well, if it's as I wish, let's do it right now." – and we did. Duncan prayed the sinner's prayer, "God be merciful to me a sinner. Forgive my sin for Jesus Christ's sake. Help me to live for You. Thank you, Lord. In Jesus'name. Amen."

Bud Kerr hugged his great friend of many years, and they wept together.

As we were leaving, Duncan said to me, "Tell Gwen, 'Praise the Lord!'" To God be the Glory.

When we arrived back at the Kerr's home, little Robbie came out to meet us shouting,

"I know what happened. Duncan gave his heart to Jesus." Robbie, too, had been praying.

TERRY FOX – A TRUE CANADIAN HERO
Terry Fox was unforgettable. We met on highway 115 south of Peterborough. I could see him coming with his entourage, so I pulled over on the shoulder of the road and waited.

The news media had told us about this young college student from Coquitlam, B.C. who had lost a leg to cancer and planned to run across the country – the equivalent of a marathon each day, on one leg – to raise money for cancer research. Seeing him in person was awesome. As I stood at the roadside, I had prepared to shout, "That a boy, Terry," but as he got near and

The Silver Bullet

The Van

The Hampton House

Painting in the Hampton House Studio

I saw this handsome winsome young man, I got a lump in my throat and tears in my eyes. I just could not speak. I have never been able to mask my feelings – I'm sure Terry could read me. There was no one else near us; it was just Terry and I – face to face. So I watched in admiration as he hobbled past.

Then I drove ahead, parked, and waited a second time. This time I was able to get the word out. "That a boy, Terry." Terry replied, "Thanks a lot." I had given my donation to Terry's brother and received my Terry Fox button. I just sat there in the car for a while and prayed.

Not knowing whether Terry was a Christian or not, I prayed for his salvation, for strength, for health, for success. A day or two later Terry was at Bowmanville. I wrote a short letter to him outlining the way of salvation and my promise to pray for him each day, which I did. I handed the letter to Terry personally while he was running.

Then a news report on T.V. and radio carried Terry's voice and I learned that he was indeed a believer. Terry always spoke with emotion. You had to listen carefully to get every word, but his testimony was there if you were able to understand him.

I painted a portrait of Terry running. You can see it in this book. I added it at the conclusion of my art from the Bible lecture. Each time I showed it in school there was an immediate standing ovation.

By this time I had pieced together Terry's testimony to faith in Christ as his Lord and Saviour. It helped me to explain this sinner's prayer clearly to students listening.

When the news came from Thunder Bay that Terry was taken to hospital there, the nation was deeply saddened. Terry's 26 mile-a-day run was taking its toll. He was losing weight and had developed a cough. As Terry neared the half way mark of his Marathon of Hope, he became so ill he was rushed by ambulance to hospital in Thunder Bay. The report was devastating. Cancer in his lungs. Terry fought back the tears. The nation prayed.

Terry lived another year and in that time gave a clear cut testimony. One thing he said was, "I want to hear Jesus say, 'Well done' as I finish the race of life." He was able to attend a ceremony at Ottawa to receive the Order of Merit from the Canadian Government.

Drawing Souls To Christ

Terry Fox was a regular at the youth meetings at a Baptist church. The pastor, Don Merritt, formally worked with Christian Service Brigade in the Hamilton area when I was a fellow pastor there. Don knew Terry well and he also attested to Terry's faith in Christ. It was a young woman from that group who was instrumental in Terry's conversion.

At his funeral Terry's minister left no doubt about Terry's relationship with Christ as his personal Saviour. Tim and I were ministering together at Millbrook Prison the Sunday Terry Fox died. The prisoners were truly saddened by the news. How wonderful that we could share his faith and assure them of his eternal salvation.

NAPANEE PRISON

One Saturday a month I traveled to minister at Napanee Detention Centre. It was a hundred mile journey one way and involved about eight hours of my time. Gerald Frizell, a real estate broker from Napanee, was in charge of the service and I did the preaching.

The service was at 7 p.m., but we went for coffee and cake at 6:30 with the men in the cafeteria. One of the guards said, "You are wasting your time tonight. We have a brand new large screen T. V. and it is hockey playoff time and the Toronto Maple Leafs are playing. No one will come to your meeting."

There was only on thing to do – PRAY! As I drank my coffee and prayed, I was suddenly aware that one of the prisoners was looking me over intently. I immediately realized this man could be one of my former art students and went over to him. He was now bearded and twenty years older, but sure enough, he was one of my boys. He asked "Were you the art teacher at Bowmanville?"

We chatted about old times at the school, and then I asked, "Did you enjoy working in my shop?"

"Oh, yes, it was great."

"Do you appreciate what I tried to do for you?"

"Most certainly."

"Well, I have a favour to ask of you. I am conducting a religious service in the chapel tonight at 7 pm. I know the hockey game is a great attraction, but I sure would appreciate it if you would tell these men just exactly what you think of me and explain how you know me and that I will be showing Biblical paintings in my presentation." As I was saying these words, I wondered why I was saying them. It wasn't like me to say something like that – I believe it was one of those times when the Lord takes over and the words are His, not ours. He knows exactly what they need to hear.

My former student's face fell. "Oh, I don't know whether I can do that or not."

"I hope you will try and I hope you will come yourself."

Then Gerald and I went to the chapel to pray. We prayed for my former student and all the men. We prayed for favour. We prayed for an audience. This request was in the miracle realm. If anyone came it had to be God who directed them. I believe God appreciates desperate prayers.

We prayed for half an hour and then it was chapel time. The prisoners began to arrive – they just kept coming. The chapel was filled and more chairs were brought in. The chapel was packed with prisoners and extra guards. The Lord moved upon them from the beginning and we had a wonderful service. When I gave the invitation to pray the sinner's prayer, EVERY HAND WAS RAISED – EVEN THE GUARDS RAISED THEIR HANDS FOR PRAYER. WOW! It was glorious. My former student also got saved. The guards were smiling. God is so good.

When we left the prison to go to our car, we were walking on air. My friend from Napanee said, "I never saw a service like this one before. Praise the Lord!"

The trip home did not seem so long this time. I could hardly wait to tell Gwen what happened and how God met so many needs. We rejoiced together and thanked the Lord.

STAN WALLACE

Stan Wallace spent time in prison and later became a great prison evangelist. Our son Tim, who has worked with Stan a number of times, considers him the number one prison evangelist he knows. Tim graciously included his dad high on the list and it was kind of him to do so. I feel highly honoured to be considered on the list and with men of Stan Wallace's calibre. When Stan Wallace sits down with his guitar to sing, it is something really special. There are few dry eyes.

Stan Wallace was a tough guy whose life was transformed by Redeeming Grace. His million dollar smile and gentle manner came after conversion and not before. Once he came to see me, while I was working at the Bowmanville Correctional School for Boys. The receptionist had known Stan since he was a boy and known as the terror of the neighbourhood. Joy called through to me and said, "Stan Wallace is here and wants to see you. Do you want to see him?" She was surprised that I said, "Yes."

Later she called back and said, "Stan was smiling. What happened to him? He is so different." I had known Joy in high school. She and her husband, and Gwen and I were good friends. I replied, "Joy, you know what happened to Stan." Then it dawned on her, that kind of transformation could only come through the new birth in receiving Christ as Saviour and Lord.

Stan Wallace has worked with me in and out of prison as a prisoner and as a free man. I just love the guy. He is one of my dearest friends, a real trophy of grace. To God be the glory!

Stan once confided to me that he was scared of our German Shepherd, "Smokie." I did not know Stan was ever scared of anything. When guests came to our house sometimes Smokie would lay down at the doorway to the living room to keep watch. Every few minutes she would give a little growl just to say, "I'm here. Make sure you behave yourself."

SMOKIE

We did not need a dog; did not want a dog, but Smokie needed a home and if she did not get one her owners were planning to have her destroyed. Our son, Tim, found out about her from one of his guitar students. Tim asked each of his guitar students, but there were no takers so he came back to us. "It would not hurt to go and see the dog would it?"

"Well, maybe not." WRONG!

Smokie was a guard dog of the first order. She was chained outside her home on a thirty foot chain. She went wild when I approached the house. I calculated by the length of her chain that I could just make it by her to the side door. I was right. Smokie was infuriated. She went bananas. I loved it. I thought this is a real dog. She won my heart. Smokie liked women, but she was selective with men.

It took a while, but Smokie became part of our family. She loved to travel with us across North America for nine years. It was easy crossing the border with her – one growl was enough to scare border guards out of their routine of questions and say, "Go on."

Smokie sure did make life interesting.

The first time I took her to the vet he said, "This dog has been abused, but she's in heaven now with you folks."

Smokie had great discernment, and she loved it when people prayed. If there is a place for dogs in heaven, Smokie will be there. Smokie loved Gwen, and Gwen kept her looking like a beautiful German Shepherd should be.

The only time Smokie was bad was when we went away and left her at home alone – and there were cookies around. Once we left the pantry door open. Smokie found a ten pound bag of dog biscuits and ate every one. She did not eat again for three days -- her tummy was so bloated she had difficulty walking.

SUPPORT FOR BAM SARASOTA BAPTIST

I remember the time when I received a letter from a church that had supported BAM with $600 per year. Gwen had already read the letter before she handed it to me. As she handed it to me, I said, "I don't want to read it." The Lord had already told me this church was going to stop supporting us so I knew what the letter would say and I did not want to read it.

Sure enough the letter said exactly what the Lord had warned me would happen. I sat in my easy chair dejected. Who would make up the $600?

Gwen said, "You're worried aren't you?"

"No", I replied.

"Yes, you are," she said.

"No I am not."

"Yes you are."

"Well, maybe I am."

Gwen said, "The Lord looked after us before we knew anything about that church and He will look after us now."

"You are right," I said.

Then I told the Lord that I was sorry for worrying and asked Him to meet our need.

A few days later when I came home from ministering in schools, Gwen handed me another letter. It contained a cheque for $1,000. And this supporter gave $1,000 each month, all year long, and still does. Bless the Lord..

Someone said, "God's work done in God's way will never lack God's support."

SNOWY RETREAT IN NOVEMBER

In over 55 years of ministry very rarely have I said no to an opportunity to serve the Lord in ministry.

One November it turned snowy and cold. I was scheduled to speak Friday, Saturday, and Sunday at a retreat held at a farm. There were thirty or so in attendance. The women were to sleep in the farm house. The men in the barn.

There was a fresh fall of six inches of snow . The cold and snow were not appealing. The thought of sleeping in the barn was not my first choice. I was one of two preachers. The other fellow preached Friday evening and left for home. I really wished I were leaving with him. I never liked being away from Gwen and I don't like the cold. The enemy really told me how stupid I was to be there. I was not looking forward to sleeping in the barn.

There was a furnace in the barn, but it was still a barn. We slept in sleeping bags on straw.

Ah, but the fellowship were great. All but one couple were strangers to me. I made some new friends.

The enemy told me it would be a lost week-end, but the results were beyond anything I could imagine. One of the young men at the retreat, Jim Wylie, was a Prebyterian theology student. When he graduated some time later he became pastor in Prince Edward Island. We kept in touch. I wrote him about the possibility of spending two or three weeks covering all the schools on the island. He set up my itinerary.

SPUD ISLAND – THE SILVER BULLET

In 1943 as a member of the commissioning crew of a Canadian Navy Frigate HMCS Sussexvale we had sailed by Prince Edward Island on our way to the North Atlantic. Now I could minister in public schools all over the island and be able to enjoy its renowned beauty as we went. Prince Edward Island, affectionately called "Spud Island", is known worldwide for its potatoes. At one time they had the contract to supply all the potatoes used at McDonalds restaurants worldwide.

We had parked our Airstream trailer at Damascus, Ohio for the winter at my cousin Lyle Davison's home. I had done a masterful job of blowing out the water lines so they would not freeze. Or so I thought.

In those days there was no causeway to the Island and the

only access was by ferry. So we towed our Airstream aboard the ferry. Immediately it was the center of attraction and was named the "Silver Bullet" by the Islanders.

When we hooked up to the water supply at Jim Wylie's home, immediately I heard Gwen screaming inside the trailer. Water was spurting from everywhere. Over the winter the lines had frozen and split. We would have to be carriers of water until we could make repairs. Rod Trite, a Full Gospel Businessman at Moncton, New Brunswick had assisted me with several presentations. He owned a huge mobile home park and RV center and he and his men did a great repair job free of charge. Thank you Lord!

The students of schools all over Spud Island were super special. They just loved Art from the Bible. They purchased hundreds of prints. In one school village we figured almost every home would have one of our prints as a constant reminder of God's provision of salvation.

At one rather primitive school we gave the presentation in the basement. The dirt walls made it somewhat less inviting than other places we had ministered. Perhaps you pray a little harder and more desperately in situations like that. To my surprise and great delight, the presence of the Lord could be felt so strongly. When I returned later to see how many prints the children had ordered it was almost a total sell out.

At St. Patrick's School on an Indian reservation, each student had made a little gift for me. I was able to reciprocate by giving each of them a free print. In each school presentation we made the way of salvation clear and plain. I also explained my own conversion at age 17 and the prayer I prayed. From letters received we got statements like, "I gave my heart to Jesus today," and "I opened my heart's door to Jesus." Often we use the painting of Christ at Heart's Door to show how Jesus does not force His way into our lives, but stands knocking.

At Summerside high school, where the world renowned Canadian singer Anne Murray had been a gym teacher, in the midst of our Art from the Bible presentation the principal whispered in my ear, "We have a bomb threat." So we left the building until it was determined there was no danger and then resumed our presentation.

I recall overhearing one teen say to another, "That was some good." Had I not spent seven years in the Maritimes I might

Drawing Souls To Christ

have misunderstood the meaning, which is "That was great."

One man we met on the ferry, took me on a tour of the Island. There were Gospel Text scripture signs all over the island. My new friend became angry as he read each sign out loud. Suddenly, I realized why. Each quotation was judgment. One sign said, "The wages of sin is death." It should have included, "But the gift of God is eternal life."

My friend took me to his family's home where there was a bunch of people sitting around a huge kitchen table. We sat with them. The owner of the home was building a large steel sailboat in the back yard. It was magnificent. The welds were perfect, just like the kind on Indianapolis racing cars. His reason for building was to keep him away from the bottle. He was an alcoholic and trying to find deliverance his way.

When I spoke of boats with him, I got around to Noah building the ark. He didn't believe that nor did any of the crowd.

There is such a thing as the laugh of faith. I did it. I good humouredly said, "Whether you believe it or not does not change the truth--truth is truth." Suddenly they all got angry, at least a dozen of them. It was time to leave. Had I messed up? I don't think so. Dwight L. Moody said, "If your preaching doesn't make people sad, glad or mad, it isn't effective." They were mad! They would remember the illustration of God's ark of safety with Christ as the door, the only way in to safety. They were ready to literally throw me out when I left.

Recall the man at Bon Echo Provincial Park, the former WWII sailor, who threw boots at fellow sailors who knelt to pray? Remember how this really brought conviction to his heart and led him to Christ? We prayed it would be a similarly effective witness.

At the close of the day as we drove past a beautiful old white Presbyterian church my new friend said, "My grandfather built that church." Indeed! Now I felt I understood why the Lord had me spend the day with this man and his relatives. It was for the sake of His servant of many years ago.

You may not win them all, but you sometimes win those you did not realize were won.

SIGNING AUTOGRAPHS CAN HAVE
SURPRISING RESULTS

"The highest form of worship is obedience
If you hear, what will you do?"
Elizabeth Elliott

When one student asks for an autograph, they almost all ask. I have made it a habit to pray about each autograph. I ask the Lord for guidance about which scripture verse to write along with my signature.

Most are written on scraps of paper. Is it significant or are they just thrown away later? Some are – but not all.

More than one teacher has remarked about how the verses written suited the student exactly. When God is in it, that's the way it should be, and is.

Somewhere near Goderich, ON, a Christian lady was concerned about the spiritual welfare of the little girl next door. The girl's family had no time for church. The lady continued to invite the little girl to go to Sunday School with her, but the little girl never wanted to go. One day the lady was surprised and overjoyed because the little girl came to see her and asked if she could go to Sunday School.

The lady was curious about why Sally wanted to go to Sunday School that day. Sally said, "Come with me and I will show you." She took the lady to her bedroom and showed her a little piece of paper pinned to the window curtain. It was the Bible verse with my autograph. Sally said, "This man came to my school and showed us paintings and told us about Jesus and that's why I wanted to go to Sunday School."

How many thousands of autographs we have signed in Canada, U.S.A., Jamaica, Colombia, and Ecuador? I have no idea. How far reaching the impact only the Lord knows.

THE BLANK FACE

We have made 5,000 prints each of Christ at the Heart's Door, Jesus the Good Shepherd, and The Way of the Cross. These are available to students for one dollar and to prisoners free. Thousands of these prints have been distributed around the world.

A teacher in New Liskard, ON told me about a boy in his class who purchased a print of The Way of the Cross. The next day he brought a photograph of himself to school, cut out the face, and glued it into the blank face in the print. The blank face represents you.

A girl in Orangeville had her print framed and hung in the living room of her home. When guests looked at the painting, she would say, "I'm in that painting," and would tell the story and point to the blank face. That girl's mom and dad became prayer partners and strong financial supporters of BAM. When they died, they remembered BAM in their will. Bless the Lord.

NORTHERN ONTARIO

My Full Gospel Business Men (FGBM) brethren in Northern Ontario invited me to minister in their area for a month. They decided to share me a few days each in their homes, thus lessening the load for any one family.

One of these segments was with a bachelor preacher whose culinary skills were almost non-existent. The first meal with him was something less than exciting, but as we were eating, he opened the fridge door where a large bowl of fermenting tomatoes could be seen. "I have these stewed tomatoes that should be used up. I think I'll warm them up for dinner, brother."

"Lord, how do I get out of this one?" was my prayer. Suddenly I thought of a solution. "How about going to a good restaurant for dinner tonight after we finish ministering at the schools? I would like to take you as my guest."

The preacher's face beamed, "I'd be delighted," he replied. Preachers love an invitation to dinner. When I represented Gospel Light across Canada, I invited scores of preachers to dinner. I can't remember any one of them refusing. I do recall one who said, "I can't go with you today, but if the invitation stands good for tomorrow, I'll be glad to meet with you."

I had completed a day of schools and was looking forward to speaking at Montieth Prison near Kirkland Lake after supper. I was cold and a wet snow was falling. As I tried to start my trusty Volvo station wagon, it absolutely refused.

Knowing the local Pentecostal preacher was a former auto mechanic, I called him for help. He tried to fix the points. It did not work.

One of the local FGBM volunteered to take me in his station wagon. I was soaked through to the skin and shivering. I had a change of clothes, but I needed an overcoat. He had an extra one. It would fit someone twice my size, but that was okay. It was good to be warm again and on my way.

I had no idea the prison was so far away. Enroute a transport truck kicked up a big rock that crashed through our windshield and showered glass all over us, leaving a gaping hole in the centre of the windshield.

When we arrived at the prison, a guard told us there was something special on for the prisoners that night and probably no one would come to our meeting. I began praying harder. A handful came, six or seven. But I have often given presentation for one person at a service station or wherever the opportunity presented itself. Jesus often spoke to one – why should we do differently?

When the invitation was given I asked those who had never received Christ as Lord and Saviour to pray the sinner's prayer with me. "Heavenly Father, I ask you to forgive my sins for Jesus sake. Thank you, Jesus, for going to the cross for me and taking my place so that my sins can be forgiven. I invite you Lord Jesus to come into my life and to be my Saviour and Lord. Help me to live for you, in Jesus' name. Amen."

Immediately following the prayer, one of the prisoners spoke out, "Where did you get that prayer?"

"Why? I asked. "Did something happen to you when we prayed it?"

"Yes," he exclaimed with joy. "I just felt that darkness went out of me and left me and that light came into me and joy."

The prisoner on his left said, "Me, too."

And then the prisoner on his right said, "Me too!" To God be the glory.

Was it worth the effort? There was joy in heaven and in our hearts as well.

ASHEVILLE, N.C.

Jack Lehman was the keynote speaker at a Christian School teachers' convention at the People's Church in Toronto. The master of ceremonies recommended our Art from the Bible presentation and asked me to stand so that people could recognize me.

When the session was over, Jack Lehman came directly to me and gave me his card. "If you are planning to come to the Asheville, North Carolina area, please contact me in advance and I will set up a schedule of Christian Schools in our area." I wrote him but didn't hear back. A year later, I got an apology from Jack. Their school had burned down, but was now rebuilt. He scheduled a week of schools for me in the area. He also provided a cabin in the woods with a refrigerator full of good food. Gwen and I just loved it there. Gwen was recovering from a car accident and required a few chiropractic treatments, but we were still able to visit Bitlmore House and go over to the Ben Lippen School that Jack ran, for some meals together. The school is just ten miles from Billy Graham's home. The mountains are absolutely beautiful. One of my favourite spots on earth.

Gwen had wanted a convection oven and Sears in Asheville had a good one on sale, so we bought it. We always enjoyed doing things like that together. I remember that very happy day as we walked together through the mall listening to "It's a Small World After All," a song a good friend sang just a few weeks previously in Canada, in great weather realizing what it would be like back home in February. We usually made one missionary journey to warmer places each winter.

There is something about Art from the Bible that appeals to students of every age and interest. I remember a group of teen boys at Candler, N.C. who helped me load my equipment after the presentation at their school. It wasn't so much the words of appreciation they spoke as much as their attitude. This had been a special time for them – an experience they would never forget. They seemed to sense that and their whole being expressed it. It was a special moment for me, as well, as I sensed that the Lord had ministered to them as a group and individually as well. Perhaps some doubts were forever settled. Perhaps the wonder of God's love in redemption was strengthened. Perhaps the need for wholehearted commitment to Christ and the challenge to seek first the Kingdom of God in every area of life became real to those considering life's purpose and goals.

A school principal said, "Today my students got a glimpse of how each one of us can honour God throughout life in our chosen profession – no matter what that profession may be." To God be the glory.

Mountain people live close to God in nature. That week amongst them in North Carolina was an awesome adventure in Christ.

MRS. K's SHAWL

Gwen helped me with driving, but while I was driving, she was busy knitting, crocheting, or making something for somebody.

She loved giving things to people. In Oklahoma, she gave a shawl to a millionaire's wife one evening when we had dinner at their home.

The lady, Mrs. K was so overwhelmed, she cried. She said, "No one ever gives my anything. They think I have everything."

It was one of the most remarkable reactions to receiving one of Gwen' gifts we ever had. Gwen was no respecter of persons. Everyone was on the same level.

She also loved the unlovely people with equal intensity, and she made time for them.

The K's had given us the use of their beach house for as long as we wanted to stay. It was Gwen's genuineness and natural love that people felt. She respected everyone, and no one above the other.

GOOD COOKING

My mother was a professional cook. She worked as a cook for millionaires.

When I was away in the Navy in World War II, Gwen lived with my parents, and she learned how to cook like my mom. Her roast beef and gravy with roast potatoes, vegetables, and Yorkshire pudding was indeed "Fit for a King."

Gwen seemed to be always looking for an excuse to put on a big dinner for friends. Many visiting preachers rejoiced over an invitation to stay for dinner. Gwen went out of her way to invite those with special needs.

She took to heart Titus 2: 3-5, and took time to teach younger women how to be a good wife. She tried to help married couples who were having difficulties and recruited me to counsel with the men. She did not give up. She prayed and persisted to victory.

In our home church she always found time to counsel teens and college age girls. She was open and frank about everything. They just loved her. She had an encouraging word for each one.

As we traveled in ministry through the American mid-west, we were driving through Oklahoma City and Gwen read a sign out loud –COWBOY MUSEUM, WOW! I wheeled the Volvo around and we spent an hour or so in one of the finest art galleries of the world. There were paintings by all the great western artists. Remmington, Russell, von Schmidt, McCarthy, even Norman Rockwell. What an inspiration! I knew about the museum, but was not aware that it was on our route. Those are special blessings the Lord provides to delight His children.

In Chickasaw, Oklahoma, we so enjoyed the name that we stopped and shopped. There was a fantastic sidewalk sale. We bought ice cream cones for ten cents. We bought clothing at ridiculously low prices. It was fun. For a person who as a boy grew up on the great western films of the late 1920s and early 30s, visiting the American west was like going home. In our "Amazing Adventure in Christ," the Lord allowed us to travel all over North America to behold the beauty of God's creation.

In San Francisco I remember looking across the harbour and recognizing Alcatraz prison on that little island. As we crossed the Golden Gate Bridge I felt – this is the greatest structure I have ever seen that man has made – until Eureka! I saw the Redwood trees towering 365 feet into the heavens. Then in a souvenir shop, we bought a piece of redwood with a poem imprinted on it. It reads:

The Redwoods
Here sown by the Creator's hand,
In serried ranks, the Redwoods stand
No other clime is honoured so,
No other lands their glory knows.

The greatest of the Earth's living forms,
Tall conquerors that laugh at storms.
Their challenge still unanswered rings,
Through fifty centuries of kings.

This is their temple, vaulted high,
And here we pause with reverent eye,
With silent tongue and awe-struck soul,
For here we see life's proper goal.

To be like these, straight true and fine,
To make our world like theirs a shrine,

Sink down, Oh, traveler on your knees,
God stands before you in these trees.

By Joseph Strauss

When I read the poem, I sensed the man who wrote it felt exactly as I did. Then I found out that Joseph B. Strauss was the designer and builder of the Golden Gate Bridge.

As you seek the Lord, He will be found of you. As you see Him in nature, He will reveal Himself to you. Enroute to ministry, we saw the Grand Canyon in Arizona and the painted desert. We brought home a chunk of petrified forest wood that feels and looks like stone. We floated in Great Salt Lake in Utah. We were impressed by the mountain named the Great White Throne. What an awesome reminder!

We ministered in Oregon and were charmed by Portland, the City of Roses. I bought a beautiful pair of brogue shoes for $6.50. They never wore out. I kept them for almost 40 years. Just like the wilderness provision. Our son, Paul, loved to eat at John Bunyan's Restaurant in Portland. There was a stature of John Bunyan about thirty feet high outside.

Gwen and I traveled pulling a house trailer across North America more miles than we could remember. We used three different trailers and one RV. One day in Florida we stopped to get a good look at a Conestoga Wagon like the early settlers used. I took a photo of Gwen beside it. As I did so, I thought about our modern day Conestoga wagons and how Gwen and I had criss-crossed the continent so many times. It has been an "Awesome Adventure in Christ."

1980-1881

"IT'S A MIRACLE YOU ARE ALIVE!"

Dr. Ewart was our neighbour at the Newcastle Beach on Lake Ontario where we lived. He was also our family doctor. He usually had a half-smoked cigar clamped at one side of his mouth while speaking between his teeth out of the other side. He did not waste words. He told it the way it was. He was thorough in what he did. He was one of those unforgettable characters who always made you smile. You had confidence in him when he was at work.

For Dr. Ewart to say, "It's a miracle that you are still alive!" was to realize the seriousness of what you had gone through.

For him to repeat this statement three times during his examination made you realize that God had preserved your life in circumstances that usually prove fatal.

Gwen had gone shopping and had been gone too long. I was at home and getting a little anxious about her return. Then the phone rang. "Is your wife's name Gwen? I don't want to alarm you, but she has been involved in an auto accident. She is all right, but your van is a wreck."

"How can she be okay if the van is a wreck?" I asked. I took details of the location and sped to the scene.

It was a head-on collision of two vans at an intersection. Both drivers were women. The other lady was covered with hot dog mustard, a whole gallon bottle had burst, and she got it all over her. Gwen and the other driver were walking around the scene and the police were investigating the accident.

Gwen said, "I am okay. I just have a broken blood vessel in my hand." Strangely the other driver had identically the same injury.

At the hospital Dr. Ewart found that the seat belt had caused a two inch bruise right around Gwen's body. It was just like a two inch black belt. It was incredible. The force involved caused the blood vessels to rupture. Had a vessel in a vital place been ruptured she would not have survived. Thank you, Lord, for your protection. To God be the glory!

The automobile dealer was ready to write the van off, but as money was in short supply, we chose to have it repaired instead.

BERTRAND

I met Bertrand at Lorton Prison in Fairfax, Virginia. Bertrand was a very fine boxer, built like Mr. Universe. I saw him boxing in the prison gym. His handsome face was unmarked. He could avoid a punch like Mohammed Ali in his prime.

The gym was adjacent to the prison chapel where we expected to minister that night. But the Black Muslims had taken over the chapel for the night, and we were told to have our meeting elsewhere. But where?

A guard suggested the cafeteria. Would there be anyone there? Well, a few might wander in for a coffee. It would be a catch-as-catch-can situation. A handful of prisoners had gathered with me. They were upset about the change in location.

I tried to calm them, saying, "Let's just wait and see what the Lord will do."

I set up my easel in the cafeteria with "The Via Delorosa" painting displayed hoping to attract some attention from those who would wander in for a coffee. And prayed!!

It worked. Bertrand, the boxer, stood three feet in front of the painting enthralled by the scene. As I moved beside him, he pointed to the head of the figure of Christ with the cross, and said, "I see blood. The blood is caused by the crown of thorns."

"What is the crown of thorns?" Bertrand asked. Was he putting me on? Had he no knowledge of the Way.

"What are the marks on his back?"

I explained the scourging and the bleeding wounds. As I explained the Way of Salvation, he listened with great interest. He had never heard the story before. I asked him if he would like to pray and invite Jesus into his life as Saviour and Lord. Bertand said, "I don't know how to do that. I have never ever prayed a prayer in my whole life." I explained to him that prayer is talking to God – just as we talked to each other, we could talk to God. He bowed his head and we prayed. "God, be merciful to me a sinner. I want you to forgive me because Jesus took my place. Lord Jesus, I invite you to come into my life and be Saviour and Lord of my life. Help me to live for you. Thank you in Jesus name."

How many millions today have never ever prayed? Everyone prayed every day in school fifty years ago. What have we lost by taking prayer out of our schools?

I had coffee with Bertrand to keep him there until our meeting got under way. Then, I said, "Let's join them." And he did.

One of the inmates had a guitar and led the singing. Some who were believers clapped their hands as they sang. Bertand sang, but kept his hands at his side.

Then we sang, "The joy of the Lord is my strength," and Bertrand began to clap with the others. One of the fellows caught it just as I did, and smiled. "He's got it." I felt good about it, too.

One of the prisoners gave Bertrand his Bible.

When the meeting concluded, a large group of prisoners had gathered to see Bertrand and tease him about becoming a Christian. What you do in prison is known almost before you do it.

He spoke a language they all understood, by his very manner he was saying – laugh if you like, but I am not ashamed.

I am not ashamed of Jesus. I am not ashamed I prayed that prayer.

One of the prisoners later said, "Bertrand never came to a chapel service before. If we had met in the chapel, Bertrand would not have been there." Surely the hand of God was in this. To God be the glory.

THE LITTLE GIRL IN TORONTO

Some time after Bertrand's conversion (possibly a year) I was preaching at a Pentecostal church in Toronto. I showed the paintings and told the story of BAM's work in schools.

At the conclusion of the service a little girl came up to me and said, "You were at my school." She seemed so small and so young that I thought she was making it up – imagining that she was in school. So I asked her which school she attended, and sure enough, I had been there about three months previously. Bendale School.

Then the little girl's mother came up and said, "When my daughter came home from school the day you were there, she told me the story of Bertrand the prisoner. Then she said, 'Mommy, I have a friend who makes fun of me because I am a Christian and because I pray. But from now on, I am going to be like Bertrand. I am not going to be ashamed of being a Christian. I am not going to be ashamed because I pray'."

Shortly after this incident, I was speaking at Aylmer, Ontario and told the story of Bertrand and also the little girl. Later a teenage boy came to me and said, "Last year I was living in Ottawa and you came to my school. You told us the story of Bertrand, but why did you not tell us about the little girl?" He felt they had been cheated.

When I explained that I had not met the girl then and did not know her story, he understood and was satisfied.

That the student remembered the presentation so well a year later shows something of the keen interest in seeing Art from the Bible with its message of salvation. This is evidence of God's answer to prayer. We always pray for God's favour and anointing and for His blessing upon each person seeing and hearing the message.

Something else. The teen age boy was interested in the message the second time and recognized the difference when a new story was added.

When school principals asked, "Do you have time for coffee?" whether I did or not, I made the time.

It was often a personal cry from the heart. One wrote later, "You will never know what our coffee conversation did for me."

When you try to read faces you may be dead wrong. It was a school in Quebec. The principal who had been watching the presentation seemed deeply disturbed. She left the auditorium in a hurry, apparently in anger. Would she send a disapproving report to the school board?

Whenever possible at the conclusion of a school presentation, I seek out the principal to say, "Thank you." I found this principal at her desk in tears. The Lord was speaking to her. She was under deep conviction.

Almost twenty years later a retired school principal said to me, "I remember the paintings and your message at my school. They spoke to my heart. My life was affected by that experience."

A Cobourg, Ontario principal who saw the presentation at his school was so deeply moved that he and his family began to attend and then actively participate in a local evangelical church. Later, when I was preaching at the church one Sunday, the pastor told me that the principal and his family delayed their departure for holidays so that the family could see and hear Art from the Bible.

PRAYER MUST PRECEDE EVERY FACET OF MINISTRY

It was September and a new school term. As I sat in my station wagon, I was making my first call seeking to line up my first presentation that term. My prayer is always, "Lord, give me favour with the principal."

I was nervous. It wasn't easy to get out of the car and go in to see the principal. Not all received you graciously. Some were rude and openly hostile.

To my surprise the secretary was a Christian I knew. She smiled and that helped.

The principal was down the hall. I did not recognize him as someone I knew. When he looked up and saw me he raised both hands in the air and said, "The answer is YES!" I had not even asked the question. Then he said, "I was V.P. at the Grove School last year. I saw your presentation there and I want you here." God hears the heart's cry. He opens doors.

THE MYSTERY CUSTODIAN AT TRENTON

Thousands of custodians saw and heard the presentation over the years since 1976 when we began.

At a Trenton, Ontario school when the two presentations were completed and I was packing up ready to leave, the school custodian came to me, and said, "I don't know what kids got out of that presentation, but I sure know how it affected me. It was a spiritual eye opener to me. I will never be the same again."

The way of salvation is clearly explained along with how to pray the sinner's prayer.

Some weeks later when I was traveling that way again, I called in at the school hoping to see the custodian. I hoped to be of spiritual help and encouragement. He was not there.

When I inquired about him, no one knew him. He had just filled in one day to replace a custodian who was away. Just one day – and that day God spoke to him and his life was forever changed. That was not by chance. To God be the glory.

BREDNER SCHOOLS TRENTON

A male teacher at one of the Bredner schools Trenton Air Force Base invited me to lunch at the Officer's mess. Ever after that I made that a requirement of my visit to those schools – which was about once every two years. It was as good a dinner you can get, a far cry from the Navy mess halls of World War II.

During lunch, the teacher said to me, "I guess the most important thing in life is to receive Jesus Christ as Saviour and allow Him to be Lord of my life. Your art presentation challenged me to do that today."

That teacher became a special friend and we had a number of lunches together at AFB Trenton through the years that followed.

Gwen, Dr. Kendrick Hughes, NASA scientist, and wife Nina)

Stan Crookall meets Colonel Jim Irwin who walked on the moon.

Once, I met NASA astronaut Colonel Jim Irwin, who had been speaking at FGBMFI Toronto. My painting of an Astronaut walking on the moon was used as a backdrop to add interest and to show just what it was like. After the meeting Jim autographed my painting.

Meeting Jim Irwin, who walked on the moon and searched for Noah's Ark on Mount Arrarat was fabulous.

The Toronto Star reporter photographed Jim and I together in front of the painting. That was another surprise.

Jim talked with me about his moon walk, his heart problem

due to over-exertion on the moon, and about his quest to find Noah's Ark. I asked him if he had a message for the school children at Trenton Air Force Base. I told him that I would be speaking there the next week. He did indeed. It was "I believe it was more important that Jesus Christ walked on the earth than that I walked on the moon."

At the Bradner School I began my Art from the Bible lecture with the NASA painting, pointing out Jim Irwin's signature. Then I told them that I had met him just days previously and that he had given me a message especially for them. Did they want to hear it? They could hardly wait. It was a blessed experience.

Some parents were in attendance at the presentation. One sent me a beautiful letter of appreciation. She was grateful that her children could see and hear the gospel through fine art in such a meaningful and unforgettable way. To God be the glory!

Each presentation is preceded by prayer. The anointing of the Lord is vital. The anointing is what makes the presentation meaningful and effective.

DORCHESTER

Dorchester prison stands back from the New Brunswick highway like a formidable fortress. Its turrets, towers, and high gray walls loom menacingly cold and uninviting. It is a step backward in time. It sends shivers up your spine. You want to leave before you arrive. It makes you think of all the men who spent years in such a place.

Our first visit there was May 9, 1977. It was our birthday. Gwen and I were born the same day and birthdays throughout our 60 years together were always special. When doors for ministry open, you step through and take advantage of the opportunity, birthday or no.

Ministering in a notable prison on your mutual birthday may not seem exciting to some. To us it was a chance to fulfill our Lord's command to visit those in prison and it took priority over everything else. "Seek ye first the Kingdom" had always applied in situations like this. There would be time for festivities later. We rejoiced. There were no regrets.

A good chaplain has a tremendous impact on prisoners and upon the prison itself. Dorchester's chaplain, Rev. Pierre Allard, was one of the best. He had been used of the Lord to make chapel services special for the prisoners. The large chapel was well filled for the service.

As Pierre led, we had barely begun the service when Gwen tugged at my coat sleeve, excitedly. "That man in the centre at the back. He has to be the biggest toughest looking man I have ever seen in my life!" She was right. Wow! He stood out like King Saul, head and shoulders above the rest. A giant of a man. His shoulders were as broad as I had ever seen. His cut away shirt sleeves revealed huge well muscled arms. His huge head was shaved, back when that was not the style and gave the appearance of power. His open shirt revealed a neck well beyond size 17.

The prisoners sang "Happy Birthday" and made us feel welcome in their midst. That took our attention momentarily away from the colossus at the back.

When it was my opportunity to share, I used my brand new painting "The Way of the Cross." As I explained it, the prisoners listened and watched with great interest. The scene is the Via Delorosa, the center of interest is Jesus holding the cross. His back is torn and bleeding from the lash. He wears a crown of thorns emblematic of the curse of sin. He is on His way to Calvary where He will be nailed to the cross and die for our sin.

In the crowd there is one figure with a blank face. That figure represents you. It represents me. Jesus is indeed taking my place. He is dying for my sin so that I can be forgiven and reconciled to God.

The invitation to come forward to receive Jesus as Saviour and Lord is given. To our surprise and delight, there was an immediate response as prisoners came forward and stood all across the front of the chapel to pray. The first man to move forward was the giant at the back. He stood with head bowed right in the centre. When I reached out to embrace him, I could see that there were rivers of tears coursing down his cheeks. There was actually a puddle of tears on the floor at his feet.

With deep emotion he said, "I did not know that Jesus did that for me." How thrilling to see this man along with the others take such a courageous stand for Christ. We prayed together as the now gentle giant committed his life to Christ.

Gwen and I left Dorchester confident that the new converts were in good hands with the chaplain. It was a momentous birthday for Gwen and me.

Drawing Souls To Christ

After visiting prisons literally coast-to-coast in Canada. I concluded that Pierr Allard was one of the finest chaplains in Canada. Some twenty years later it would be my pleasure to visit him in Ottawa in his office where he had become Head Chaplain for Canada. I was delighted to see him in that position. I talked with him about the giant prisoner. Pierre knew his name and said he was doing well. He worked at a half way house for former prisoners.

I have learned the lesson of Ezekiel – not to be afraid of faces no matter how menacing. God softens the hardest hearts and the bravest of men. Some have been waiting a lifetime to hear the Good News. Why indeed did they have to wait so long? Personally at 17 when I heard the gospel for the first time, I asked, "Why did not someone tell me this before?" Each time I preach I realize that there may be some who are as I was, just waiting to hear.

Ten years later, our son Paul, become an Associate Warden at Dorchester Penitentiary and I ministered there again.

Art from the Bible has a tremendous appeal wherever shown, but it is especially VERY SPECIAL in SCHOOLS and PRISONS. That's what it was designed for and that is where God called us to minister.

God is not looking for ability as much as availability. Our plans can be rescheduled when duty calls. As a small boy I remember singing:

Dare to be a Daniel,
Dare to stand alone,
Dare to have a purpose firm,
Dare to make it known

Where duty calls or danger,
Be never wanting there.

I could not understand the words. It did not make sense not to want to be there. In time I realized it meant BE THERE!

HOME LEAGUE – LONDON
Do you ever have a tendency to write someone off because they don't seem interested or capable of grasping what is going on?

At a women's home league meeting at the Salvation Army Citadel in London, Ontario, there was a very old lady who seemed to be out of it. She seemed to be dozing off to sleep. Then suddenly she exclaimed, "What is Billy Graham doing in that painting?" Billy Graham was indeed in the painting. Most could not figure out who he was even when I asked. But I had not asked. I was absolutely amazed that this dear lady, sitting back about fifteen feet from the painting could recognize the tiny figure. You just see the head and shoulders about four inches high. I painted Billy Graham in the crowd with head bowed and hands clasped in prayer, just as he does after giving the invitation for people to come forward. I felt it gave me an opportunity to quote him as he says, "You must come to the foot of the cross." And to recognize him as the greatest evangelist of our time.

FEEDBACK

We always appreciated feedback from the teaching staff. A public school principal in Belleville, Ontario stated before his entire student body, "I have never ever in my life before seen and heard so much good information in 45 minutes..." A principal in Burke's Falls, Ontario said, "I believe that what my students saw and heard today will be indelibly registered on their hearts and minds and never to be forgotten for a lifetime."

In Manatee County, the principal of the largest, most up-to-date middle school I have ever seen, with a student body of 2000, said, "This is the best presentation we have had here. I thoroughly enjoyed it. It dealt with all we are trying to teach our students about art. The religious side was there and you recognized that, but it was dealt with in a way that did not create any problems for me."

One of his art teachers said, "You dealt with everything we want our students to know. I thought it was terrific." Another art teacher said, "More of our kids need to see and hear this. We hope you will come back again. My wife teaches at Palmetto Elementary, she was just thrilled with your presentation there." A third art teacher said, "I think it was wonderful the way you witnessed to our students."

A high school art teacher in Crystal River, Florida said, "You have shown me this afternoon that the Bible is a book I should be reading. I am going to start. You reached at least one person here today and that is me."

In Bogotá, Colombia a group of parents wrote, "When our

children came home from school they told us about the beautiful Bible paintings and the beautiful words that were spoken. We want to thank you for coming to Colombia to teach our children these beautiful things."

Methodist saddle bag preachers had a lot to contend with, how much better to drive the vehicles of today. I have always admired the old Methodist saddle bag preachers and wondered how they would do what they did on horseback. How much better to arrive in a comfortable automobile or van, especially in the frozen north in below zero temperatures.

How often have I sat there for a few moments of prayer and meditation before informing the Principal of my arrival and watched fifteen or twenty or more school busses arriving loaded with students who will make up our audience to see and hear Art from the Bible. "Oh Lord, bless them, open their hearts to understand your wondrous plan of redemption. Grant your favour and anointing. May many receive Jesus as Saviour and Lord as they hear for perhaps the very first time the Good News of the Gospel of Redeeming Grace."

RESPONSE FROM CHRISTIAN SCHOOLS

Jeremy S., principal of a Canadian Christian school of 1000 students said, "This is the best presentation we have ever had. You did not take for granted that every one of our students had committed their lives to Christ. And the message was plain enough that students could respond to receive Christ as some of them did today."

A school principal in Candler, North Carolina said, "I was thrilled that my students today saw how God can be honoured in every profession and God's plan of redemption shared effectively."

At first when we began Bible Art Ministries, we went only to public schools, but at Christian Retreat in Bradenton, Florida I met one of the leaders of a Christian school organization who pleaded with me not to forget the students at Christian schools. We listened to what he had to say and decided to include Christian schools as well. It has been our delight to visit many hundreds of Christian schools as well as the multiplied thousands of public schools across Canada, The United States, Jamaica, Colombia, Ecuador, Argentina, and now hopefully Spain as well.

Wherever we have ministered, the Lord has provided people to support and help us reach the people of their area for Christ.

On our first missionary journey to Florida we met Marie Budd. She graciously opened her home to us and became a close personal friend. She was a wealth of information about schools in the area. Marie had been in charge of the cafeteria at one of them.

Marie Budd kept on bugging me to visit Manatee County schools. Marie knew the need. After three years of trying, the superintendent finally said "yes," and some twenty-three schools agreed to have Art from the Bible presentations in their schools. A number of the schools have 900 or more students.

Each year while I visited private and Christian schools, Marie Budd kept on bugging me about getting into the Manatee County public schools. It took three years of praying and trying, and finally the doors were opened to Manatee County and Sarasota schools.

At the same time a lady at a Sarasota Baptist church gave us a pile of directives for school principals from Dr. Turlington, Director of Education, for the state of Florida. After reading through more than 200 pages, I finally found exactly what was needed to convince local school superintendents and principals that it was okay to grant us permission to present Art from the Bible in their schools.

Dr. Turlington wrote: "Religious paintings may be shown in schools as long as the paintings are not allowed to remain in the schools at the conclusion of the lecture." Hallelujah! That did it.

This lady, whose name I cannot recall, had attended every parents meeting at her children's schools for many years to obtain these directives. Her prayers and her persistence paid off.

MIRACLES ALONG THE WAY

Marie Budd had a personal friend named Garnet, a member of Marie's Alliance church. who was facing surgery to remove both her knee caps. She struggled to walk using two canes.

Marie said, "I am going to take you to see Garnet and you are going to pray for her, and the Lord will heal her!" Wow! Nothing like getting put into a situation like that.

We arranged a meeting at Marie's home. About half a dozen friends from the Alliance church came along with half a dozen

Drawing Souls To Christ

Canadian friends, including Doris Moffat, Gord Ballenger and Mr. and Mrs. W. V. - .

I asked Brother W. to give a testimony, and he talked about the Baptism in the Holy Spirit and speaking in other tongues. The friends from the Alliance church were getting uneasy and so was I. So I asked my wife Gwen to tell how the Lord had healed her knowing that she would steer clear of the controversial issue of speaking in tongues. Wrong! That's not what she did. Four from the Alliance church got up and left. My first thoughts were, this is a disaster, but then I realized that perhaps the doubters were leaving to create a better climate for healing to take place.

When it came time to pray for Garnet, I asked everyone to turn to Mark 11:24-26. We read it together. "Therefore I tell you, whateer you ask for in prayer, believe that you have received it, and it will be yours. And when you stand praying, if you hold anything against anyone, forgive him, so that your Father in heaven may forgive you your sins. But if you do not forgive, neither will your Father who is in heaven forgive your sins." Then I felt led of the Lord to have Garnet read it out loud. I felt the Lord was saying, "Have her read it again." Then "Again." This time as Garnet read verse 26 it seemed a burden lifted, and we could pray for Garnet's healing. We laid hands on her and prayed for her healing, knowing that she was facing surgery the next morning.

After prayer, Garnet struggled to get out of the chair to stand to her feet and her sister said, "I told you nothing would happen!" Wow! It didn't look good.

Immediately I stated, "Now let us remember God's promise and read it again." Then I said, "Sometimes the Lord heals instantly and sometimes it is in an hour or so, sometimes longer, but keep believing God to heal you! And don't give up!"

Garnet struggled out the door with her two canes and her unbelieving sister still sure that nothing happened.

Early the next morning the phone rang. It was Garnet. She said, "I have just returned from a two mile walk without my canes! I have cancelled the surgery. The Lord healed me!" To God be the glory!

Marie knew it all along. It's great to have friends like that.

Marie was constantly finding people for us to pray with and places to present Art from the Bible.

TIMMINS

We had an exciting missionary journey planned to cover three weeks of schools, prisons, Full Gospel Business Men's meetings, and a whole lot more, beginning in New Liskeard and including Timmins, Kirkland Lake, Cobalt and Cochrane.

Gwen went with me for the first week then went on to visit family while I carried on alone.

For the first week we were guests at a medical doctor's home. The doctor's wife was an enthusiastic, charismatic Christian. She had arranged my schedule for the week.

I tried to have a meaningful after-dinner chat with the doctor, just he and I, for half an hour each evening. The doctor thought Christianity was a crutch he didn't need.

The doctor's wife told us about a young kindergarten teacher who was in the hospital with a serious back problem and in terrible pain continually. She said, "I'm going to get her out of the hospital and into our home and you are going to pray for her and the Lord is going to heal her." Wow!

Later when the doctor came home from the hospital, he talked with me after supper. In the course of our conversation he said, "My son is a born-again Christian."

I asked, "Is that good?"

The doctor replied, "For him it is."

"What about you?" I asked.

"Oh I don't need that crutch," he answered. The doctor went on to tell me about the teacher with the back problem. He said, "My wife is crazy. She is going to get her out of the hospital and bring her here to our home. We can't do anything for her in the hospital and we can do far less here."

Lala the school teacher was in such pain the first day that she didn't want to talk to anyone. The next morning Gwen went into her room to see her and Lala was willing to have us visit her. We had been praying for Lala.

We read the word and talked about everyone's need to know Christ as Lord and Savior. Lala was all mixed up with transcendental meditation, but the Lord opened her heart and she prayed the sinner's prayer. Hallelujah.

Then we read about Jesus healing people and asked if she would like us to pray for her healing. She was ready.

She slipped one hand from under the bed covers to Gwen and the other to me. We held hands and prayed. Then I went off to schools for the day.

An hour later, Lala was out of bed dressed and jumping for joy. She had no pain and had perfect mobility.

We waited with eager anticipation for the doctor's return for dinner that evening. When the doctor walked into the dining room and Lala was standing at the head of the table radiant, excited, and ready for teaching at school the next day, I watched the doctor do a triple take. He was indeed shaken. He knew better than anyone that a miracle had taken place under his own roof.

We understand that very soon after this, the doctor came to believe that he needed the same faith his wife and son and his patient Lala embraced.

The doctor's wife had scheduled me to visit ARC Industries three days in succession. I wondered why. But on the third day when I gave the invitation to pray the sinner's prayer to receive Christ as Lord and Savior, every handicapped person there asked for prayer. Then I understood it was no mistake. You just cannot find words to express the joy felt when something like this happens.

It is a confirmation that you are in the right place at the right time. It is a confirmation that God can be trusted to do what He has promised. It is a direct and immediate answer to prayer. If the reader has any doubts about God's interest in all things and all prayer, we hope the numerous examples of God's answers about so many things will reassure you.

I called to see the Director of Education for the area. He had one of our Art from the Bible presentations video taped. He was impressed by our teaching methods and the quality of our presentation. He offered me a job, but as a regular art teacher, without using Biblical references. My salary with Bible Arts Ministries was $200 per week. He offered me $1000 per week! When my Board had asked, "What is the minimum wage you can get by on?" I stated $200 per week. I was getting a small pension of $200 per month in addition to this, as a superannuated teacher. The director did not know what my income was. He just knew it was a lot less than he had offered. But money wasn't the issue.

When God calls you to do what you are doing, you don't change without His confirmation. That would be disobedience.

The director wanted me to teach art in schools throughout his school section. He also wanted me to teach his teachers new methods of teaching. I was honoured by his offer. He made me feel good about the quality of our presentation.

When I preached at the Full Gospel Businessmen's banquet at New Liskeard, I became reacquainted with the Rev. Peter Williams whom I had known previously at Ottawa, Ontario. Peter had loaned me a priceless three volume set of paintings by the great French artist Toussout. The artist had spent a decade in the Holy Land researching authentic records of the crucifixion and this material helped me tremendously in my paintings of the crucifixion and the resurrection. I had shown the painting of the crucifixion at the Saturday Full Gospel Businessmen's Fellowship International meeting but Peter Williams was unable to attend. The audience was so appreciative of the painting. I felt somewhat apologetic when I shared the resurrection painting at Peter Williams' church the next day, but to my great surprise the people who had seen both paintings preferred the resurrection. It was, by the way, my wife Gwen's favorite.

At a rally for native Indian young people, the Lord ministered to hearts in a very special way. In response to the invitation to receive Christ, young people lined up from wall-to-wall across the room. Such was their repentance and commitment that there were literally puddles of tears on the floor where they stood. To God be the glory.

At Haileybury, the students sat on the floor in a long wide hallway. It wasn't the best setting. As I was wondering how well the presentation was received, a group of students gathered around me. One said, "I thought it was great." Another said, "I did, too!" Another said, "I thought it was terrific!"

A little girl wanted a print of Christ at Heart's Door and also The Good Shepherd. The principal whispered, "I don't think her parents can afford the $2.00." I gladly gave her both prints. Then the principal said, "She has leukemia and we appreciate your gift especially to her."

At New Liskeard a local minister told me, "My daughter came home from school all excited about Art from the Bible." And she had said to him, "He's not like a minister." The minister asked her, "What do you mean, 'He's not like a minister?'" Her reply was, "He's not boring."

A local medical doctor got in on a presentation along with his two sons. One son had seen an earlier presentation at his school. He wanted his dad to see it with him.

Joining the teachers for coffee in the staff room I got their reaction. "Good job. We hope you come back again. Our students really loved this Art from the Bible Presentation."

WE DID NOT PLAN TO GO TO JAMAICA,
BUT IT WAS PART OF GOD'S PLAN.

Here's how it happened. One day when Gwen and I were visiting our daughter Marjorie in Peterborough, we stopped in to see our old friends Lucien and Claudia DuMoulin. When they arrived in Peterborough from Quebec some twenty years previously, their four small children could not speak English, but those kids knew how to express their love as they ran to greet you and hung on to an arm or a leg and just would not let go.

Hugette, the oldest, was now a teacher. She was at home this day and concerned about employment. "Please pray for me," she said.

Hugette had resigned her position as a teacher of French language in order to teach the next year in a Christian school her church planned to open. But the church had decided at the last minute to cancel their plans.

Hugette was out of a job and her vacated position with the Peterborough schools had been filled by someone else.

As Gwen and I prayed, I found myself saying, "Please Lord, surprise Hugette with something beautiful and something she does not expect."

A day or so later, John MacFarlane, my right hand man on our Ottawa Valley Evangelism Team, and I were visiting Cobourg Pentecostal Camp and ran into Mrs. Ian Schliefer who was Headmistress of a Christian school in Jamaica. John had met her on a trip to the Holy Land a few years previously. When John explained our work in schools with Bible Art Ministries, Mrs. Schliefer immediately asked, "Would you happen to know a Christian teacher who would come to Jamaica to teach?" Immediately I thought of Hugette. Within three weeks she was in Jamaica and thrilled to fulfill a lifelong dream of going there.

After teaching in Jamaica two or three months Hugette wrote, "Why don't you come to Jamaica and visit our schools with your Art from the Bible Presentation? We can help you line up some schools and you and Gwen can stay at my cottage here."

That is how we decided to go to Jamaica, but getting there

was quite an experience in itself.

To get there required two miraculous interventions.

First Miracle - To Obtain Permission To Cross the Border.

Gwen's sister Marge and her husband Stan Burditt were Salvation Army Officers, and like all Salvation Army Officers, were moved every few years often long distances to take up another appointment. Right now they were stationed in Windsor, Ontario at the Windsor-Detroit border. We stayed overnight at their home in Windsor. Early in the morning, I was reading Luke chapter one and verse thirty-seven seemed to pop off the page to me, "For with God nothing shall be impossible." Dr. Henrietta Mears' suggestion for daily Bible reading is to read prayerfully until God gives you a special verse. That will be your message for the day, for you, and for all you meet today. I wondered what this would mean for us today.

We arrived at the border at about 7 a.m. The American customs official seemed hostile. He was afraid we were going to raise money in the U.S. We were taken before the senior customs officer. She was more hostile and said, "You cannot enter the U.S., you must go back to Canada," and we were turned back. Wow! It is a humiliating experience involving several police guards who treat you like criminals while the crowd looks on wondering what you could have done wrong.

What about Jamaica? But our verse was, "For with God nothing shall be impossible." That meant crossing the border, too.

At Windsor, the Canadian side of the border, we pleaded our cause. The Canadian official said, "This is a retaliation game you are caught in. We get tough on an American so they get tough on a Canadian and you are it. My advice is to wait until the changing of the guard at 8 a.m. and try again. But tell them you were stopped and why, because you will be in their computers and if you don't tell them they will really throw the book at you."

We did a lot of praying and went back to the U.S. Detroit border at 8 a.m. It wasn't any better. An official grabbed my briefcase and found a letter from a Canadian school principal asking for five fine art prints for $1 each. Big Deal. But it was to them.

I explained fully that we were going to Bradenton, Florida

for two weeks then to Jamaica for February, and back to Miami and then home. "No way!" he said. He was not going to let us cross the border.

There were five or six customs guards with guns in holsters who fired questions at me all at once trying to trip me up in my statements. It was tough.

I had taken my brother-in-law Major Stan Burditt with me to vouch for our integrity, but nothing doing, they treated him as rudely as they treated us and commanded, "You sit over there, we don't want to hear anything from you." We were shocked. It was like Rodney Dangerfield. We got no respect. But we just stood there praying and reminding the Lord about His promise of Luke 1:37.

Finally the customs official in charge took the five or six other officials into an anti-room and they discussed the situation. I could hear him shout, "I'm not going to let them cross!"

Wow! Then he came out and said, "I'm not going to let you cross, you must go back to Canada." I just stood there face to face with the angry official. I said nothing to him, but I was silently praying, "Lord you promised nothing shall be impossible. Please help us to get across the border."

We stood silently face-to-face for what seemed like ten minutes and I just looked at him while I prayed.

Suddenly he shouted, "O.K. I will allow you to cross the border, but if you are found here after two weeks expires you may be deported to Canada and never allowed in the United States again."

Wow! Home free! I didn't ask any more questions. We just took off. I said, "Thank You!" to the Lord and to the official.

God is faithful to His promises! Only God could soften that hard heart and cause that official to be willing to loose face before his men after boldly declaring he would not let us cross.

Second Miracle: Arrive Alive

After two weeks in the Bradenton-Sarasota area schools, we were off to Jamaica. We were flying with Christian Air Service out of Sarasota.

Don Lee told us that they did not have any airplanes of their own. They borrowed a plane when needed. He had said that for a flight of this distance over open ocean we needed a twin engine plane. That made sense. But the only plane they could get was a single engine Beachcraft Bonanza.

Gord Ballenger, Doris Moffatt and Marie Budd went with us to the Sarasota airport. They were appalled when they saw the tiny plane. Gwen and I were kind of shaken, too. But it would get worse.

We could not get our larger paintings into the plane. We had to settle for three small ones and our chalk drawing equipment. It would be difficult, but the Lord would make a way.

We took off in dense fog. Our pilot, Don Lee, had never flown that plane before. Our wheels had just left the runway when the cabin door flew open. Oh, joy! We landed and got the door secured then tried again.

As we lifted into the dense fog, our pilot wiggled the wings and it was real scary. Then we levelled off and we were on our way. The fog was so thick you couldn't see three feet ahead of you.

Mr. D. owned the plane and he came along, having business in Jamaica. He was a big man. He could fly a plane on visual flight rules, but he couldn't read instruments and fly in fog.

As we approached West Palm Beach, Mr. D thought we were flying upside down and got in a panic. Lee assured him we were O.K. What a relief when we touched down on the runway. It could have been disastrous if Lee hadn't handled it right. The owner was about to grab the controls.

At West Palm Beach airport, we rented an inflatable lifeboat, and refuelled the plane. The fog was lifting. As they stowed the life raft in the plane, we had a few questioning thoughts.

As we were about to board the plane, the owner said that he would like to try to fly the next leg of the flight. What can you say when the fellow owns the plane.

A Beachcraft Bonanza is a neat little plane, but it sure is small. Our course was charted to fly around Cuba to avoid Castro's MIG jet fighters Lee had encountered on a previous flight.

We had flown about a hundred miles over the Atlantic in the area of the Bermuda Triangle and Gwen decided to share the lunch she had prepared. Then suddenly we flew into a large cloud. Immediately we were being pelted by hail. It sounded like being struck by a staccato of a hundred pounding hammers. The water poured over the wings and fuselage like going through a car wash. It dawned on me that we couldn't go on

Drawing Souls To Christ

Refuelling at Inauga Island

like this for long. Right. Suddenly we just dropped out of the sky and straight down.

I gripped the right armrest as I was suspended about six inches above the seat, held down only by the seatbelt. Gwen held onto my left wrist in a vice grip. A steel wrench was flying around over our heads and I tried to ward it off with my foot. Gwen was praying out loud, "Jesus...Jesus...Jesus." I'm sure we were all praying. I prayed, "Lord, we didn't come out here to drown in this ocean. We came to share the Gospel with kids in Jamaica. Please help us."

We had been flying at 7000 feet. We had dropped like a stone to five hundred feet. Just as suddenly, we levelled off and flew straight ahead. Wow! We settled back down and were sort of getting back to normal when I thought about the lunch. "Hey Gwen, what about the lunch?" "Don't talk to me about food. If we ever get there I'm staying, I'm not coming back!" she replied. She needed some space.

Soon we were running short of fuel and had flown into the heavy rain of a tropical storm. We were over the island of Inaugua in the Bahamas. Was there an airstrip? Yes! Was there gasoline for sale? It looked like it.

As we touched down the runway was under several inches of water. A crop duster plane flew in right on our tail. Scary again.

The other pilot was concerned about another crop duster who

had been flying with him but was now lost in the storm. We stood there and prayed. Then we heard the drone of an aircraft and, praise the Lord, the lost plane found its way and landed.

We phoned for gasoline and in about an hour the gas attendant showed up. The gas was expensive, $200.00. A twin engine plane used by drug smugglers that had been shot up by police lay abandoned at the side of the runway. They had refuelled and tried to take off without paying for the gas. The police were crack shots. One bullet struck a tire and another bullet struck one of the engines. We made sure to pay.

The weather cleared and we were on our way again. We were flying close to Haiti and the Dominican Republic when darkness fell, about 7:00 p.m. The sky was black as ink. Our two pilots were pouring over maps with a flashlight. We were flying at seven thousand feet and the mountains were nine thousand feet high. It was important to miss them. Scary again! We did a lot of praying.

As I looked at the map I could see that if we missed Jamaica we would be lost over the Caribbean.

Our pilots determined we would arrive at Kingston, Jamaica in twenty minutes. Thirty minutes later we were still flying in the black darkness. Pray again, remember God's promise in Luke 1:37 For nothing is impossible with God. It sounded to me as though our engine was sputtering. Imagination? No. I was hearing right. They frantically adjusted valves and soon the engine purred again. "Thank you, Lord." But we were lost. We tried to contact Kingston, but couldn't reach them. Scary again. Pray!

Then down into the darkness there was a single light. Don thought it might be a ship. But then the blackness again. Keep praying. Then radio contact, but our pilots had not registered the flight plan to Jamaica. Jamaica didn't want to give permission to land. Oh, boy!

When we did land we came in right behind a four-engine jet that had just taken off. The turbulence was awful. We hit the runway, and then bounced about twenty-five feet into the air. Gwen blurted out, "Hallelujah! That's close enough, we can make it now."

We were suddenly surrounded by soldiers with machine guns. They thought we were smugglers. We were ordered out of the plane and marched to police headquarters. They didn't convince easily. It took about an hour to get OK'd to stay.

Then Hugette and Ian Schlieffer appeared. They thought we

were coming in a larger plane and couldn't believe we came in that little fellow. .

When it was time, we returned by Air Jamaica. One flight with Christian Air Service was enough. Gwen was greatly relieved.

We had left Sarasota at 8 a.m. We arrived at Kingston at 8 p.m. Twelve hours, what a flight! We thank the Lord for His protection and deliverance in that memorable flight. Thank you, Lord.

Ian Schlieffer had set up a fantastic itinerary for us. He said, "You have my best Land Rover and my best driver to work with you for a whole month, and I will pay for all of the gasoline." Gasoline was $3.25/gallon when in North America we were paying about $0.50/gallon. The driver, Clive Lazarus, a native Jamaican, was a fine Christian. He played guitar, sang and led singing. He was also my bodyguard, but I didn't realize that at first. I was unaware of the dangers faced traveling in the interior.

It had been quite an adventure so far. It would prove to be a most rewarding missionary journey. Bless the Lord! We would see several hundred come to Christ.

Our first meeting was Sunday afternoon at a Methodist young people's rally. I drew a stick-man Bible story. I was the only white person in the packed building. Stick men are drawn in black chalk. As I drew the first figure, I wondered how an entirely black audience would respond. What if they didn't like it? What if they were offended?

As I glanced back at the audience, there was silence for a few seconds and then they roared with laughter. They loved it.

I had prayed much for weeks and the presence of the Lord was so real, but no one responded to the altar call. I couldn't understand it. Disappointed, definitely.

The next day I met the man who had been the leader of the youth rally. He immediately became ecstatic about yesterday's service. "But, no one responded to the invitation," I said. "Oh, that is where you are wrong," he said. "After you left I gave another invitation and everyone in the building responded." It was glorious. To God be the glory! It was like a revival. I could see it would be necessary to learn Jamaican ways.

The next day (Monday), we were off to schools and Richmond Prison. My schedule was loaded. Sometimes we visited five schools in one day with extra meetings at night. We loved it.

Clive Lazarus, my driver, bodyguard, helper, song leader, guitar player, soloist, is one of the finest Christian workers we have ever met. He and I bonded immediately. The Lord had put us together for a Gospel adventure we would forever cherish and never forget. Clive was thirty years old, I was fifty-six. The year was 1978.

We ministered in schools large and small throughout the island. The larger schools ranged from 500 to 1000 students. There were no chairs in the school auditorium. Everyone stood. They could pack 1000 students into a small space that way.

At Kalabar Boys School in Kingston, there were about 900 students. The assembly service droned on for half an hour before Clive and I had an opportunity to minister. The school chaplain spoke at length using impressive vocabulary, but everyone was bored to distraction. I was praying, "Oh Lord, please somehow take over in this service and open the hearts of these students to take in the message and receive from You exactly what they need. Please save this hopeless situation and make it glorious."

I had about 25 minutes to speak. I drew Jonah, my favourite stick man story. Wow! God answers prayer. The place came alive. The way of Salvation was made plain and I gave an opportunity to pray the sinner's prayer. Then came, to our utter amazement, thunderous applause that lasted and lasted and lasted.

Gwen was outside in the Land Rover. She exclaimed, "What happened in there? I never heard applause like that in my life." Was it five minutes or was it more? We will never forget it. God answered prayer immediately and dramatically. To Him be all the Glory.

I had given the drawing to a ten-year-old boy. I didn't know it, but he happened to be the son of the Ambassador from Nigeria. Later as we were leaving, we passed by his classroom and he was standing at the front of the class with the drawing and they were discussing it together with great joy.

At another school during recess, I noticed many students had purchased some sort of pastry in a brown paper bag. They seemed to be enjoying it. "What is it?" I asked Clive. "Patty mon," was his reply. "Could we buy one?" I asked. "Yea mon," he answered. I gave Clive some money. He asked, "What do you want to drink?" "Oh I don't need a drink," I replied. Clive put his head on one side and had a puzzled look but was off to make the purchase. One bite of the Jamaican patty made my hair sizzle. Clive laughed with delight and ran to get me a drink. We would share many patties over the next several weeks together.

At Richmond Prison, the chapel was about one-third full with many others standing outside looking through the huge open windows.

We began our service. Clive led the singing and sang a solo and soon the men outside were climbing through the open windows, and the chapel was full.

Six men walked forward to receive Christ as Saviour and Lord when the invitation was given. Bless the Lord. That takes courage in prison.

When we got back to Canada, I related the story of the six men getting saved at Richmond Prison. A man from the audience asked, "What follow up do you have for men like that?" I told him that I couldn't possibly do the work I do and follow up all the converts, but God can and I believed He would. The man was skeptical and disbelieving.

Months later I received a letter from Clive Lazarus telling us that the local Methodist minister in whose home we had dinner the next day had followed up on those men and each one had been baptized in water. Praise the Lord! Thank you, Jesus!

One day as we were driving from one school to another, we passed a large high school. I asked Clive if we were scheduled to go there. But he said no, that it was not in our itinerary.

Clive had been a student there and he knew the principal. We decided to try. When we talked with the principal, he said, "I am so sorry. It would take me at least twenty minutes to arrange to have your speak." In twenty minutes we were speaking to one thousand students. Wow! Only in Jamaica. To God be the Glory!

IT'S JUST AN EARTHQUAKE

Radio news always gave a long list of robberies and killings. Most homes had bars on all doors and windows plus a big fence and two guard dogs between the fence and the house. When I asked why two dogs, the answer was, "If they kill one, we still have one left."

One Saturday we slept at the home of a deacon as we were to speak at his church in Kingston the next morning. In addition to the wall, two dogs and bars on the doors and windows, there was a steel grill between the living area and the bedrooms.

When I asked, "Why?", they explained it would take thieves twenty minutes to break through that door and hopefully help would arrive before that was accomplished. Pleasant dreams.

On Sunday morning as we left the church there was a great commotion and the police were shooting at two thieves on the rooftop. A man who purchased the last package of cigarettes in a store was accosted by a man with a gun who demanded the cigarettes. When the customer refused, he was shot and killed.

The next Saturday we were sleeping in Hugette's cottage, on the Christian School property. There were no bars on the windows, not even a lock on the door, just an old style latch like in the cowboy movies. At midnight, all was quiet when suddenly the door latch began to jiggle. Gwen's hand grabbed my wrist in a vice grip as she exclaimed "What's that?" I was hoping it was not "Da Tief" as I groped under the bed to find my machete. Then the whole house shook. I knew what it was. I sighed with relief: "It's only an earthquake." We went back to sleep.

The next day we saw cracks in buildings and other damage caused by the quake.

YOUTH RALLY – JAMAICA

My schedule was as heavy as I can ever remember. Ian Schlifer had set it up for me and he had every day booked. Sunday, I was scheduled to speak twice in the morning, once in the afternoon, and again in the evening. I had already made school presentations, three to five a day, all week, and spoke at a Youth For Christ Rally Saturday. We were traveling hundreds of miles by Land Rover.

Few roads were paved, and many had never seen a grader. The Land Rover had good clearance; we often straddled chickens loose on the road, but never hit one. We dodged a lot of people, too. Chickens, goats, and people all took to the roads as though the cars would miss them, and they were right most of the time.

It was Sunday afternoon and I was speaking at a Baptist Youth Rally. I was in the midst of drawing a stick man Bible story and feeling so tired. I was actually questioning why I was there. I was thinking, "These kids know the Gospel. They don't need me here." And then I gave the invitation to receive Christ and seventy-five teenagers responded. Suddenly I was not tired anymore. I was praying, "Lord, forgive me for not realizing the great need of these kids."

We saw hundreds come to Christ all over the island. Bless the Lord. It was an awesome adventure in Drawing Souls to Christ.

JAMAICA

Water and sunshine have always been an enjoyment to me. I love the beach and the swimming pool. Where we stayed in Jamaica at the school , there was a swimming pool. Each day when I got back from schools, if it wasn't too late, I was in the pool for a refreshing swim.

Ocho Rios has one of the world's finest beaches. The cruise ships anchor just offshore and passengers come ashore in small launches. The famous falls are there.

We had enjoyed a great time at a Christian school and just had time for a brief swim before lunch. While swimming, a large fish brushed against my leg. I knew there were barracudas in the area so I made a hasty exit from the water. Clive was beside me and chuckled, but suddenly the fish brushed him, too, and he reached shore before I did, with his eyes and mouth wide open. We had no idea what kind of sea monster we were dealing with.

As we relaxed and ate our lunch, I noticed Clive had tears running down his cheeks. "What's wrong?" I asked. "Nothing wrong, man, nothing wrong. I have just been thinking that these weeks we have spent together are the greatest days of my life."

At the last school, I had to speak outside. A crop dusting airplane was zooming low over the surrounding banana plantation, but not a single student turned to watch the plane. God had given us favour with the students. They chose to watch and listen as I drew a stick-man Bible story. And it seemed that everywhere we had been throughout the island students responded to receive Christ as Saviour and Lord. As we left the last school, a teenage boy said, "Come back, sir. Come back."

YOUTH FOR CHRIST RALLY

One Saturday evening we were ministering at a Youth For Christ rally in a small building miles from nowhere. As I waited to preach, I was thinking about how isolated this was, how far away from home, and then they began to sing. "We have come into His house and gathered in His name to worship Him." This

A school presentation in Jamaica

hymn was written by Bruce Ballanger, son of one of my best and closest friends, Gord Ballanger. It was not-the-first time I heard this sung in a distant place, and was always a warm reminder of home and people praying for us. In that rally I felt led of the Lord to make the message as challenging as I possibly could. It was evident to me that there was a great spiritual battle going on in the hearts of many of these young people. And when the invitation was given, those who came forward to receive Christ were weeping and very definite about their commitment to Jesus Christ.

THE DANGER WAS REAL

Only days after we left Jamaica, Clive Lazarus, our driver/ helper/body guard, was attacked by several gunman who were about to kill him when suddenly the police arrived. We thank God for protecting our wonderful brother and for His protection over us as we had traveled those many miles all over the island preaching the unsearchable riches of Christ. To God Be the Glory! This incident was a reminder of how real the danger had been. Most Third World countries have special tourist areas where people are well protected by police. The tourists are unaware of what things are like in other parts of the country.

Chapter 12

South American adventure

The Lord in His great wisdom and grace brought two young men from Bogotá, Colombia and a patriarchal missionary couple from Canada to meet at Gospel Outreach Church in New Port Richey, Florida. His purpose: to unite us in a great missionary venture into the schools of Colombia, Ecuador, and Argentina.

That all four, myself Stan, my wife Gwen, Omar Rincon, and German (pronounced Herman in Spanish) Rozo were given artistic ability was not by chance but part of God's plan.

Both young Colombians became like sons to Gwen and me. We in turn became mom and dad to them.

While I taught Omar and German Bible and Art, Gwen loved them, fed them, and made our home their home. Her qualities of faith, hope, encouragement, and prayer brought a new dimension into their lives. Her very special lemon tarts and oatmeal cookies had a special appeal to Colombian pallets.

German had arrived three years previous to Omar. They lived together in a large one room apartment. Omar was just learning to speak English. He wondered what that large sign with letters three feet high GOSPEL OUTREACH CHURCH on the side of that large building meant. German explained it was a church. Omar was interested. German said, "We will go there next Sunday."

After four Sundays, Omar had grasped enough of Jerry Magliulo's sermon to understand how to be saved. With his poor English he felt incapable of answering the altar call to be saved, so he prayed at home.

Omar knelt in true repentance and invited Christ to come into his heart and life. Then he concluded his prayer with, "If you can use my life, I surrender it to you to use." Little did Omar realize how God would take his life and use him to become a great evangelist and soul winner.

German Rozo was attracted, by the music, to a Gospel church in Bogotá about a week before he came to America. It was there he found salvation.

It has been said that you do not become a missionary by traveling to a distant land. You become a missionary where you are before you go.

Omar and German attended 6:30 a.m. prayer meeting services Monday to Friday at Gospel Outreach Church. They visited sick people in hospitals. They were part of Gospel Outreach's door-to-door visitation once a week. What they did was done quietly and without fanfare. I had to dig and question to find out.

As a brand new Christian, Omar worked at Jade Fountain Chinese Restaurant five days a week and part time at Hooters, where waitresses were scantily clad. After a few weeks he decided that Hooters was not the place he should be, and quit.

Gospel Outreach had a children's church called Kids' Factory. Omar volunteered to help and worked there faithfully until he returned to Bogotá to work with Bible Art Ministries.

Somehow in addition to all this, Omar attended enough night classes to gain a high school diploma.

When God called Omar in 1992 to go back to Colombia to minister to children, he was ready to go. We were able to pay his salary through Bible Art Ministries and Omar, with the help of Pastor Ron Rager, established Hope House, an orphanage for street kids.

In February-March of 1993, it was German Rozo's turn to answer God's call to return to Colombia to join Omar at Hope House and also to minister along with him in schools, prisons, and the community.

By this time, German had been coming to our home almost every day of the week. He never outwore his welcome. We were always glad to see him come, and reluctant to see him leave.

Whatever German saw that needed to be done, he wanted to do it. He had worked in construction and as a metal worker. He worked fast and hard. What a joy to have him as a helper. When he left the Jade Fountain Restaurant, they had to hire two men to take his place.

German next worked at Kinjo Japanese Restaurant. It was not all roses there. John, one of the chefs, was a karate expert. German was only half John's size, but he was muscular and John wanted to fight him.

John tried to provoke German into a fight every day by trying to trip him when he was carrying dishes. He would put a chalk line on the floor and say, "Now if you cross over that line, we fight."

When German told me about this, I said, "Let's pray about this." We prayed that God would give German favour with John and make John his friend instead of enemy.

The very next day when German came to our house, he was so excited. "Guess what, Daddy, last night in the restaurant, John tried to trip me and I said, 'John, I don't want to fight you. I want you to be my friend. I have a friend who is an artist who paints pictures of Jesus. He would be glad to give you one. I could bring it tomorrow.'"

To German's amazement, John said, "I would like that. Tomorrow is my day off, but I will come in to get the picture." Later John called German over and gave him a special shrimp dinner, the kind he knew German loved.

That instant answer to prayer blew German away. He would never be the same again. In that moment God becomes more real and we take a leap in faith. It's like facing the lion and the bear before facing Goliath.

The next day there was another problem, but not with John. It was with Kinjo, the owner. Kinjo got mad at German and as German put it, "Kinjo said bad words at me."

I was aware that German had made some small Gospel texts and put them up on the walls of the restaurant. I was also aware that German had reprimanded Kinjo for swearing. I explained to German that you don't put signs up without permission and you must be careful in what you say to the boss when he is wrong. German understood things a little better now. Well, we prayed about John and God answered that prayer, so we prayed about Kinjo.

The next morning, German was all excited when he arrived at our house. "Guess what? Last night in the kitchen at the restaurant, Kinjo got down on his knees before me in front of all the staff and said, 'German, I'm sorry for what I said to you.

I don't want you to leave. You are my very best worker and I want you to stay'." Wow! Another instant answer to prayer. German's faith was soaring like the eagles.

A day or so went by and German had another problem. He said, "Last night as I rode my bicycle home from the restaurant, God spoke to me, and I'm scared."

"What did God say to you German?" we asked.

"God said, 'German what are you doing here in America making money, when your people in Colombia don't know me?'" He concluded: "Stan, I'm scared."

When you are praying always, that is just what you are doing. It becomes automatic. I was silently praying. "Lord what do I do about this?" The Lord indicated that we should offer to support German through Bible Art Ministries and offer him the opportunity to go back to South America and work with Omar. But there was a complication. Elizabeth Vargas had been waiting in Colombia six years, waiting for German to return to marry her. She was a devout Roman Catholic, but she was not born again. As I prayed, the Lord gave me the assurance that this would be okay and that Elizabeth would quickly come to know Christ as Saviour and Lord. Thank you Lord!

German was ecstatic. When Gwen and I accompanied him to Bogotá a few months later, we arrived on Saturday night. The next day I preached at an Evangelical church and Elizabeth was there. It was my privilege to declare the way to Elizabeth in that message. She said later, "It's so much easier to understand the Bible when you use paintings to explain it. This was the best explanation of salvation I have ever heard." To God be the glory!

ONE IN EIGHT MILLION

Our group traveling to Bogotá consisted of German Rozo, Pastor Ron Rager, Doris Moffatt, Gwen, and me. We flew on Zuliana Airlines. It was the best price, but never again did we want to go on Zuliana. The paint was peeling off the fuselage, the carpets were thread bare, and the seats were badly worn.

While German was working in Florida for six years, he paid his fiancé Elizabeth Vargas' tuition through high school and university. Now that he was at last coming home to Colombia she was overjoyed. But there would be three delays due to circumstances beyond our control. When German phoned

Drawing Souls To Christ

Elizabeth to announce the third delay she began to cry. Then German began to cry because friends and family had thought that German was now making excuses and really wasn't coming. Finally Gwen and I got on the phone and all was well.

I sat with German. He had the window seat. As we left Miami, German looked longingly out the window and tears rolled down his cheeks. I didn't understand his tears until we arrived in Bogotá. The moment we landed you could feel the oppression.

German loved Florida. He knew that having been in the U.S.A. as an illegal immigrant he may never see his beloved Florida again.

The flight to Bogota involved landing at Mariciabo, Venezuela and Medallin, Colombia enroute. Each time the plane lands there is a great shout of relief from the passengers accompanied by applause. The airport runways have huge pot holes and bumps. Take off and landing is something else.

Bogota airport is a dangerous place thieves work in packs. If your bags look interesting--Look Out!

During the flight, Gwen and Doris sat beside an attractive young Spanish senorita named Rita. Rita was traveling on business from California. She was dressed too well for travel in Colombia. She wore a beautiful red leather coat and far too much gold.

Gwen witnessed to Rita about the Lord and helped her understand more clearly what it meant to be born again. Rita was a native Colombian and like so many others not understanding the way of salvation through Christ alone.

Gwen gave Rita her Personal Workers New Testament that contained much good reference regarding salvation and the Christian life. Gwen prayed with her and they prayed the sinners' prayer. Rita got off the plane at Medellin.

Two or three days later, Ron Rager was on the street in downtown Bogotá and heard a woman calling his name. It was Rita. She told a scary story of leaving the Medellin airport in the family car with her mother and chauffer. On the road they were ambushed by thieves. Her mother was shot and she was robbed of $4000 plus credit cards, etc. She said, "The only reason we survived is that Gwen prayed for me on the airplane." Rita's mother also survived. Bogota is a city of eight million – was it simply chance Ron met Rita there?

ART FROM THE BIBLE PRESENTATION

Omar had been in the Colombian Army for two years and ran the orphanage military style. This worked very well. We tagged him with the nickname General Omar. Soon there were ten boys under General Omar's command. Omar taught the Bible every day along with singing Gospel songs and choruses. Soon all ten boys received Christ as Saviour and Lord. To God be the Glory.

Jon Jyro did not know his birth date or age. They decided he was eight years old. He was asked to select his own birthday. He chose December 25th. Ten years later three of that original group would become full time missionaries. Jon Jyro was one of them.

Both Omar and German have artistic ability and enjoyed studying art as well as the Bible. German enjoyed learning to draw stickmen. The day came when German gave his first stick man Bible story. He was so nervous we decided that he and I would do it together, so I told the story while German drew the various scenes. The next time he would do both. Soon he was adding his own style of humour and the teacher was learning from the pupil with delight.

VISITING BOGOTA SCHOOLS
PRESENTING ART FROM THE BIBLE

At school entrance. Not seen are the 3 armed uniformed guards protecting the school

Drawing Souls To Christ

Our first school presentation in Colombia (Stan and Omar)

Our first school proved to be an exciting experience. Omar Rincon and I boarded the bus with our equipment and headed for the school. We disembarked three blocks too soon so we had to walk farther. We had to cross a roaring creek of water about twenty feet wide. The bridge was a medium size tree trunk. It was something like walking a tight rope. With equipment and paintings it proved a challenge at 72 years young. You pray continually in this type of ministry, and prayer becomes a continual communion with the Lord. I guess that is my definition of "Praying without ceasing. " This develops an awareness of God's presence. He is always closer than hands and feet and closer than breathing. When you become conscious of God in this way, others sense His presence too. Unbelievers may not know how to define it. Numbers of teachers have said, "Something very special happened here today. I don't know how to describe it, but it was very special."

Also involved in this is the anointing and favour of the Lord. It is vitally important to pray for this always before and during ministry. Try doing things without it. You will soon notice the difference. It is the difference of ministering in the flesh and ministering in the Spirit.

After walking the plank so to speak, we had an uphill climb of several blocks to the school. The school building was an old house, modified by tearing out walls. Some of the bricks were still heaped up here and there. How they ever packed all those students in that tiny two-story house is a mystery. There was no room large enough for the presentation, but there was an outdoor amphitheatre carved out of an earthen hill and sodded with green grass that served our purpose well as the photo will show.

When you are accustomed to ministering in the market-place you learn how to make do with what is available "Praying Always". The wind was fairly brisk. It would have blown our painting easel down had we not recruited two of the larger boys to hold it securely in place. Fortunately they had a PA system of sorts, so with Omar Rincon as my Spanish interpreter we made the best of what we had and prayerfully gave our Art from the Bible presentation. The students loved it. To God be the Glory!

Suddenly, Omar recognized his brother's two children among the students at the school. What an unexpected blessing. We had made the message of Salvation plain and in taking the message to this school had reached Omar's own family as well. Bless the Lord! Omar and numbers of other Bible Art Ministries missionaries would in the years to follow see many thousands of students, teachers, and school principals receive Christ as Lord and Saviour. Praise the Lord!

During February and March of 1993 Omar Rincon, German Rozo and Stan Crookall ministered in twenty schools in and around Bogota. We visited schools of every size, great and small, some primitive and some as up to date as you would find anywhere including the most exclusive private Colegio Nueva Granada. Pastor Ron Raeger went with us to most of these schools and filmed the presentations. Unfortunately we were robbed at the airport in Bogota on our way home, and our camera and films were stolen

WHAT IT WAS LIKE MINISTERING
IN SCHOOLS IN COLOMBIA

Children are precious everywhere. When you love them they love you back. Young children love to draw. Art from the Bible has an added spiritual dimension. Faithful prayer warriors support us through asking the Lord to bless the presentations. They are praying for the Lord's favour and His special Anointing. Those ministering pray before each presentation and are depending on God. It is an atmosphere of worship. It is the Lord who makes it special. It is the Lord who creates interest and lengthens attention spans beyond what teachers thought possible. It is the Lord who stirs the hearts of students to arrive home from school with excitement about what they saw, heard, and experienced.

The parents of students at a large public school in Bogota got together and wrote: "When our children came home from school they told us about the beautiful Bible paintings that were shown and about the beautiful words spoken. We want to say thank you to you for coming to our country, and to help our children in this beautiful way."

Colombian children are skilled with their hands. They write and draw exceptionally well. Many had pencil and paper and tried to draw what they were seeing. They asked and answered questions well. They grasped the way of salvation and were not ashamed to pray when the opportunity was given.

We traveled to the schools by taxi, by bus, and by a brand new Isusu Trooper SUV loaned by a Spanish businessman and his wife. We met this couple in an evangelical church where we preached our first Sunday in Bogota. After a few trips in the Isuzu we decided it was too great a risk to drive it on some of the back roads for fear of damage to the vehicle, and because it was a prime target for car highjackers.

The road back from one rural school had a narrow bridge about 50 feet long and about 12 feet wide with no guard rails. It was two tree trunks with 12 foot planks nailed across the middle. It hung over a deep gorge. But the real problem was a hole about 8 feet long and four feet wide in the centre. We enquired but there was no other way. While we waited and prayed an old bus came along. The wary bus driver summed up the situation in a glance and with great bravado zipped across the bridge without batting an eye. Wow. If he could do it we could--and with the Lord's enabling we did.

Buses in Third World countries are either the latest model Mercedes or something from the distant past. You have to be 80 years old to remember the buses with a decorative back porch. Well, there are still some of those around. The baggage is piled high on the top of the bus. You wonder how they do it. By the way some of the taxis in Bogota are old Studebakers. Studebaker stopped making cars in 1966. Most taxis are painted bright yellow. They need to be the way they zip in and out of traffic and deliberately go through red lights.

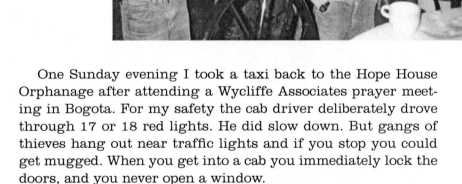

ttrance to Hope House
rphanage, Bogota,
olombia

**Former Street Kids
Hope House**

One Sunday evening I took a taxi back to the Hope House Orphanage after attending a Wycliffe Associates prayer meeting in Bogota. For my safety the cab driver deliberately drove through 17 or 18 red lights. He did slow down. But gangs of thieves hang out near traffic lights and if you stop you could get mugged. When you get into a cab you immediately lock the doors, and you never open a window.

Chela Mindosa had driven me to the prayer meeting, but we were not sure it was the right building. I expected to see a big sign Wycliffe Associates. But there was no sign. There was a formidable steel fence and an armed guard in the guard house. When I asked the guard if this was Wycliffe Associates building, he did not want to answer me, but when I mentioned Hank Koop's name, he said, one moment and called him on the phone. Some years before, rebel soldiers kidnapped Chet Bitterman, a young Wycliffe missionary translator, possibly from that same spot and a few days later killed him.

The 44 missionaries at that prayer meeting were nearly all Americans. They were big handsome young men. I was impressed by them and their courage. Not long after that, the rebel forces threatened to kill them all if they did not leave the country immediately. The rebels then kidnapped five men, some from Wycliffe and some from New Tribes Missions. The ransom demanded was in the millions. When the ransom was not paid most of the five were killed. As a result most of the translators were forced to leave Colombia. The rebel armies are told that American missionaries are all CIA agents. Many rebel soldiers were former street kids who had been hounded by police who had seen the police kill some of their fellow street kids. They became brutalized and had no mercy.

While in Bogota it was our privilege and delight to minister with Art from the Bible at a special school for missionaries' children. We were scheduled to visit another school in the jungle, but the missionary plane was under repair and we could not go.

What a privilege to minister to the children of missionary parents. When I do, I try to honor their parents and express my personal appreciation for the sacrifice the parents and children make to take the precious Gospel to those who have never heard.

Once while ministering to children of missionaries at the Gowens Home in Perry Sound, near Toronto, to my great delight I had an opportunity to chat with the teenage son of Gordon Bishop, who was a missionary with the Sudan Interior Mission. Gordon Bishop and Harold Germaine were the two missionaries we met in Sackville in 1948 and were challenged by them regarding foreign missions. It is a small world after-all.

We visited public schools mainly, but we also visited Roman Catholic Schools, private schools, and wherever there is an opportunity to minister. Some schools appreciate us giving students an invitation to receive Christ as Saviour and Lord. Some schools do not give that opportunity. But wherever we minister we ask the Lord to help us to make the way of salvation plain enough for even the youngest students to understand the way. We have received letters from students telling us that they committed their lives to Christ in this way. To God be the Glory!

At Colegio Nueva Granada, the most elite private school in Bogota, they teach in English,, so I did not need an interpreter. The school was hundreds of steps up the side of the mountain. Half way up there was a landing and a bench where I sat down to rest. It was just Omar Rincon and I this day. I asked Omar to go up and see if we could meet somewhere else. I didn't think I could make it any further up those steps. Moments later Omar was back accompanied by the psychology professor who wanted to carry me up the steps. He looked about 60.years old.

Omar with the psychology professor at Collegio Neuo Grande

There was no other place to go. In almost 30 years I had never before given up in a difficult situation like this. Omar put his arms around me and we prayed. Bogota is situated on a plateau a mile high, with these steps up from there. The Lord helped us and we made it. The psychology professor carried half of our equipment so that helped.

The students were all in good shape. They had to climb those steps every day. We had a great presentation with them. One young man asked, "Would you please explain what it means to be born again?" That is like saying, "Siccum," to a dog. What a precious opportunity. I pointed to Nicodemus in the Crucifixion painting and explained how he was pointing to Christ on the cross, telling Joseph of Arimathea. "Now I understand what Jesus meant when He said, As Moses lifted up the serpent in the wilderness, even so must the Son of man be lifted up: That whosoever believeth in Him should not perish, but have everlasting life." I explained how the people had murmured against God and were bitten by fiery serpents and were dying, but when they looked up to the serpent made of brass which God told Moses to make, they were healed. So Christ Jesus was lifted up on the cross at Calvary so that all who believe in His sacrificial death and the shedding of His precious blood for the forgiveness of our sins can be and are then born of the Holy Spirit. This is the second birth referred to by our Lord Jesus Christ as being born again.

In closing , when I thanked the psychology professor for inviting me to speak to his students as I reached out to shake his hand, he reached out both of his to grip mine and said, "Oh no, it is not you who thank us, but we who thank you!" Bless the Lord! Those are moments to be remembered for a lifetime. Was it worth the effort? It surely was. These students were the children of the president and political leaders of the nation, by this time of writing perhaps leaders themselves. Oh what privileges God gives to you and to me to go before princes and kings with the story of redeeming grace. Thank you Lord!

BASEBALL CAPS FOR THE BOYS
AT THE HOPE HOUSE ORPHANAGE

A former American baseball player, who attended our church in New Port Richey, gave us 10 special big league baseball caps for the former street kids at the orphanage, which I gave them. They put them on immediately with great interest and excitement. Then they asked, "What is baseball?" Everyone in Colombia knows all about soccer, but baseball was something new to many. When we visited schools at recess or noon hour you had to beware as a dozen or more soccer balls whizzed every which way across the school yard.

The next day I was on my way back to Florida. Gwen and Doris Moffat had returned earlier as Doris became ill in Bogota. I left the Bible paintings in Colombia for Omar and German to use in thousands more schools, not only in Colombia, but in Ecuador and Argentina as well. Over the following years they would have the great joy of praying with multiplied thousands to receive Christ and to enroll them in The Mailbox Club Bible correspondence courses.

For one not fluent in Spanish traveling alone can become a problem when announcements are made by stewardesses who do not speak English. An announcement was made in Spanish that I did not understand. Then everyone disembarked at the Mariciabo, Venezuela Airport. Everyone, but me, that was. I thought it strange that I was the only one going to Miami. Then a stewardess confronted me with animated gestures. She was really getting frustrated. Then she hit a word I could understand, "VAMOOSE, VAMOOSE!!!" So I vamoosed off the plane as they brought the drug sniffing dogs on board. When the search was completed we were able to board the plane again for the flight to Miami.

At Miami a very large black customs lady did not like my passport, and gave me a difficult time. I was glad that I knew Gwen would be waiting for me at the airport to vouch for my eligibility to get through customs. The customs lady told me to "Sit there and wait," but when she disappeared, so did I. Soon I found Gwen. How good it was to be together again.

JAILHOUSE CONVERSION

One day as German Rozo was escorting the boys from the orphanage to their school three thieves attacked the boys to steal their baseball caps. German ever watchful and ever wary immediately stood in the gap. When one of the bandits drew his knife, German gave him a knuckle sandwich to the jaw. The thief turned and began to run. German can run. He runs for exercise. It is a good thing to be able to run if you live in Bogota. Bogota has long been considered the most dangerous city in the world for crime. German chased the robber for ten city blocks. The robber ran right into the arms of a policeman. That seemed safer to him than being caught by German.

The policeman took both German and the robber to the police station, German apologized to the robber for hitting him. German went on to explain that he was a Christian. As German explained what being a Christian is, the robber and the policeman both trusted Christ as Lord and Saviour. Some weeks later as German was taking the boys to school they met the newly converted robber. He joyfully explained that he now had a good job and robbed no more.

Drawing Souls To Christ

ALARIO THE CRIPPLED-ARM STREET KID

In the photo German Rozo is inviting Alario to come to live at the orphanage. But Alario is part of a gang of older street kids who tolerate him because people give him money when they see his handicap. Then the bigger boys rough him up and take the money from him.

The average life expectancy of a street kid is 15 years. Alario was 13. I asked German to try to keep track of Alario and keep trying to recruit him for the orphanage. Alario told German that he had been in a home at one time but did not like it. He preferred to live on the streets.

Street kids sleep on the street sidewalks during the day in plain view, for safety. The police will not kill them during the day when people are around. But at night the street kids hide for protection. One day, German had sad news about Alario. His body was found, floating in the river. He was 15.

How tragic. But think of the boys who were willing to accept the challenge to yield their lives to Christ and learn to love and serve Him. Of the original 10 boys at Hope House, ten years later 3 of them were serving the Lord as full time Christian workers. There is hope for street kids. Indeed Hope House was well named. The fields are white unto harvest... "Pray ye therefore the Lord of the harvest"..........Omar Rincon and German Rozo faithfully discipled the boys and like Onesimus they too became profitable. Glory to God!

As time went by, others took over the work at Hope House when Omar and German began to work full time in schools and prisons... Jon Jyro one of the original group of ten, worked full time for several years with Bible Art Ministries Jon's specialty was painting scripture or gospel signs. These signs are located everywhere, in stores, in schools, in restaurants, in places of business and industry etc. Some large signs grace walls near major bus transfer points. God's word is quick and powerful and sharper than any two-edged sword. One employer said, "This sign convicts me of being unkind to my employees; I must change my attitude toward them, and treat them with kindness." Jon joined the Army for a couple years, but has now returned to work part-time with Bible Art Ministries.

PREACHING ON THE BUSES

When Julio and Kelly Velez started working with Bible Art Ministries in August 2000, We began the practice of preaching and giving out gospel tracts on the buses. Bogota, with eight million citizens, has a large bus system. People do not react the way Canadians or Americans respond to certain issues. Bus drivers appreciate German and Julio's ministry on the buses. It may surprise you to learn that most Colombians not only ac-cept a gospel tract graciously, they read it.

But what can the reading of a gospel tract accomplish, you might ask? In Japan, after World War II, Captain Mitsuo Fuchi-da, leader of the fighter-bomber squadron that attacked Pearl Harbour, read a gospel tract written by Jake DeShazer, one of the captured Doolittle raiders who bombed Tokyo. The tract gave the account of DeShazers torture by the Japanese, but how his conversion while in prison changed him so that he could love his enemies and later spend his life as a missionary in Ja-pan seeking to win the Japanese to Christ. Machida as a result of reading the tract committed his life to Christ and became a missionary to his own people, eventually joining DeShazer in evangelistic crusades throughout Japan.

On a missionary journey to Argentina Julio Velez and Ger-man Rozo were thrown off a train for preaching. They caught the next train and continued preaching unmolested. Try preach-ing on a bus or a train. As I write, I'm thinking of the most dif-ficult place I can think of for trying to get the message across. For me it has to be a lumber camp in Northern Canada. Next would be the seemingly hundreds of hospitals where I have tried to minister to critically ill people amidst the business of hospital staff and visitors.

In lumber camps you go to the dining tent and preach while the men gulp down their food. If you try to eat with them and then preach you will never make it. Lumberjacks are the fastest eaters I've met. Once while working with the Rural Life Mission, I took Evelyn Ellison with me to sing. Big mistake, no one could hear her. Being a chalk artist is an advantage in lumber camps. As the men see the Bible story drawn, the words spoken become clearer above the din of dinner.

BAM MISSIONARIES ADAPTABLE

German Rozo arrives at Toronto International Airport for a well-deserved rest and Canadian visit.

You have probably heard it said that a preacher should be ready to pray, preach or die at a moment's notice. He should also be adaptable and versatile. We must be ready to do what we have never done before when the opportunity comes up. Our missionaries are like that. When German Rozo saw large Gospel Text Signs in a state of disrepair, he found out who had made the signs, and obtained permission to repair them. One had letters several feet high. It was at a bus transfer point where thousands of people passed by every day. This is how our Gospel Text Sign venture began, as mentioned in another chapter of this book. My father, Thomas Rylands Crookall, was a top notch sign writer back when all signs were hand painted. He worked for E.L. Ruddy Signs, the largest and best in the business. My Dad would be proud of B.A.M.'s sign department. My Dad painted signs each week for local churches, and I delivered them the moment they were dry. Churches were very sign conscious in those days, and the churches were filled with people, especially Sunday night.

When my father painted signs I would stand motionless as close as he would allow, and watch every brush stroke. If I shook the floor I would hear about it. You didn't mess with my Dad. He was a World War One Canadian Army Veteran and a strict disciplinarian. My Dad fought in the big battles at Vimy Ridge where he was badly wounded. When old army buddies would come to visit I would listen to the captivating stories they told. My father was proud to have both of his sons volunteer to serve king and country in World War II. We both served in the Canadian Navy. For me my time in the Navy gave me time to grow as a believer. I spent much time in prayer. I learned to be praying always. I learned to pray about everything. My wonderful wife at home in Hamilton, Ontario was also growing as a Christian. She too was learning to pray, and to become the greatest prayer warrior I have known. Her marvellous letters were like epistles. It was during the last six months of my time in the navy that God called me to a life of full time Christian service. It was a struggle for me to surrender. I didn't tell Gwen at first, but she was probably away ahead of me. She knew me well enough to sense the spiritual struggle I was having and indeed was going through the same struggle herself. A husband and wife are one and the Lord surely speaks to both at the same time. Gwen had a special gift from the Lord--patience to pray for her husband, and allow him time to catch up to her spiritually while still maintaining his position as spiritual leader. What a treasure. How unselfish. How precious.

At the times we were going through important decisions, I was amazed that she could so quickly stand with me in perfect agreement. Now as I look back I can see that sometimes she had prayerfully been waiting years for me to catch up to her spiritual level on these issues.

John Horton, a fellow cadet at the Salvation Army Training College, was a World War II hero, having served in the famous 8th Army all the way through North Africa, Italy, and

Drawing Souls To Christ

Normandy. He could see these special qualities in Gwen. John was single, and looking for the Lord's choice of a life partner. Many times he would poke me in the shoulder as men do to get a point across. Then he would say, "You lucky stiff - you don't know how lucky you are to have a wife who is so special." Many years later others would recognize that Gwen was such an equal partner in everything the Lord led us to do.

Our Salvation Army training stressed soul winning. That is a priority in all of our various activities in Bible Art Ministries. That is why we preach on the buses, why we paint Gospel Signs, why we take Art from the Bible to schools and prisons and even venture into the marketplace where people are.

There are only two kinds of people, SAVED and LOST. If you are not saved through faith in the finished work of Christ then you are lost without Him. It is important to make the most of each opportunity. We have to make the Way of Salvation plain. We must faithfully warn as well as tenderly win.

The joy of leading souls to Christ is spiritually rejuvenating. There is nothing quite like it. As the Bible says, "The Joy of the Lord is our strength." It is the winning of a battle for souls in a very real warfare. When those who come to faith in Christ are children or young people it is a whole life saved.

When it comes to referring to numbers of souls saved I always think of David numbering the people and hesitate to give specific numbers especially when they are in the multiplied thousands.

DISTRIBUTION OF GOSPEL TRACTS

Arnold Scott of Oshawa, Canada has distributed tracts and Bibles worldwide for more than three decades. I remember personally working with him at the Oshawa Fair during the 1970s. Arnold is one of those unsung heroes who goes about quietly and faithfully serving in the thick of the battle just as he fought in the Canadian Army during World War II as he earned almost every campaign ribbon and medal issued through all the heavy fighting. We worked together serving in the Oshawa chapter of Full Gospel Businessmen and Arnold could always be counted on.

Arnold has supplied many thousands of Spanish Gospel Tracts to our BAM workers in Colombia, Ecuador and Argentina for many years. I can imagine when we all get to Heaven, someone asking, "Wow! Whose great mansion is that?" And the answer will be, "Oh, that is Arnold Scott's place." Arnold has also been a great BAM prayer supporter since we began in 1976.

My favourite tract is The Four Spiritual Laws, written by Bill Bright, founder of Campus Crusade for Christ. This little booklet condenses God's wonderful plan of salvation into four steps. It deals with the meaning of salvation, decision for Christ, and how to live the Christian life. Law 1 is: God loves you and offers a wonderful plan for your life. Law 2 is: Man is sinful and separated from God. Therefore, he cannot know and experience God's love and plan for his life. Law 3 is: Jesus Christ is God's ONLY provision for man's sin. Through Him you can know and experience God's love and plan for your life. Law 4 is: We must individually receive Jesus Christ as Saviour and Lord; then we can know and experience God's love and plan for our lives

The following explains how you can receive Christ:

YOU CAN RECEIVE CHRIST RIGHT NOW
BY FAITH THROUGH PRAYER.

Prayer is talking with God. God knows your heart and is not as concerned with your words as He is with the attitude of your heart. This is a suggested prayer:

"Lord Jesus, I need you. Thank You for dying on the cross for my sins. I open my heart to receive you as my Saviour and Lord. Thank you for forgiving my sins and giving me eternal life. Take control of the throne of my life. Make me the kind of person You want me to be. In Jesus' Name, Amen."

Bill Bright was one of Dr. Henrietta Mears' students in her College and Careers Class at Hollywood Presbyterian Church in Hollywood, California. Dr. Mears was the co-founder of Gospel Light Publications. As recorded in an earlier chapter, it was my honour and privilege to work for Gospel Light for a number of years and to learn much from Dr. Mears. She had an acrostic, GROW:

G Go to God in prayer every day. (John 15: 7)

R Read the Word of God every day. (Acts 17: 11)

O Obey God every day. (John 14: 21)

W Witness for the Lord every day. (Matt. 4: 19; John 15: 8)

If we follow this plan for life we will grow spiritually every day!

Drawing Souls To Christ

BIBLE ART MINISTRIES Connects with
THE MAILBOX CLUB

Omar Rincon our first Colombian missionary who began ministering in his native Colombia in 1993 found out about the MAILBOX CLUB International and began using their lesson materials with new converts in the school ministry. Omar arranged a meeting with John Mark Eager, son of George Eager, founder of Mailbox Club, at Word of Life in Hudson Florida. This led to Mailbox Club supplying Bible correspondence courses for thousands of school students our missionaries met while ministering in public, private and Christian Schools. Now we had a follow-up program to help new converts to grow in their new-found faith, just as Gospel Light does with Sunday School Curriculum. An important feature is the questions dealing with the student's understanding and grasp of what it means to be a Christian and how to grow as a believer. Volunteers who mark and return the lessons are trained to answer spiritual needs. Little rewards add interest and encouragement also.

Stan Crookall and George Eager, Founder of the Mailbox Club, at Valdosta, Georgia

George Eager, founder of the Mailbox Club International, and Stan Crookall, founder of Bible Art Ministries International, have much in common. They were both born in 1922. They both served in the Navy in World War II, George in the American, Stan in the Canadian. They have both ministered extensively in public schools. Both have discipled others including family to work in the ministry with them. The discipling was not intended for the purpose of working together. That was just how the Lord worked things out. What a delight it is for a father when that happens.

"Drawing Souls To Christ" is what Bible Art Ministries is all about. The never-dieing soul of each person, young or old, is precious to the Lord. It is of infinite value. Christ Jesus declared it is more valuable than the whole world. "For what shall it profit a man if he gain the whole world and lose his own soul?"

MISSIONARY ADVENTURE IN EQUADOR

January, 1956, the Christian world was shocked by the martyrdom of five American Missionaries killed by Auca Indians near Shell Mera, Equador. (Jim Elliot, Nate Saint, Ed McCulley, Pete Fleming, Roger Youderian). Nate Saint, the pilot of the missionary airplane, was brother to Phil Saint, an outstanding Gospel Chalk Drawing Artist whose book on the subject was the best I had ever read. This made the death of these men more personal to me. We had not heard of Christian martyrs for many years so it was front page news around the world. As a young pastor I was deeply moved. I remember praying, "Lord what can I do? How can I help?"

Joyce Pene ministering in Equador

Drawing Souls To Christ

Now, half-a-century later, Joyce Pene, one of our young Bible Art Mission workers, was living in Quito, Equador, ministering in schools. And Omar Rincon, based in Bogota was on a missionary journey which included the Shell Mera area. Omar was flown in to minister in a small mud hut school in the jungle very close to where the five young Americans were slain as they sought to evangelize the Aucas. Wow! My prayer of half a century ago was being gloriously fulfilled. God does not forget. He remembers far better than we do.

Omar used my Biblical paintings to explain Redemption's wondrous plan to Auca children. When he gave the invitation to receive Christ as Saviour and Lord some 24 or more responded. So, when they were ready, Omar marched the group down to the river and baptized them. To me that is really exciting. Our aim is to provide a good Art and Bible lesson that will also draw many souls to Christ. To God be all the Glory!

Third world countries emphasize the three R's: reading, writing, and arithmetic. Their development of hand skills surpasses that of our North American students. They are better at art and drawing. Their ability to print well and to write legibly makes art more appealing to them.

SARAH CROOKALL'S HEALING OF SPINAL BIFUDA

We had invited our son Tim and his wife Lisa to have dinner at Teddy's, our favorite bistro (restaurant) to celebrate: we had just learned that Tim and Lisa were expecting their first child. As grandparents we were excited. But suddenly there was a serious problem with the pregnancy and Tim phoned to cancel our dinner date.

The doctor had ordered some tests. The results were alarming. The unborn baby had a 99% likelihood of being born with Spinal Bifuda. The complications and multiple surgeries required were cause for great concern. The doctor's recommendation was abortion. Two of Lisa's family agreed with the doctor's recommendation. Tim and Lisa did not favour abortion. The pressure was mounting. All concerned were prayerfully considering this critical decision. Gwen and I drove over to Tim and Lisa's home to talk and pray with them. We had met Betty Baxter and heard her wonderful story of God's miracle healing of her incurable back problem when she was a child of nine or ten years of age. – similar to what our unborn grandchild would face.

We had The Betty Baxter Story on tape. As a child she was bedridden and unable to walk. Her body was twisted like a pretzel. Then one day as she was praying, God spoke to her, and told her that on a certain Sunday afternoon, at three o'clock, He would heal her, and she would be made perfectly whole and would be able to walk. Betty told her mom about this, and asked her mom to go and buy a nice dress and shoes for her because she was going to go to church the evening of the day she would be healed. She also wanted the dress to be hung up and the shoes where she could see them as a constant reminder of God's promise to her until the day of her healing.

Betty's mom hoped she could get the car out to go to town without her husband knowing, but he stopped her and had to know where she was going and why. When she told him the whole story, he said, "Now isn't that too bad. All this time Betty has been so sick and in such pain, but her mind has never been effected by it--and now her mind has gone!" But Betty got her dress and shoes nevertheless.

Often while we are waiting for God's promise to be fulfilled, things get worse instead of better. Such was the case with Betty. Her promised healing was some eight or ten months away. In the meantime she became very ill and her condition worsened considerably, but Betty held on to God's promise and looked forward to the day she would be healed and wear the new dress and shoes to church. When that special day arrived a number of friends had arrived to be with them for the occasion. At precisely three o'clock that promised Sunday with every door and window shut, a wind began to blow throughout the inside of the house and Betty Baxter's twisted body straightened as God fulfilled His promise to her and healed her, making her whole. To God be all the Glory!

Betty put on the new dress and shoes and walked. She went to church that evening. The church was packed with people as news of Betty's healing had spread far and wide.

Forty years later, Gwen and I met Betty Baxter at Evangel Temple in Toronto. She was a beautiful statuesque lady, poised and graceful, still praising God for His mighty promises and glorious fulfillment. She had often given her testimony at Oral Roberts' great tent miracle crusades.

We played the tape of Betty Baxter's healing that night before we all laid hands on Lisa and prayed. I can't remember the prayer, but remember God's answer with thanksgiving to the Lord. The next morning Lisa, her mother, Gwen and Tim and I all felt the assurance that the baby would be normal at birth. And she was.

About two years later, Pastor Jerry Magliulo of Gospel Outreach Church held little Sarah Crookall in his arms at an Anti-Abortion Rally at Sims Park in New Port Richey, Florida and told the story of her birth. Today as I write, Sarah is a beautiful twenty year old young lady. To God be the Glory!

I wish I could remember more of the beautiful things she said about spiritual matters as a young child. I do remember her advice to Smokie, our big German Shepherd dog. Smokie was hesitant about climbing the open steps of a basement stairway where she had experienced some difficulty previously. Sarah was at that time only inches taller than Smokie. Sarah's words were priceless, "Smokie, you have to learn to face your fears".

Smokie was a tall German Shepherd who weighed 100 pounds. Smokie had been to obedience training and knew all the obedience commands. Sarah knew them as well. It was hilarious to see Smokie's reaction to a command from Sarah. Smokie's pained facial expression clearly was, "Do I really have to do what this little kid commands?"

Sarah always had to have a ride in the back carrier of Grama Gwen's three-wheeler bike. We always had to blow the car horn while driving under an overpass bridge. We always had to "Feed the lake" with pebbles while at our cottage at Cobourg Camp. We always had a Bible Story and prayer. And Sarah's prayers were beautiful. "Many are the afflictions of the righteous, but the Lord delivereth him out of them all. I Am the Lord Your Healer."

MATTHEW BRYDGES HEALING

One crisp spring morning we were on our way to give an Art from the Bible presentation at Renfrew Christian School. Renfrew is a small town northwest of Ottawa. Beth Deacon was the principal and we knew that we were in for an exciting time with her students. I usually travel alone, but this time Doris Moffatt, Marion Hayman, my wife Gwen and our grandson Chris were with me. Both Doris and Marion were long time prayer supporters and interested in seeing our latest series of paintings.

We also planned to visit Marie Brydges and to see her six year old son who was enrolled at the school. Marie had been pianist and soloist with Bill Prankard Ministries and both Marion and Gwen and I had been part of that team. It is a long drive and we could hardly wait to get there.

Driving distances and fitting in to school schedules calls for pin point timing. Serving in the Navy in wartime was great preparation for being prompt.

When we arrived at the school we were disappointed to learn that Matthew was not there. He was at home, sick. We learned of his very serious affliction with allergies. We also learned that the Brydges had a special house built of materials which would not cause allergy problems for Matthew. It was that serious. Both Matthew and his Mom had never slept through a single night since he was born because of the allergies. Gwen and I had gone through many years when our daughter Marjorie might have a grand mal epileptic seizure at any time, but this was far worse. We could empathize with Marie and her husband Bobby. Six years of awakening time and time again every night. Parents do these things in love, thankful that their child survived the night. It had probably been a rough night, and both Matthew and his Mom were recovering.

Each and every presentation of Art from the Bible is special. Kids are special at every age and learning level. The opportunity to ask and answer questions gives them the chance to open up to find important answers about art, about God and the Bible and problems very real to them. In a public school in Bowmanville, Ontario a boy about 12 asked a number of questions and each time he raised his hand amidst the many other hands that were raised I sensed the Lord directing me to allow him to ask or answer the question. Usually I don't allow one student to monopolize this opportunity, but this seemed to be of the Lord. To my amazement, at the conclusion of the presentation this boy was selected as the person to thank me for coming to their school. He did a terrific job of it to the delight of his teachers and fellow students. Then privately several teachers and the principal told me how very special the presentation had been. They had seen a miracle take place in their midst and they knew it. This particular student had gone through 7 grades in their school without being able to ask or answer a single question ever before. It was a breakthrough that amazed the entire staff and student body. Great is our God and greatly to be praised. To God be the Glory! How important prayer is and how God loves to answer prayer. How thankful we are for every prayer warrior on our Bible Art Ministries team of prayer supporters. Just as the worshipping trumpeters and singers went ahead of the Israeli army into battle so we need our prayer warriors every moment of every day.

Getting back to our visit with Marie and Matthew, we talked about many things. Gwen related how a young woman in Peterborough who had the same allergy type problem as Matthew, and lived in a specially built house as the Brydges had made to protect Matthew, was gloriously healed in answer to prayer. Matthew took that in, but said nothing. Before we left, we joined hands and formed a prayer circle. Included in the prayer was a prayer for Matthew's healing.

The next day, Marie and Matthew were down town shopping. Suddenly, Marie felt an inward voice saying, "Buy Matthew a treat to eat". But if Matthew ate it, he would fall down in convulsions. The prompting persisted. Finally, Marie felt it must be the Lord, so she bought a banana. Nervously he broke off a very small piece and Matthew ate it. Matthew did not fall down in convulsions so Marie gave him a larger piece of banana. Matthew was still alright. She gave him the whole banana. She bought a piece of cake. Matthew ate the whole thing without a problem. That night Matthew slept through the whole night without waking. So did his parents. The first time in six years. Hallelujah! That was some two decades ago, and Matthew is still well and strong. How great is our God and how great to be praised.

Soon after we began Saturday services at Pembroke a very unusual fellow showed up. He was the first to arrive that night and would be the last to leave. In fact, from there on he would always be the first to arrive and the last to leave as long as we held services there. We greeted him warmly. He said, "I'm an ex con. I just got out of Millhaven.

My name is Ernie Hollands. I'm living with Grant Bailey and working in his store." Wow! Ernie had been a bank robber. He had been charged with shooting a policeman, the gun went off while the two of them grappled for it. He had spent over 15 years in prison, and had escaped three times.

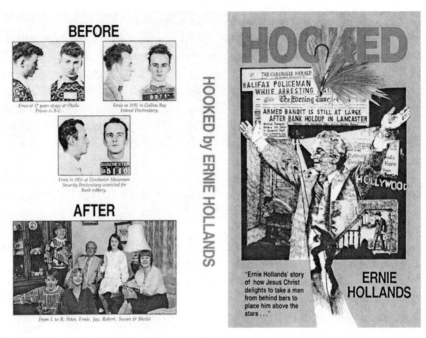

Ernie Hollands Bank Robber Converted

Having worked at the Bowmanville Correctional School for ten years I had seen some great transformations, but also some sad disappointments. I hoped Ernie would not disappoint his mentor Grant Bailey. We would do our very best to do our share of discipling whenever we could. In our Salvation Army training I had learned to meet our Sunday converts on Monday morning and walk to work with them wherever possible. As a pastor I had learned to help people get started right.

As a shy seventeen year old, I had my share of questions after I was converted, but I was embarrassed to ask for help. I had learned how to get to the questions more easily for others. Dear old Major Mercer always asked every Sunday, "How are you getting along with the Lord?" And as a young convert I needed help, but his approach scared me and I just blurted out, "Fine" and wanted to get lost. If he had told me how to study my Bible, how to pray etc., he could have helped me more.

Whenever I was near Pembroke, I would do my best to have a visit and prayer with Ernie prior to our Saturday evening service. When the Lord directed me to begin Bible Art Ministries and discontinue the weekly Miracle Services, I was concerned about Ernie. How would this affect him?

To my great surprise when I went to see Ernie at his apartment, intending to tell him about this change, Ernie beat me to it. He began to tell me how he felt led of the Lord to move out into a prison ministry. Wow! I wondered if he was ready for that. Time would tell. It did. He was ready. When God directs it works. When it is our idea alone that is another story. Ernie Holland's Prison Ministry took him all over the world in time, even to Russia.

Our paths crossed many times in many different places. A few times we ministered together. One Full Gospel Businessmen's chapter scheduled us both for the same meeting. That was different.

Soon after Ernie began going to prisons I dropped in to see my son Paul in his office at Joyceville Prison near Kingston, Ontario. Paul flipped a business card across his desk to me. It read, A witness for Jesus; Ernie Hollands. Paul asked, "Do you know this fellow?"

My answer was, "I sure do!"

Paul didn't often waste words. He asked, "Is he for real?"

To which I replied, "You had better believe he's for real!"

"Okay" Paul said, "I'll give him a chance to speak here." That may have been Ernie's first opportunity. Prison managers are very cautious about former inmates coming in, they can be a valuable resource, but managers first want to make sure the person is "solid" and not just playing a game. Once you prove yourself and get a recommendation it is so much easier to get an appointment elsewhere.

Ernie was small of stature and very quiet when I first met him. He developed into a great preacher who could use his voice very effectively. The Lord used him to win many prisoners to Christ. Ernie had a late start at learning the Scriptures and in many things, being about fifty years of age when he met the Master that glorious time while in prison. In order to learn Scripture verses, Ernie would write a verse on the palm of both hands in ink each day. Each time our paths crossed I wanted to see Ernie's verses for that day's learning.

Ernie decided that he needed a wife, so he asked the Lord to give him a ready made family, a widow with young children. Shortly after his prayer he was speaking on television and a preacher's widow with three children was watching the program. The kids loved Ernie and exclaimed to their Mom, "That is the man we want to be our Daddy!" Not long after this, Ernie was the speaker at an FGBMI banquet that the little fatherless family attended. They met and soon there were wedding bells ringing. We were so glad for all in this very special family. Later a little girl was born to the family, making it complete. The family settled in Peterborough, Ontario. A bank manager lived on one side of them, and the chief of police lived on the other. Ernie showed great respect for the police and honoured them wherever possible.

During one of his bank robberies, the bank manager fired five shots at Ernie at point blank range and missed. Later, after his conversion, Ernie called in at that bank to tell the manager about his new life and his soul winning ministry. Ernie asked, "How did you miss me when you fired those five shots at me?" The bank manager replied, "I couldn't find my glasses". One bullet went right through Ernie's suit jacket.

Ernie became a great soul winner with a world-wide prison ministry. To God be the Glory.

When I learned that Ernie was speaking in Peterborough about the year 2000, I went to see him. Sadly I learned that he had contracted hepatitis through a blood transfusion. As we embraced in parting, Ernie said, "I may not be here tomorrow, but I know where I'm going, Praise the Lord!" Three weeks later Ernie went to be with the Lord. What an abundant entrance this mighty warrior would receive. How wonderful to have the privilege of knowing him and being able to call him brother and friend.

DETERMINING THE WILL OF GOD
(Tom Harmon's Bible School Application)

Back in the hard times of the great depression (1929 to 1939) we sang an encouraging chorus:

"Got any rivers you think are uncrossable?
Got any mountains you can't tunnel through?
God specializes in things thought impossible,
And He will do what no other power can do."

Never take "no" for an answer until you have prayed about it!

Drawing Souls To Christ

During the mid-seventies at the zenith of the charismatic renewal, a group of four young men who were converted at about the same time all joined a truly great church, Grace Cathedral in Whitby, Ontario. In the course of time, three would become ordained ministers and the fourth, our son Tim, became a gospel musician, motivational speaker and Bible teacher. He also ministered in schools for Bible Art Ministries for seven years. In the beginning he worked with me, then later developed a music presentation entitled, "The History of Modern and Gospel Music."

Tim's friend Tom Harmon, one of the four, felt called of the Lord to go to Bible School to train for full time ministry. Tom was going to Peterborough to apply at the Pentecostal Bible College for the next school term beginning in September.

A few days later, when Tim told me that Tom had been told that there were several hundred applications ahead of his, and he should consider applying next year, I became concerned. I had known others who waited and when it became more difficult due to the birth of children they never did apply. Tom had accepted that it was God's will. When I talked with Tom I asked if he had actually made out an application. He had not. I believe it was of the Lord that I told him I did not believe he could accept the postponement as God's will unless he really filled out an application and was officially turned down by the School.

Tom went back and filled out an application, and guess what? He was accepted for the session beginning in September, ahead of several hundred others. We did some praying. God answered! Hallelujah! Tom became a great pastor, and the Lord enabled him to build a new church that continues to grow as the Lord adds to the church.

What if Tom had not applied? Our friends Ken and Verna M--- had the same call from the Lord, but waited and each year it became more difficult, until finally it did not happen. When the Lord directs our path it is imperative to step out in faith. Well meaning people may give advice, but God's ways are past finding out.

Robertson of the 700 Club likens life to the game of football. When the offensive line opens a hole in the defensive line, there are only split seconds in which the running back can get through to score before the opening is closed, and the opportunity is lost.

Spiritual discernment is that sense of knowing when to act, and when not to. It is usually learned by drawing nigh to God and obeying His leading. When we fail to realize it, it is a lesson to obey the next time. As Samuel said to King Saul, "To obey is better than sacrifice."

TIM AND BAM

Both of our sons Paul and Tim have played an important role in Bible Art Ministries.

Tim worked with me on the road for a year or so. Then he went back to college for a couple of years studying music at Berkley in Boston, and later at Humber in Toronto.

Upon graduation, he worked with Bible Art Ministries for six years. He expanded our focus, by developing and presenting a musical version: "The History of Modern Music," and how gospel music developed through the years until now. Tim included a number of gospel songs that he had personally written. This is my favourite, he wrote when he was 18:

In the Beginning
Tim Crookall

In the beginning He made beauty everywhere
All was just, perfect, and fair
He gave the gift of life to man
He had for him a perfect plan.

But in the garden Adam chose sin
That's when the downfall of man did begin
He brought a curse upon the race
Because for sin a price must be paid.

Chorus
Oh, how He wanted our love
Not robots made of steel
So He gave us
A free will.

But God still loved us with an everlasting love
He sent His Son to Earth, He left His Home up above
He became a perfect man
His blood would pay the price of sin.

Drawing Souls To Christ

Jesus came to this lonely, empty world
He was a friend to all who loved the truth
"Love your enemies," He said,
If a man is hungry make sure he's fed

Self-righteous, religious people hated Him
Because He was honest and He told them of their sin
They wanted to live in their lives
So they nailed Him to a cross and they watched Him die

Oh, but Jesus fooled them all
He rose up from the dead
And you can hear His voice call
"I'll set your spirit free."

When this life is over there will be beauty once again
For everyone who simply follows Him
It will be just, perfect, and fair
There will be beauty everywhere.

In his presentations he included "Rainy Night Conversion," which is the dramatic story of his personal conversion. He traveled extensively doing this until the Ontario government passed legislation to forbid the Bible in our public schools in 1991.

Tim is a great actor. I didn't think he was listening when he was a child, but he can act out my stickmen sermons from those days which preceded BAM. His music presentation included a few quick costume changes and a wig. The students loved it. Tim's ministry was very valuable

When the committee to rule on Religious Education headed up by Dr. McFarland came to Cobourg (Northumberland, Newcastle Board), both Tim and I presented twenty-minute papers to show why we need religious education in public schools. Both Tim and I had spent a considerable amount of time preparing and praying.

Personally I spent more than a week on research and preparation. I learned that public education began in Canada, under the Reverend Doctor Egerton Ryerson, a Methodist saddlebag evangelistic preacher (1803 – 1882). Dr. Ryerson became the first Director of Education in Ontario, and the school he founded in 1841 in Cobourg, Victoria College was later moved to Toronto and is now a distinguished part of the University of Toronto. Ryerson University was named after him. Throughout the public school system, God was honoured in the curriculum, and Scripture portions were memorized. (e.g., Psalm 1, Psalm 23, I Corinthians 13, Isaiah 53) when I attended public school in the 1930s.

Reading assignments featured character building stories based on Biblical truths of honesty and integrity.

The observation was made that the incidence of crime, drugs, etc, was much lower, and no one ever heard of guns and killings in schools.

It didn't take a space scientist to realize that Dr. McFarland and his committee had been appointed to do away with religious education in the public schools.

When I concluded reading my paper, Dr. McFarland leaned across his reading stand, and said, "Mr. Crookall, do you think all Christians are all good people? – What about Jimmy Bakker and Jimmy Swaggart?"

When Tim concluded his paper, Dr. McFarland said, "You remind me of the story of the Good Samaritan. You are like those who pass by on the other side."

Tim's reply was, "Oh, no. You have it all wrong, I am trying to be helpful like the Good Samaritan was."

This tribunal conducted hearings in each school board area throughout Ontario. Only Dr. McFarland and his committee knew what was recommended and said in each school board area. When the Board concluded their hearings, they recommended to discontinue religious education in Ontario public schools. The church was silent on the matter. The churches allowed this great freedom of religion to be removed without a whimper. Alas, one more freedom that many of us fought for in WWII was lost. Prior to this ruling, the law stated that two class periods per week should be used for religious education.

It had been our personal privilege to teach the religious education period in many rural schools in the Thunder Bay and Geraldton areas. Also in Hamilton, Ontario during the 50s and 60s. At that time local ministers were invited to do this without remuneration. Those who did it looked upon it as a great opportunity and privilege. While a pastor in Hamilton, Ontario, I was asked to do double duty in schools there as the ministers in a certain area of the city were not willing to volunteer. "Where there is no vision, the people perish."

Those who volunteer to fight for their country must leave their comfort zone and some must sacrifice even life itself for the cause they believe in. The Christian warfare requires the same and more as we serve the King of Kings and Lord of Lords.

We have allowed liberal arrogance to rob us of our Christian heritage of prayer and Bible in our schools. As the great Irish Statesman Edmund Burke observed (circa 1785): "It is necessary only for good men to do nothing for evil to triumph."

When I was a pastor in the 1940s, 50s, and 60s, our Ministerial Associations in the cities where I ministered stood against evil, and with God's help, stemmed the tide of evil. Unfortunately, today's ministerial groups are not so inclined.

At the school board meeting in 1991 in Cobourg, I do not recall a single minister in that area, other than myself, presenting a paper and not more than twenty people attended that meeting. This school board represented 85 schools. If the committee took that to mean that the masses were not interested, perhaps they were right.

PAUL AND BAM

Our son, Dr. Paul Crookall, worked for Correctional Services Canada for 27 years. He had a distinguished career beginning as a case manager and concluding as Senior Advisor to the Commissioner, with prison warden and hospital CEO along the way.

Upon retirement, Paul took over as Secretary-Treasurer of BAM in order to make life easier for Mom and Dad. During this time, he was able to assist in obtaining permission for our native Colombian missionaries to come to Canada for a combined holiday and missionary venture, to meet our supporters. No small feat, we assure you – since both German and Omar had been illegal aliens in the United States, before their conversions. I had previously personally talked with the Canadian ambassador and local members of Parliament to no avail.

Paul continues to be a valuable member of our BAM Board, managing the finances, producing the newsletter, managing the website (www.bibleartministries.com) His God-given talents are appreciated as a consultant for the ministry. His experience as a writer and editor has been most helpful. We certainly appreciated his advice and assistance during the writing of this book.

EVERYONE NEEDS HELPERS

There are so many who have helped by contacting schools and scheduling presentations of Art From the Bible, who have prayed for us, who have contributed financially. To recognize all who have done this, this book would have to be a thousand pages. Each one has been greatly appreciated. Perhaps if I mention a few, it may encourage those who feel a little timid about facing such a task.

Dewar and Mae Norman were God's gift to us to open doors to hundreds of school presentations in the Goderich, Ontario area.

Dewar was a big bear of a man, but gentle and a wonderful friend. He had been a cheese-maker. The Norman family had operated a cheese factory and Dewar was the last of the line. He was now retired and the factory had been sold. Dewar and Mae became spiritually alive and active through their association with Full Gospel Businessmen. Mae was a retired school teacher, respected and loved by the thousands she had taught and those she had worked with. She had a burden to get the Gospel to school children. Tiny in stature, but full of enthusiasm for serving the Lord, she was a go-getter. Dewar shared her burden and worked with her in all she did.

Some time after Gwen and I met the Normans in 1976, we received a letter from them asking if I could come to Goderich to minister to schools there.

I asked Mae if she could schedule two or four schools and gave her a time slot to work with. She found it a little intimidating, but was encouraged to try and prayed about it. I didn't hear from them for several weeks and wondered if I had asked too much. But, a letter came with four schools lined up and an invitation to stay at the Normans' home while working in those schools. Dewar and Mae went with me to the schools and were so thrilled about the presentations and the response of students and educators alike. They wanted to line up more and more schools, which was really appreciated. Over a span of two decades, they scheduled hundreds of schools.

The Normans home became a home-away-from home for me, and Gwen too on occasion. Meals at the Normans were always very special, and the box lunch I took each day while visiting schools. Every meal had cheese, including breakfast, and it was the best cheese.

Literally multiplied thousands of students saw and heard

Drawing Souls To Christ

Art From the Bible with its clear message of salvation due to Mae and Dewar Norman's prayerful efforts. Many will rise up in Glory to call them "Blessed." Goderich is on Georgian Bay and in the snow-belt. We usually scheduled schools there for the end of winter. Fellowship was an important part of a visit with the Normans. That was very special.

ANOTHER EXAMPLE

At Strathroy I had been invited to speak at a beginning church. While there, I asked the pastor if there was someone in his congregation who could schedule schools for me in the area. He introduced me to Bev and Jean Elliott. Mrs. Elliott is another one of those people who gets things done. I asked her about calling to see a few school principals and scheduling some presentations. Her immediate reaction was, "I don't know about this." That is a good reaction because it shows that a person is aware of some of the problems and work involved. She said that she would pray about it.

During a dozen or more years that followed, Jean Elliott scheduled literally hundreds of school presentations. Year after year I would spend a week in the Strathroy area and give twenty presentations each week to thousands of students. To God be the Glory!

AND ANOTHER....

I met Jim and Susan Creaser at a plowing match in western Ontario.

This is the photo of the Plowing Match crowd and typical tented city.

We attended events like this with a display explaining our school and prison ministry. Jim Creaser was a school teacher at Burks Falls, Ontario. Year after year he would line up a week of schools for me. Jim and I actually ministered together at a Korean college-and-careers week at a resort at Wasaga Beach one summer. Jim is a great guitarist-singer with a tremendous repertoire of Gospel songs.

BIBLE ART MINISTRIES: QUO VADIS?

Where are we going? We have always been lead by the Lord step by step, and we seek to continue serving and obediently following His leading.

New opportunities are opening up in far-away countries through the amazing computer-related helps we can provide. We produce DVDs for a computer learning program in schools in Africa, as students study art and the Bible through computer lessons. Missionaries in Kenya, Ghana, and Siberia are working with us now, using our paintings and prints. The opportunities are tremendous.

We also work in cooperation with The Mailbox Club Bible Correspondence Courses. There are thousands presently learn-

The Korean college and career group

ing the Bible this way in Colombia, and several thousand who have graduated from the courses. Elizabeth Rozo in Bogota supervises volunteer workers in sending out the lessons, marking the completed lessons, and providing certificates of completion and managing award celebrations.

Paul the Apostle wrote to the church at Thessalonica (2 Thessalonians 3:1) "Finally, brothers, pray for us that the message of the Lord may spread rapidly and be honoured, just as it was with you." We ask for your prayers, brothers and sisters in Christ.

EPILOGUE

In writing this book, I could see how all the things that took place came together to fit in to God's plan for our lives.

I vividly remember Dr. Peter Hoogendam, my pastor, teacher, and friend, using tatting as an illustration – tatting is a thing of the past, but fifty years ago everyone knew about it. It was needlepoint or fancy work with colored threads sown on a piece of cloth kept taut by two wooden overlapping hoops. One side was a thing of beauty, but the back was a series of knots and cut threads. Looking at the back, it seemed like a mess – but life can look like that. Eternity alone will reveal the full beauty and God's overall plan.

Bible Art Ministries and our Art From the Bible presentations went through the three stages Bill Gothard speaks about:

(1) the birth of a vision,

(2) the death of that vision, and

(3) the fulfillment of the vision.

God gives talent and abilities, but He expects us to develop them by studying and hard work mingled with prayer.

There are many Christian artists who draw and paint, producing a message on canvas. There are more preachers who use words to paint scenes on the canvas of your mind. In Bible Art Ministries, both paintings and words are blended together in a unique way to tell the greatest story ever told – designed and blessed of God to "Draw Souls To Christ."

Today I had lunch at Jesse Lund's Amigos Café. Jesse told me about a teenager who remarked about the print, "The Way of the Cross," which hangs on the restaurant wall. She spoke of the blank face in the painting that represents you. She had heard the painting explained by me at her school. Art From the Bible has a double-barrelled approach weaving both subjects together for an impact to be remembered for a lifetime.

The viewer and the hearer is the blank face in the painting. The message is that God's great plan of salvation in Christ is for you. God offers His precious gift of forgiveness and reconciliation. It is our responsibility to receive His unspeakable Gift.

"If thou shalt confess with thy mouth the Lord Jesus, (Jesus as Lord,) and shalt believe in thine heart that God hath raised Him from the dead, thou shalt be saved."

For with the heart man believeth unto righteousness and

with the mouth confession is made unto salvation." (Romans 10:9,10)

As stated in the beginning of the book, my wife Gwen wanted these stories recorded for others, to encourage you who read to come boldly to the throne of Grace in prayer knowing that "with God nothing shall be impossible." (Luke 1:37)

Stan and Gwen Crookall, Sweethearts since 1939 and labourers together with God. Our Life motto Matthew 6:33, "Seek ye first the kingdom of God and his righteousness, and all these things shall be added unto you".

For all that is good and great and wonderful in this book, to God be all the glory!

For He alone is worthy!

Visit our website: **www.bibleartministries.com**
Inquiries and donations can be made at
P.O. Box 4460 Stn E, Ottawa, ON, Canada, K1S 5B4
Telephone 1.613.565.7117

CPSIA information can be obtained at www.ICGtesting.com
Printed in the USA
LVOW08s0232030813

346045LV00002B/11/P